The Cultural Dialogue

The Cultural Dialogue
An Introduction to
Intercultural Communication

Michael H. Prosser University of Virginia

Houghton Mifflin Company   Boston

Dallas   Geneva, Illinois   Hopewell, New Jersey

Palo Alto   London

Printed in the U.S.A.

Library of Congress Catalog Card Number: 77-89049

ISBN: 0-395-24448-X

*To Carol Mary, Michelle Ann, Leo Michael, and Louis Mark,
constant contributors to my cultural dialogues*

Acknowledgments

Thanks cannot adequately repay those who have influenced one's developments and interests. The debts are especially heavy in a field such as intercultural communication, whose major thrusts are just beginning to be clarified. The first academic friend who seriously challenged me to develop an expertise in international and intercultural communication was Robert T. Oliver. My developing interest in communication at the international and intercultural levels received many insights from his work. William Howell dared to recommend and promote the study of international and intercultural communication for the speech communication profession at a time before it was popular to do so. He has also consistently sought a broad integration of various interdisciplinary approaches for the study of intercultural communication.

Edward Stewart, for whom much of the material in *The Cultural Dialogue* is but a modest footnote, has gone further conceptually than perhaps anyone else in outlining how intercultural communication should be studied seriously. Many of the concepts explored in this book have been suggested by Stewart himself. David Hoopes, a practitioner-friend, has sought for the last several years to stress the divergent interests of theory and practice in intercultural communication.

His leaning toward the practical orientations does not diminish their relationship to the theoretical aspects of intercultural communication. Finally, by his life style, his writing, and his insights, Jack Condon has left me envious of his thorough understanding of the various dimensions of intercultural communication.

The systematic, scholarly advice and assistance which Houghton Mifflin provides its authors from colleagues in one's field is most rewarding. Among the scholarly reviewers for *The Cultural Dialogue* who have provided varying measures of assistance have been Nemi Jain, LaRay Barna, Kenneth Bryson, Jess Yoder, Terri Elliott, and most important, Sharon Ruhly and Eileen Newmark. The last two persons have advised me particularly well. Their insights have played a very important role in the completed manuscript.

Since my ideas have been tested with various other colleagues and students, many thanks are also due them for forcing me constantly to reconsider the central focus of intercultural communication, its limits, and its parameters. So often, they have made me realize how little I know even now, how many sources I still need to read, and how many more intercultural experiences I need to undergo. It becomes clear that *The Cultural Dialogue* becomes mostly a synthesis of the insights of others. Nevertheless, I am hopeful that these insights will prove useful and challenging.

Contents

Preface

Men and women have been communicating culturally through time and space since the Ice Age. Culture and communication are both ongoing and inseparable processes—anthropologist Clifford Geertz states that without humans, there would be no culture, but without culture, there would be no humans. In this sense, we have literally created ourselves. As builders and users of symbols and tools, we have separated ourselves dramatically from other animal species. We engage in social discourse and build our culture. We act upon and shape our culture through our ability to communicate. We communicate both unconsciously and deliberately when we seek to influence the beliefs, attitudes, values, and behavior of others. Whenever we communicate, we rely entirely on our cultural background. We tend to be more successful interculturally when we understand and appreciate the special character of members of other cultural groups and other cultures as a whole.

It is the principle of similarities and differences on which much of intercultural and crosscultural communication rests. Intercultural communication can be defined simply as that interpersonal communication on the individual level between members of distinctly different cultural groups. Crosscultural communication can be defined simply as the collective communication between cultural spokespersons of different cultural groups or between whole cultural groups. This principle of similarities and differences, along with such other issues as control, conflict, technology, cultural stability and change, and cultural imperialism and dependency, all play a major role in establishing and affecting the relationships between communication and culture. Part One will concern itself with such principles and issues.

The role which the components of communication play in any contact between communities or culture is important. Part Two will stress these components. When we seek to isolate a communication event for a detailed analysis, we need to consider how the interacting components work within the event. Chief among all of the components is the message. Messages require focused interaction and function in various ways. They powerfully affect our cultural communication. Their selection and control become a significant factor in relating communication to culture. Other important components of communication include the participants; communication codes, both verbal and nonverbal; and the channels and media of communication.

Cultural components and linkages specifically help to develop the interacting relationships between communication and culture: this is the main subject of Part Three. Such theoretical orientations toward culture as cultural evolutionism, cultural functionalism, cultural history, and cultural ecology allow us to distinguish specific cultural units which interact with communication interculturally and crossculturally. An emphasis on values and value orientations suggests it as the most cultural of cultural forms. Among the most individual aspects of culture, subjective culture is the study of human cognitive processes. Within the emphasis of subjective culture, the role of perception becomes an important element.

In Part Four, we shift from a synthesis of key theories and their applications to an actual cultural dialogue between a group of American and Japanese professionals at an intercultural communication workshop in Japan. This section offers a practical application of many of the theories and examples cited in a rewarding but somewhat difficult intercultural setting. The use of a dialogue between Americans and Japanese offers us an opportunity to see individuals from essentially contrasting cultures interacting.

Both communication and culture are complicated processes. Their interaction is constant, whether by accident or by deliberate plan. Technological advances have made it impossible for us to avoid continuous and intense contact in social interaction within and between cultures. Some of us serve crossculturally as spokespersons. Some of us are already bilingual and bicultural. A few of us can be expected to become multicultural persons—people on the boundary between our cultures and other cultures—in a state of tension between the cultural norms and restrictions imposed upon us by very different cultures in which we are involved. We are likely to be participants in cultural dialogue for most of our lives.

Tho purpose of *The Cultural Dialogue* is not only to provide a humanistic view toward communication theory and practice as an important aspect of our humanness, but more importantly, to place communication, both unplanned and deliberate, within the context of the cultural setting. If we have indeed created ourselves by building cultural structures, those cultural structures and barriers are developed within and between cultures by our ability to communicate. We communicate because our cultures have provided us with the ability to use and make symbols and tools. Culture and communication are always seen in a framework of interaction. This interaction can be called the "said of social discourse." It shapes and molds our cultural dialogue, both with members of our own culture and with members of other cultures.

M.H.P.

Introduction
Basic Concepts in Communication and Culture

It is our nature to communicate. All humans from the beginning of time to the present, and in every culture or geographical grouping and setting, have had the innate ability to communicate. Other living species and certain machines communicate, but they do not necessarily duplicate the quality of human communication. Among living species, we still accept as basic that humans are the only genuine symbol-building, -using, and -manipulating animals, and the only genuine tool-building, -using, and -manipulating animals. Only we can make tools which build tools. Despite recent dramatic scientific discoveries in studying other forms of animal communication, our ability to work with symbols and tools remains unique. Our machines have already demonstrated an ability to think and work faster than we can, but they are set into motion by the original manipulation of humans using our symbol systems.

Several premises emerge. Communication and culture are both processes. Communication, like culture, is a human necessity. Communication always occurs at the human level, both intrapersonally and interpersonally when human interaction is involved. Certain communicative acts are involuntary, causing the communicator never to exercise total control of the communication event. At the same time, culture itself makes it possible for every human being to exert partial control over his or her culture and communication. Often we seek to control or influence the attitudes or behavior of others in a positive or negative way.

Communication and culture are inseparably linked. Both are of primary importance. They become linked through communication within our own cultural setting, and through intercultural communication. Thus, intercultural communication becomes a subset of communication and of culture. Cultural communication occurs interpersonally and collectively.

Culture and communication are processes

Life, culture, and communication are ongoing, changing, and evolving processes without precise beginnings or endings. All such processes may be isolated artificially to study or analyze *as* processes. Still, such processes are essentially part of the long-term history of the individual, the culture, or human history. Most of us develop self-concepts throughout our lives, in the context of the cultural environment around us. Somehow, the total development of our own individual culture and culture at the broadest human levels has played an important part in leading us to our own self-identity. As individuals, we are constantly changing. To paraphrase Heraclitus, a Greek philospher of the sixth century B.C., "You can't step in the same river twice." Such change is almost imperceptible in a minute-to-minute, hour-by-hour, day-by-day basis. Children always worry that they aren't growing or becoming heavier or stronger; adults worry that they are aging too quickly when that actually happens very gradually, as most processes do. No matter what the process, it is ongoing. We constantly create our cultural traditions, norms, and values and pass them on to others through the ongoing process of communication and social discourse.

We communicate whether or not we wish to

We have no choice about whether or not we wish to communicate. When we interact with other humans, we communicate. Intrapersonally, our nervous systems engage us constantly in involuntary communicative actions that help our bodies function biologically and allow us to fulfill our primary mission as symbol-and tool-builders, -users, and -manipulators. While these nonvoluntary communicative actions may be unconscious to us, others may note them and may be consciously influenced in some way. In turn, their consciousness of our unintended communication may lead to conscious communicative feedback or reactive behavior. We are never in total control over a communicative event, partly because it is a part of a longer process, and partly because if we had total control over every situation, we would be gods rather than men and women. Various forces are at work to prevent total control over communicative behavior. The Watzlawick/Beaven statement (1967:5) is sensible and persuasive, especially in the interpersonal setting: "In the presence of another, all behavior is communicative." Watzlawick and Beaven did not say that all behavior is only communicative, but that behavior consists of everything a person does in every situation in which the smallest element of interaction can take place. This interaction includes voluntary actions and symbol manipulation, as well as involuntary actions. The level of perception may be very small, but at least a minimum amount of awareness must be present for interpersonal communication to take place. All the communicators in a given event, especially on the interpersonal level, can be influenced both by voluntary manipulation of symbols or actions of one communicator, and by his or her involuntary actions. At the same time, the recipients of the message can also influence the initial communicator.

Ruesch and Bateson (1951:5-6) stress that communication refers not only to verbal, explicit, and intentional transmission of messages. They conceptualize communication as including all those processes by which people influence one another, based on the premise that all actions and events have communicative aspects as soon as they are perceived by another human being. The premise implies that such perception changes the information which an individual possesses and therefore also influences that individual. Ruesch and Bateson accept not only the inevitability of communication whenever humans interact, but also its essentially influential nature. In Western studies of communication, the conscious, intended, and persuasive influence has always been a prime consideration. Most communication at the interpersonal level is two-way, or circular, in orientation. This implies the effect of feedback to the sender's message, and may be multidirectional, with an ebb and flow in interaction constantly taking place. Like the initial message, the feedback may be provided unintentionally and unconsciously, or with the deliberate attempt to influence the initial message-sender. Even interpersonally, feedback may be minimal, sometimes because a monologue may be occurring instead of a dialogue. Although we are most interested in dialogue, as the book title suggests, monologue is also important. Especially at the collective level of communication, monologue reduces the opportunity for feedback or makes it formal and ritualized.

The preceding statements lead us to two different but complementary definitions of communication. Based on the Watzlawick and Beaven statement, slightly modified, that "in the [perceived] presence of another, all behavior is communicative," we can identify it as an ongoing, unconscious, unplanned interaction. At the same time, taking the statement of Ruesch and Bateson, or the statement of Gerald Miller: "In the main, communication has as its central interest those behavioral situations in which a source transmits a message to a receiver(s) with conscious intent to affect the latter's behaviors" (1966:92), we can also define communication as focused, planned, purposeful, instrumental interaction. We can see that intercultural communication often fits the first definition because it is often an extension of interpersonal communication which has aspects of being highly spontaneous and often unplanned. Crosscultural communication, however, seems to be more likely an aspect of the purposeful, instrumental communication identified in the second definition. While intercultural communication involves much two-way interaction, crosscultural communication has more of a collective element to it, in which the interaction is more likely to be one-way, from a cultural spokesperson to another, or where an entire culture is interacting in some way with an entirely different culture.

Condon and Yousef approach communication functionally. That is, they ask in what ways communication chiefly works. They list six such functions: small talk, relating and receiving information, cartharsis or tension release, ritual, affective (emotional) communication, and instrumental communication (1973:29-32). If we evaluate these functions on the basis of the two definitions of communication proposed above (spontaneous, unplanned communication and purposeful, planned communication), we note that elements of both definitions are possible in each function. Predominantly, however, we are likely to say that small talk, tension release, and affective communication more closely characterize the first definition, while relating and receiving information, ritual, and instrumental communication more closely demonstrate the second one. The view which we have taken throughout this text is that much communication is accidental and unplanned. At the same time, much communication is purposeful and planned. Both types of communication play a regular role in our lives.

We act upon culture through communication

Culture is often defined as the traditions, customs, norms, beliefs, values, and thought-patterning which are passed down from generation to generation. Implicit, too, in a definition of culture is the ability to *control* one's environment at least to a partial extent. As humans, we never can control our cultural setting entirely, but the very nature of culture is that it consists of those characteristics which make us truly human within a specific social setting. Thus, although all humans are normally blessed with the same biological characteristics, it is our specific culture which allows us to determine partially how we will utilize normal biological functions. For example, all normal men and women have the innate ability to eat, sleep, move, and undertake other bodily functions. It is culture, however, that teaches us how to manipulate our biological environment to make it our cultural environment also. While animals react to culture, we act creatively upon it.

Communication and culture are so closely bound together that virtually all human social interaction is culturally linked. Even when we engage unconsciously or consciously in intra- or interpersonal communication, our own cultural background affects all of our actions and reactions. We have relatively little choice about much of our cultural heritage and background: we carry our cultural baggage with us and cannot isolate ourselves from our cultural roots. Still, it is possible either by accident or through design, for children to be moved entirely out of the culture into which they were born, and into a totally new culture. They may never recognize that they were once members of an alien culture. Biologically, such children inherit certain traits which will affect their cultural development, but the new cultural environment itself may be more important in such a case. The adult who seeks to drop old cultural habits to take on new ones can rarely do so completely, especially if "culture penetrates to the entire roots of one's nervous system," as Edward Hall argues in *The Hidden Dimension* (1966). Since a major aspect of cultural transmittal does include the passing down of cultural traits, it is clear that many of these contributions affect the individual largely unconsciously.

It is a given fact that all humans possess a similar potential for complementary communicative and cultural development. These developments are always affected by many factors. Culture transcends time and space. The age in which a person lives, the locality, the climate, the geography, and many other factors deeply influence the way he or she communicates as a cultural being.

The rich variety of the human character evolving in different time sequences and localities is a feature which both unites us and pulls us apart. Many studies have illustrated that the more that people have in common with each other, the less likely they are to suffer serious breakdowns in communication or cultural distortion. Unfortunately, despite the closest personal and cultural affinities, communication breakdowns and cultural distortion continue to be frequent. When the differences among members of distinct cultures become intensified, it is no wonder that greater tensions develop.

Our sophisticated modern world has potentially reduced itself to McLuhan's "global village" by the rapid expansion and distribution of communication networks such as the telephone, communication satellites, and jet airplanes. Generally, we are unable to communicate personally with all other humans alive today. Nevertheless, it is now possible to communicate collectively with more people in the world simultaneously than existed in the entire world a few centuries ago. It is estimated that the 1976 presidential debates were viewed by 100 million Americans and many other millions in 105 additional countries. As more and more control is exerted over communication and culture through the human applications of technology, an understanding of communication and culture and their linkages becomes of paramount importance. Throughout *Cultural Dialogue* we shall concern ourselves with these interrelationships.

References

Condon, John C., and Fathi Yousef, 1975. *An Introduction to Intercultural Communication.* Indianapolis: Bobbs-Merrill.

Hall, Edward, 1966. *The Hidden Dimension.* New York: Doubleday.

Miller, Gerald R., 1966. "On Defining Communication: Another Stab." In *Journal of Communication.* 16.

Ruesch, Jurgen, and Gregory Bateson, 1951. *Communication: The Social Matrix of Psychiatry.* New York: Norton.

Watzlawick, Paul, and Janet Beaven, 1967. "Some Formal Aspects of Communication." In *The American Behavioral Scientist*, April, 4-8.

Part One
Fundamental Issues in Intercultural Communication

In order to link communication and culture, one must understand a series of critical issues involved. These issues will be developed throughout the book and represent a few essential elements of which any student of culture and communication should be aware. The emphasis of Chapters 1 and 2 will be an exploration of these issues, and throughout the book we will return to the issues as they help to clarify communication and culture interacting.

Central to the study of communication among members of different cultures is the *principle of similarities and differences*. All cultural groups share certain traits but differ enough so that we can describe the world as being made up of many distinct cultures rather than just a single culture. This is not to deny the possibility of an emerging world culture. If all cultures were precisely the same in all their characteristics, we would not need to consider the important study and practice of intercultural communication.

A second issue is the *principle of conflict in communication and culture*. Whether or not we wish to accept the Biblical notion of the prototype parents, Adam and Eve, and their great fall from divine grace, almost every theory of the development of humanity includes the idea that we seem constantly to be in conflict. If all communication were perfectly conducted, we would have the state of ideal harmony. This, however, is a fantasy: there is constant conflict within the culture itself between those who seek absolute control over others so that their interpretation of culture will dominate, and those who wish to interpret their culture differently.

A third issue is the *principle of communicative and cultural control.* Control within a culture leads to the consideration of a fourth issue. This is the effect which *technology* has on culture and on social discourse. Technology, in fact, becomes an overriding issue of the twentieth century.

A fifth issue is *cultural stability and cultural change.* It is often discussed in terms of the ultimate survival of the culture. A culture which maintains absolute stability is much like the culture in which total assimilation is required. Absolute stability also leads to atrophy and deterioration. As culture is process-oriented, some change is regularly necessary. A culture experiencing too drastic a change loses its own potential for survival.

A sixth significant and related issue is *cultural imperialism and cultural dependency.* Members of a culture or society often seek to assure their own survival and that of their culture by a forced extension of the culture beyond the normal boundaries of time and space. When such groups attempt to recreate the direct or indirect adaptation of their own cultural norms, such efforts lead also to the forced dependence upon the dominant culture by others who must accept the dominant cultural norms.

All of these issues—*similarities and differences, conflict, control, technology, cultural stability and change, and cultural imperialism and dependency*—involve important cultural and communicative links, both at the interpersonal-intercultural levels, and at the collective-crosscultural levels.

CHAPTER 1

Similarities and Differences,
Conflict and Control

In this chapter, we will explore more fully three issues which are important to the study of communication and its relationship to culture, especially as it affects communication between individual members of different cultures or between individuals of different cultures in the collective crosscultural sense. These issues are *the principles of similarities and differences, conflict and communicative and cultural control.* These issues (and others to be discussed in Chapter 2) will be discussed as they relate to communication in different cultural settings. They are important as they relate to specific communication components within and between specific cultures. The communication event can be seen as a total culture communicating, or as a major communicating situation of the culture itself. The culture's messages, its communicators, its codes by which the messages are presented and interpreted, and its channels or media serve as other important communication components.

The fundamental issues can also be viewed in the context of major aspects of culture, including such cultural components as perceptions, stereotypes, prejudices, beliefs, norms, values, and thought-patterns.

Major reasons for studying intercultural communication

Edward Stewart (1974a) calls the principle of similarities and differences the central focus for the study of intercultural communication. If we lived in a simple and isolated society, we would be constricted in the context of the norms, traditions, and values of that single culture. The heavily technological thrust of the modern world, however, has made it possible for us to deal with members of other cultures regularly, and for spokespersons of our culture to deal normally with the spokespersons of other cultures. Today, the media can bring the simplest societal culture into our home and can take the most advanced culture back to the simple culture by way of the transistor radio. We sometimes believe that distant cultural groups are strange, wrong, or exotic; they simply may be different.

Stewart suggests that the value of similarities, rather than differences, is considered so important that it has been one of the basic assumptions in American thought, social life, and communication. We tend to think that the more similar two persons are, the better they should communicate, whereas differences hinder communication and may promote communication breakdown. Stewart stresses that in some cultures, differences may be assumed necessary for communication to take place, with its success measured not by agreement and conformity, but by the opposite. Stewart claims that "it is on this issue of differences, either naturally or by acquisition, that intercultural communication rests its claim for identity." By focusing on the actual or perceived cultural contrasts and on the communicative contrasts between members of different cultures, Stewart suggests that intercultural communication becomes a most urgent extension of human communication itself (1974a: 4-5).

In a way, both the "typical" American and the "typical" Japanese, if such persons can be found, are highly ethnocentric. Many Americans think that their national cultural characteristics are so extraordinary that all foreigners wish to become Americans or to adopt our customs. It is true that a broad cultural adaptation of American customs and values has occurred in many other cultures. Part of the reason for this cultural transfer has been an admiration of American technology. The very notion of an *American* way of life in contrast to Canadian, Mexican, or Latin American, is itself ethnocentric. On the other hand, in their ethnocentricity, the Japanese tend to think that their national cultural character is so unique that it can't be copied adequately. Many of them hasten to accept our cultural patterns when dealing with

Americans rather than insisting, as Americans do, that we learn their patterns. This may be the result of the importance in Japanese culture of the value of harmonious relations.

At the conclusion of the Japanese/American cultural dialogue reported in Part Four, the comment was made and echoed by the Japanese participants that they expected far more contrasts in our two communicative styles than actually occurred. The similarities became more evident than the differences because the four Japanese participants had become highly Westernized, and the four Americans had regular contact with Japanese participants. As a group, there were many similarities to compensate for the differences. Still, the differences were sometimes very clear. Based on a lengthy study of Japanese and American communicative styles, Dean Barnlund has concluded: "In short, the differences are so sharp across a wide set of attributes that it is hard to avoid the conclusion that these cultures are nearly exact opposites" (1974:55). Had there been no significant bicultural differences for the Japanese and Americans to explore through their dialogue, there would have been no special need for the dialogue as an intercultural communication workshop.

"Communication" and "culture" as explicit Western and implicit Eastern terms

The need to define and study communication and culture explicitly is essentially Western, and even more essentially characteristic of the United States. When the study of rhetoric or persuasive communication began seriously in the pre-Christian Egyptian, Greek, and Roman eras, it was believed so important that it was treated separately from other important topics, such as ethics and politics. The Greek and Roman writers wrote directly and widely about the dominant role of oral communication for the societies of their day. This trend has been followed by other Western writers interested in communication and persuasion. In the ancient East, the great philosophers consistently interwove implicit concepts about these subjects in their writings. Robert Oliver (1971) suggests that both ancient Western and Eastern cultures accepted the importance of communication and persuasion. In the West, the subjects were considered so important that they had to be treated separately; in the East they were considered so significant that they had to be subsumed in the context of other important writing.

Oliver points to several basic differences in the approach to communication in the early Western and Eastern cultures. In ancient Western cultures, the purpose of discourse was to promote either the welfare of the speaker or his audience (at that time, both speakers and their audiences were essentially male). In ancient Eastern cultures, such as those developing in India and China, the purpose was to promote harmony. This difference caused Western writers to emphasize a highly personal communication event with stress on the individuality of the speaker and members of the audience. The message in this tradition was marked with argumentative and persuasive fervor, and was conducted with much emphasis on analytical and logical development. The notion of individuality in the Western tradition led to a belief in the equal potential of anyone who wished to speak, and frowned upon selecting a stand-in for important speeches. This Western stress on individuality finds its culmination in contemporary North American cultures today where perhaps a chief cultural value is the role of the individual (1971:1-11).

At the same time, the ancient Eastern tradition sought a depersonalized communication event, in which efforts were made to assure the audience that nothing in the message was original, but emanated from higher authority. The message was carefully ritualized and avoided the appearance of any persuasive fervor. The Asians, and particularly the ancient Chinese, emphasized more strongly than their Western counterparts the dual and reciprocal responsibility of speakers and listeners. They valued authority and analogy to the exclusion of formalized logical processes as the means of persuasion. They generally believed that silence, should be observed when nothing important needed to be said. Since the message more clearly stressed speakers' characters than their actions, the ancient Eastern speakers and writers held strictly to the tradition that opinion formation was primarily the responsibility of the elderly or those in authority: individuals had to earn the right to speak. Oliver concludes that the focal points of an early Asian theory of communication and persuasive discourse contrasted significantly with the focal points toward the same subjects by the early Western speakers and writers. He writes that the early ancient Eastern rhetorics "reflect a society, a philosophy, and a view of individuality that are constituents of the culture of that part of the world. Their theories of communication are an integral part of their ways of thinking and of living" (1971:258-272; 1-11).

Today in Western societies, especially in the United States, the study of communication, and specifically the study of interpersonal, oral, and mass communication, has become a very important endeavor. The study of intercultural communication as a subset of communication in general is a relatively recent phenomenon. As Stewart has suggested, Americans are taken up with the importance of communication broadly studied, and we like to stress the similarities in communication rather than the differences. In contrast, the modern Japanese have not even had terms, until recently, for such ideas as *communication apart from language*, or *culture apart from nation*, or *intercultural communication*.

In commenting on contrasting Japanese and American communicative styles today, Dean Barnlund views many contemporary Japanese cultural characteristics as parallel to those which Oliver has cited about ancient Asian cultures such as Taoism, Buddhism, Hinduism, and Confucianism. Although cultural changes are occurring, partly because of an increased Western influence, Barnlund suggests that contemporary Japanese still place the highest value on preserving the harmony of the social group. Personality is seen as a pattern of meeting real expectations, and personal strength is considered an aspect of group solidarity. Silent introspection is more highly regarded than public eloquence. Independent acts are considered potentially disruptive of social relations. The expression of strongly argumentative feelings, especially negative ones, is carefully avoided. Relationships are governed by many social and ritualistic conventions. On the other hand, Barnlund notes that Americans stress individuality, the ability to stand alone, public confrontation, personality as the emerging character of the individuality, the free expression of personally persuasive feelings, and the logical and analytical articulation of ideas in public (1974:86-96).

Barnlund suggests that when members of the two cultures engage in communication biculturally, some of the differing communicative styles clash sharply. The Japanese tend to feel the occurrence of a forced invasion of their private selves, while the Americans feel that they are cast in a pointless and obscure ritual. Barnlund compares the two communicative styles: "Insistence on full disclosure, and physical closeness, and argumentative discourse to a Japanese may appear naive and an abuse of privacy—a threat to continued relationships. On the other hand, insistence on formal niceties, on cautious exposure of positions, on physical reserve, and avoidance of disagreement may to an American appear to be mere artifice, time-consuming maneuvering, and the avoidance of honesty" (1974:86-96).

Persons from either culture who would tend to be most successful in communicating biculturally would seem to be those who are on the boundary of their own culture, in a sense, "multicultural" persons. They can cross back and forth more easily between the dominant aspects of both cultures than can more rigid, culturally bound persons. In part too, Barnlund believes that effective cultural dialogue between such contrasting cultures results from the ability to get in touch with each other, by learning to know and feel what others know and feel. To gain an empathy for other cultures, especially distinctly different ones, Barnlund insists that people must be willing to search for the truth about themselves in the context of their own cultures. By knowing themselves and their own cultures well, persons interested in effective cultural dialogue will have better perceptions of the similarities which unite members of different cultures, and the dissimilarities which cause stumbling blocks for effective intercultural communication (Barnlund, 1974:86-96).

A balanced cultural theory of similarities and differences is needed

It is just as incorrect to believe that cultural and communicative differences are of no significance as it is to believe that all such differences are insurmountable. Such a belief leads to the notion that effective intercultural communication can never take place. It is probably true, as Condon and Yousef suggest, that there probably is no real universal communicator, or one who can always communicate effectively no matter what the cultural time or place (1975:252). Nevertheless, it is inherent in the study and effective practice of intercultural communication that we learn and apply a potential balance between the two opposites, similarities and differences. One such balanced viewpoint is expressed by an influential member of an African culture who has been influenced by Western viewpoints. In an address in 1961, Julius Nyerre, Prime Minister of Tanzania, spoke before the United Nations General Assembly as a cultural representative of his own national culture, and more broadly as a cultural representative person for black African culture. His stress on what he considered key similarities among persons and the different methods for reaching common goals is strikingly well stated. His statement provides his thought on the important concept of similarities and differences:

The basis of our actions, internal and external, will be an attempt, an honest attempt, to honor the dignity of man. We believe that all mankind is one, that the physiological differences between us are unimportant in comparison with our common humanity. We believe that black skin or white, straight or curly hair, differences in the shape of our bodies, do not alter or even affect the fact that each one of us is part of the human species and has a part to play in the development of mankind. We believe that differences in our religions or our political ideologies may cause difficulties for our small minds, but do not, to our way of thinking, affect the right of every individual to be treated as a man, with dignity and honor. . . .

We believe, in fact, that the individual man and woman is the purpose of society. All great philosophies in the world do agree on this simple statement. The way they differ is how to carry out this principle in actual practice. And we believe that every country, because of the differences of history, the differences of other circumstance, is trying in a different way to organize itself in a manner that suits itself in carrying out this principle. We do not believe that on this matter an ideal solution has been found anywhere in the world . . . .

We care very much about the future of humanity; but we do not believe that the present divisions of the world are between the good and the bad. They are not even divisions based on the issues of tomorrow, that is, the relationship between the "haves" and the "have nots" of the world. The automatic assumption that one or the other of the contending major groups of States is always right, or always wrong, cannot bear examination. We believe that the propaganda which is directed at making humanity believe this proposition is a most hideous opium. (1970:824-833).

Prime Minister Nyerre's assessment stresses cultural, societal, and political relationships. The principle of similarities and differences affects all such relationships. All that follows is connected.

Conflict in communication and culture is deeply rooted

A major construct in communication and culture has been that conflict is inherently present. While it is not accurate to state that all communication and culture are oriented in conflict, there is considerable logic to Herbert Simons's assumption that communication is the means by which conflict gets socially defined, the instrument through which influence in conflicts is exercised, and the vehicle by which partisans or third parties may prevent, manage, or resolve conflicts (1974:3). The discussion of cultural conflict leads to our later considerations of control, technology, stability and change, and imperialism and dependency. As conflict relates to each of these later issues, it also assists in defining them as cultural characteristics. Since much conflict is also tied to real or perceived differences, the first issue is also joined.

We can profitably ask whether conflicts in communication and culture are deviations from the norm, or communication breakdowns, as they are often called, or whether conflict is at least necessary and inevitable as a part of general social and cultural structure. Simons contends that those social scientists who accept the first position assume "systems perspective" or "social control" orientations, and those who accept the second position believe that conflict is "influence-oriented" or "actor-oriented" because conflicts help the individual actor in the conflict to realize his or her individual interests. He states: "From a systems perspective, conflicts are to be prevented, resolved, or controlled: the emphasis is on the similarities that unite individuals, and the chief operating assumption is that scarce resources can be equitably shared and indeed enlarged through cooperative efforts. From the perspective of those with an actor orientation, however, [which he prefers] there are real, not just apparent differences of interest among men, and each combatant must fight for his own share of a limited resource pie" (1974:5). Recent writers on the subject of conflict and its resolution have begun to favor the actor-orientation approach over the systems approach.

Simons defines conflict as that state of a social relationship in which incompatible interests between two or more parties give rise to a struggle between them. This characterizes a major difficulty which occurs regularly in intercultural communication when the parties cannot agree on similarities in language codes, nonverbal patterns, attitudinal, perceptional, value-oriented, and thought-patterning cultural components. Although the systems perspective would insist that some sort of harmony be achieved, in such situations the best sort of solution may be to recognize the irreconcilable differences on certain questions and issues, and to seek harmony on less serious issues or to tolerate them. For example, in the Judeo-Christian dialogue, both sides recognize that while unity may be achieved in the recognition of God as the Maker and Father, there is no reconciliation possible on the question of whether Jesus Christ was the son of God. The message of the Old Testament is acceptable to both groups, but the message of the New Testament is not. The Jewish and Christian members of the dialogue each have different self-identities and interests. They are persuaded so differently on such issues that no final resolution is possible except by total conversion to the other point of view. Such a solution becomes a perfect resolution from one point of view, but may appear to be cultural or religious imperialism to the other point of view.

Early Peace Corps volunteers in communicative and cultural conflict

Lawrence H. Fuchs (1967:235-278) discusses the conflict which involved the early Peace Corps volunteers and their Filipino hosts. The task-oriented Americans saw themselves as change agents, utilizing essentially a systems approach to conflict resolution, and assumed that they would help the Philippine hosts to correct cultural deficiencies. Fuchs indicates that the American officials selected the Philippines for such a large influx of early Peace Corps workers because they believed the Filipinos to be pro-American, and they had already been heavily Westernized. As most of the Americans were assigned to elementary schools, members of the Philippines Bureau of Public Schools suggested that the role of the American educational aides was to "volunteer to speak a sentence with correct English pronunciation. . . . They can help in other ways. The volunteers can build science equipment and begin science clubs" (237).

Fuchs notes that the Americans' idea that culture conflict would be minimal proved very false. The Americans and their Filipino hosts simply did not approach the most important questions concerning human existence from the same cultural perspectives. The volunteers often were not even highly conscious of the "American emphasis on independence, task orientation, and personal achievements." Though they believed themselves ready for the experience, many volunteers failed to remember that the Filipinos did not share their belief that humans could control their environment. The volunteers did not understand this sense of pervasive fatalism or recognize the major Filipino notion of dependency and harmony relationships. These relationships within a formalized group emphasize reciprocity of obligation and good will in the basic group, and protection of that group against outsiders. Fuchs writes that "the value of independence in relationships and getting a job done makes us seem self-reliant, frank, empirical, hardworking, and efficient to ourselves. To Filipinos, the same behavior sometimes makes us seem to be unaware of our obligations, insensitive to feelings, unwilling to accept established practices, and downright aggressive" (242-243).

The volunteers often expressed extreme frustration and sometimes hostility, because it became obvious to them that the tasks which they came to accomplish so earnestly did not really matter to the Filipinos. Their presence mattered, but the Filipinos were happiest with the volunteers who learned that their role as change agents was less important than having a pleasurable time with their hosts. Additionally, the widespread fatalism of the barrio was expressed in the lack of emotion at the death of small children, the persistent and nearly universal beliefs that ghosts and spirits control life and death, and the failure to keep promises and appointments. The Filipinos were not concerned with the job because they believed that fate governs all human existence. The successful volunteers eventually began to accept and enjoy the individual Filipinos for what they were, without attempting to change their values to conform with what had appeared earlier as superior American values (244-247).

Many volunteers failed to reach a final stage of toleration and acceptance for the Filipino value system, and possibly left the Peace Corps early. We can speculate that they went to the Philippines believing that they could prevent, resolve, or control the value conflicts between the Filipinos and themselves so that the Filipinos would accept the new and "correct" ways of life. Those volunteers who moved through the conflict to acceptance or toleration of contrasting values may be seen as moving toward the actor-orientation. They may have realized that the conflict between values was so great that it made no sense to try to reconcile them except through acceptance and toleration. No doubt, too, those volunteers who reached a genuine empathy with their hosts were forced to assume, perhaps unconsciously at times, such Filipino characteristics as dependence within a group, shame in the presence of authority figures and strangers, deference to superiors and an assumption of deference by their own inferiors, a veiling of true opinions so that harmony would be promoted, and a "never-mind" philosophy of life. New conflicts were created for the acclimated volunteers to Filipino values when they came into contact with other volunteers with a change-agent orientation, or with Peace Corps officials caught rigidly in the American value system. Significant culture shock could be expected to affect them even upon their return home to the dominant American value system, where Filipino values were no longer welcomed.

Almost all of the key issues under consideration in the text can be found at work in the Peace Corps illustration offered by Fuchs. More recent writers on the Peace Corps' experience stress that where Peace Corps volunteers expected vast differences between cultural customs, norms and values, and psychologically prepared for these differences, they generally faced less communicative and cultural conflict than those going to apparently similar but actually very dissimilar societies. The Peace Corps experience in Jamaica offers an important example: outwardly the culture appears to be very similar to American culture, especially because of the long-term British influence there. Nevertheless, when one moves beyond the most superficial similarities, the difficulties caused by very deep differences in communicative and cultural patterns are marked and significant.

Communicative and cultural control reflects the dominant condition of humans

The control of communication and culture closely correlates with other fundamental issues in developing relationships between communicative and cultural components. In the Introduction, the point was made that we always are communicating whether or not we wish to, that in the *perceived* presence of another we always are communicating, and that communicators have only partial control over their interaction. Various outside forces prevent absolute control. Still, the higher the status of the communicator and the more complex the communication setting, the more likely will control pervasively affect communication. Norbert Wiener (1966:25-35), one of the original coiners of the modern use of the term "cybernetics," calls it the *science of communication and control*, with an emphasis on automatic control. He suggests that the seventeenth and early eighteenth centuries were the age of clocks; and *the twentieth century is the age of communication and control*. The concept of people the symbol-builders, -users, and -manipulators, implies especially in Western tradition that people are "the measure of all things." We have already noted in the Peace Corps illustration that control over communication and cultures in Eastern societies and throughout much of the world is assigned to fate or to the supernatural. Today, the metaphysics of the twentieth century is not the supernatural nor the human being, but the technology which humans have created, and the control which this technology exerts both on communication and culture.

Clifford Geertz (1973:44-51) proposes two specific ways of viewing culture. The first proposal challenges our usual definition that culture consists of the complexes of concrete behavior patterns—customs, usages, traditions, and habit clusters. Instead, he suggests that culture may be seen as a set of control mechanisms—plans, recipes, rules, and instructions (or what engineers and computer experts call programs) for the governing of behavior. The second concept is that humans are precisely the animals most desperately dependent upon such extragenetic, outside-the-skin control mechanisms, such cultural programs, for ordering their behavior.

Geertz notes that one of the most significant facts about us may be that we all begin with the natural equipment to live 10,000 alternatives for the kinds of life we live, but finish having lived only one. He suggests that the "control mechanism" view of culture begins with the assumption that human thought is basically both social and public—that its natural habitat is the backyard, the marketplace, and the town square. In these settings, Geertz claims that it is in the traffic of "significant symbols," words for the most part, but also gestures, drawings, musical sounds, mechanical devices like clocks, or natural objects which help to impose meaning upon experience, where control on the members of culture occurs. Except as new symbols are created, generally the members of culture utilize those symbols already available to the culture which can be expected to remain with the culture for a long period of time. Thus, how individual members of a culture communicate either within their culture or with members of other cultures is initially controlled for them to a large extent by the cultural setting (44-45).

As the second support for his argument, Geertz asserts that:

undirected by culture patterns—organized systems of significant symbols—man's behavior would be virtually ungovernable, a mere chaos of pointless acts and exploding emotions, his experience virtually shapeless. Culture, the accumulated totality of such patterns, is not just an ornament of human existence but—the principal basis of its specificity—an essential condition for it (45-46).

Geertz continues: ". . . by submitting himself to governance by symbolically mediated programs for producing artifacts, organizing social life, or expressing emotions, man determined, if unwittingly, the culminating stages of his own biological destiny. Quite literally, though quite inadvertently, he created himself"(46). All normal men and women have the ability to use symbols; the symbols they choose to use are culturally determined. All normal men and women are able to develop linguistic codes such as language, but which language they develop depends upon their culture. In short, both communication and culture cannot exist without control.

We will frequently develop the theme that communicative and cultural control exists in almost all of the relationships which link the two concepts of communication and culture together. A variety of specific examples illustrating these relationships will be provided. Perhaps most important in the twentieth century is the impact of technology both upon communication and culture. Technological control may be among the dominant and more frightening aspects in the development of future cultural communicators. Since technology is both irreversible and pervasive, its continued development promises vast new opportunities and problems for those seeking to communicate effectively in and between cultures, and for the cultural spokespersons between larger cultural groups. Control often has positive effects for the controller, but far less positive effects for the controlled. The manipulations of technology increase the tensions between benefits and detriments to communication and culture, and make even more persistent its presence in all communicative and cultural settings.

Summary

In Chapter 1, we have explored the opportunities and problems created by similarities and differences, conflict, and control as they affect communication and culture. We have suggested that similarities and differences constitute a chief reason for studying intercultural communication. As an aspect of this principle, we have noted that the terms "communication" and "culture" are themselves explicit Westernized terms of the United States, but are implicit in Eastern traditions. We have stressed that conflict is deeply rooted both in communication and culture. Some writers argue that conflict is to be avoided or corrected, while others suggest that it is inherently present in all cultural communication and that it may serve a positive as well as a negative function. In the example of the early Peace Corps volunteers, we have noted that they were affected both by different perceptions of similarities and differences between themselves and the Filipinos, and by contrasting views toward conflict. Just as conflict appears to be a dominant aspect of humanity and its social intercourse through culture, control also appears to be a fundamental aspect of culture. In fact, an important definition of culture is suggested by the nature of control over the members of the culture. Communication also is constantly being controlled, and even more so in the twentieth century through technology.

References

Barnlund, Dean, 1974. "The Public Self and the Private Self in Japan and the United States." In *Intercultural Encounters with Japan: Communication—Contact and Conflict.* Edited by John C. Condon and Mitsuko Saito. Tokyo: Simul Press.

Condon, John C. and Fathi Yousef, 1975. *An Introduction to Intercultural Communication.* Indianapolis: Bobbs-Merrill.

Fuchs, Lawrence H., 1967. "The Role and Communication Task of the Change Agent—Experiences of the Peace Corps Volunteers in the Philippines." In *Communication and Change in the Developing Countries.* Edited by Daniel Lerner and

Wilbur Schramm. Foreword by Lyndon B. Johnson. Honolulu: East-West Center Press.

Geertz, Clifford, 1973. *The Interpretation of Culture.* New York: Basic Books.

Nyerre, Julius K., 1970. "All Mankind Is One." In *Sow the Wind, Reap the Whirlwind: Heads of State Address the United Nations.* Edited by Michael H. Prosser. New York: Morrow.

Oliver, Robert T., 1971. *Communication and Culture in Ancient India and China.* Syracuse: Syracuse University.

Simons, Herbert, 1974. "The Carrot and Stick as Handmaidens of Persuasion in Conflict Situations." In *Perspectives on Communication in Social Conflict.* Edited by Gerald R. Miller and Herbert W. Simons, Englewood Cliffs, New Jersey: Prentice-Hall.

Stewart, Edward C., 1974a. "An Overview of the Field of Intercultural Communication." Mimeograph released by Intercultural Communication Network. Pittsburgh: University of Pittsburgh.

Wiener, Norbert, 1966. "Cybernetics." In *Communication and Culture: Readings in the Codes of Human Interaction.* Edited by Alfred Smith. New York.

CHAPTER 2

Technology, Stability and Change, Imperialism and Dependency

We will continue our discussion of fundamental issues by exploring more extensively the nature of technology's impact on culture, stability and change, and imperialism and dependency. According to such writers as Jules Henry, Jacques Ellul, and B.F. Skinner, technology may be thought of as the dominant feature of the twentieth century. They feel that we are in a period of technological determinism.

The key value of any culture is survival. As cultural norms, stability and change will be seen as being in constant conflict. This conflict is made clearer in the notion of Margaret Mead that three cultural types exist: postfigurative culture, which is traditional and grandfather-oriented; cofigurative culture, which is contemporary and peer-oriented; and prefigurative culture, which is yet to come and unknown in its orientation. We will question whether excessive stability or change can be avoided. A final major issue consists of the relationship between cultural imperialism and dependency, and whether the communication of culture is inherently imperialistic.

Technology is the metaphysics of the twentieth century

Just as such institutions as education, the church, labor, government, and the family have been major factors of culture and cultural transmission both in the past and the present, so too is technology a dominant cultural factor today. We can recall Ernst Junger's poignant post-World War I reminder that "technology is the real metaphysics of the twentieth century" (quoted in Ellul, 1964). In *The Technological Society*, Jacques Ellul expands Junger's notion by suggesting that the twentieth-century technique has overcome culture as civilization, culture as institution, culture as a specific society, and culture at the personal level. He argues that technique is civilization; it has absorbed institutions; it is the universal language; it has absorbed the sacred and its messages and mysteries; it is the new god. Ellul contends that technique has become the totalitarianism of the state. It has rendered democratic doctrines obsolete. It has created mass people and mass culture. It has caused the disappearance of community. With its mass orientation, technique and technology have left no place for the individuals who are isolated from their civilization, their cultures, their institutions, their communities, their families, and themselves (1964).

B. F. Skinner in *Beyond Freedom and Dignity*, Jules Henry in *Culture against Man*, and Ellul all agree on the fundamental principle that technology has become such a force in contemporary life that it has led to the establishment of a worldwide culture in which the important elements affecting human life, time, space, and motion have been so compacted and mutated as to become a worldwide totalitarianism with its own totalitarian propaganda. The nontechnical society or culture cannot expect to compete reasonably with the technical society. Such cultures are caught in a state of psychic mutation, and they collapse in the face of technology. Old values, customs, and norms become obsolete because of technological advances. Every civilization and culture in the past has absorbed and mastered technology, but today the reverse seems true. These authors agree that the great danger of a future culture or state emerging is that *as technology becomes the master, and therefore becomes the ultimate channel and medium of communication, the members of that culture or society will have everything that their hearts desire except their freedom and dignity.* Their cultural and individual life will be entirely pleasant, but completely controlled on a collective basis in a very strong one-way communication. Skinner argues that modern society has already reached the point where such values as freedom and dignity are simply caught in the cultural memory bank, without precise meaning or reality (1971).

Technological progress is irreversible and geometric in development

Ellul contends that in every given civilization or culture, technical progress is irreversible. Further, technical progress tends to advance not arithmetically, but in geometric progression. The meaning of these statements is that except for the arrest and retreat of an entire society, after the introduction of initial technical advances, others must follow. Future technical progress is never in doubt.

The consequences of technical improvement are not always entirely expected. A purely mechanical discovery may have repercussions in the domain of social or organizational techniques. That technical progress occurs according to geometric progression is suggested by the interdependence of the techniques on various aspects of life. Incessant discoveries take place; whole new fields are opened up to technology independently or interdependently. These become a part of the cultural diffusion made possible by other discoveries elsewhere. For example, the discovery of fusion and fission which led to the development of the atomic bomb and nuclear energy was being made in several societies and states at the same time. However, certain states had more techniques available than others, and thus proceeded more quickly (1964).

One set of discoveries leads to another. While some discoveries and techniques are the subject of intense efforts at cultural diffusion by those who possess the cultural or technical capabilities, others are jealously guarded by those who possess them, and jealously sought by those who do not have them. In the sense that cultural and technical diffusion may be unintended, or may produce unintended results, it is unpredictable. Ellul believes that as the technique and technological developments continue to spread, usually from a small group in control to a larger collective group, the role of individuals becomes weakened as the technology absorbs and masters them (1964).

Technology's commandments are "desire and consume!"

Jules Henry indicates that among the outstanding differences between the simple and more complex societies is first, the absence in the latter of what he calls *production-needs complementarity and coincidence*. The simple society generally produces only what is needed, in the quantity and at the time when it is needed. The modern technological society or culture, however, has as its motto "Desire and consume!" This causes a dichotomy also in what he calls a *property ceiling*. Where the simple society has built-in traditions and customs which typically allow its members to gain and hold little material wealth, the modern industrial society not only tends to encourage the acquisition of wealth, but as much accumulation of wealth as possible (1963).

Media and channels are multiplied in order to increase the potential messages which encourage members of the technological society or culture to desire that which they do not really need, at times when they do not need it, and in quantities in excess of their needs. More and more material wealth is accumulated with the notion that "the sky is the limit." When the transistor radio becomes a dominant medium in the simpler society, the medium and its messages powerfully urge the members of that society to begin to approach the material needs and property ceilings of the technological society. Stories are told about many simple cultures where extensive technological items are acquired without sources of energy to operate them (Henry: 1963).

Contemporary society is technologically driven and pathogenically fearful

As adults in today's world, we are the children of the technological society. Contemporary students have been educationally raised by the technological media, such as television. Typically, these students have seen more hours of video-programming before entering college than all of the hours that they have spent in the classroom—including their education from elementary school through college. Henry notes that our modern society, and the society's media, have led us to a feverish quality of life, already suggested by de Tocqueville in the nineteenth century. Henry argues that the *technological society is a driven culture, forced by drives such as expansiveness, competitiveness, individuality, and achievement. At the same time, many of us who are products of such a society believe strongly in values such as gentleness, kindliness, and generosity.* (Henry, 1963:23-25).

There is a constant interplay between the drives and the values of the technological society. This interplay is seen in the tension of our technological channels and media, and their messages. The technological society is always in a state of cultural instability, an uncertainty that Henry suggests: "feeds upon itself, for each new 'truth' becomes a new error, and each new discovery merely opens the door to new uncertainties. If you put together in one culture uncertainty and the scientific method, competitiveness and technical ingenuity, you get a strong new explosive compound which I shall call *technological drivenness*." Henry suggests that America, as a prime example of the technological society, gives a visitor, and even sensitive residents, the feeling of being constantly off-balance and asymmetrical, but the very nature of technology requires such imbalance and asymmetry: "True equilibrium—balance, symmetry, whatever one wishes to call it—is poison to a system like ours" (1963:23-25).

A major form of imbalance in Western society, and Henry believes the most important single factor in American history since the Revolutionary and Civil Wars, is a pathogenic fear of the Soviet Union. In turn, Soviet society is faced by the same fear of us. Each society and its cultural leaders fear that the other society and its leaders are preparing for the destruction of the other. This potential cultural conflict has served as a major theme in both Western and Socialist societies since World War II. The effect spreads crossculturally to allies and competitors of each society so that it has produced a general uneasiness over both time and space. Henry terms it the twentieth-century nightmare which has called forth the creation of greater communications channels and media on both sides, both in terms of more swift transport, especially for the military phases of our societies, and for more effective transmission, storage, and retrieval of information (including information received through spying on each other).

The fear of the other society calls into question the very concept of the chief cultural and societal value, survival. Every aspect of communication within and between the cultures and societies, and especially their advanced technological communications systems, leads to more and more sophisticated attempts to increase the technology for the one society at the expense of the other. Since a second major cultural and societal value is the incorporation of the young into the group, the technological drivenness in each society turns teachers, schools, textbooks, and other media which reach the young into propaganda weapons for the values of that society and against the values of the other.

In this sense, each society seeks cultural imperialism and superiority for its values and drives at the expense of cultural dependency for others who come into the orbit of its influence. Henry suggests that this pathogenic fear forces the young of such societies and cultures to dream of succeeding at any cost, while at the same time facing the nightmare of failure. Such drives and fears also lead the cultural leaders to seek absolute control over cultural and individual thought-patterning. This control in turn leads to an attempt to manipulate communicators, the messages available, the codes used for the messages, and the channels and media used to conduct the messages. Henry defines the technological culture's influence as control over all aspects of communication in the culture itself: "To say that culture 'teaches' puts the matter too mildly. Actually culture invades and infests the mind as an obsession." Henry calls the central emotion in obsession fear, and the central obsession in education fear of failure. In order not to fail, most students in both Western and Socialist societies are willing to believe anything, and not to care whether what they are told is true or false. "Thus one becomes absurd through being afraid; but paradoxically, *only by remaining absurd can one feel free from fear*" (1963:244-251).

Which is more dangerous—cultural stability or change?

At the broadcast level, authors like Daniel Bell and Charles A. Reich view culture as paramount because people construct reality in their own minds, confirming and dramatizing it by behavioral rituals. Bell argues: "Culture has become supreme for two complementary reasons. First, culture has become the most dynamic component of a civilization, outreaching the dynamism of technology itself. . . . Secondly, there has come about in the last fifty years or so a legitimation of this culture impulse; . . . the idea of change and novelty overshadows the dimensions of actual change. . . . Thus our culture has an unprecedented mission. It is an official, ceaseless searching for a new sensibility" (1970:17). Reich sees culture as the true source of revolutionary change since today's politics deal only with the "trivial and ephemeral, and it is only culture that puts in issue the true political questions that confront us." Reich believes that politics, economics, and technology are constrained by existing institutional structures, existing methods of resource mobilization and commitments, and the inertia of the existing balance of interest groups with the panoplies of policy powers, vetoes, and initiatives. In contrast, culture is free to create new rituals of protest, and it dramatizes the real scope of values. Within the realm of culture there is little resistance to expressive symbols and forms, and in effect, cultural abstractions provide a low-risk, flexible, and universal forum where any new value or ritual may seek an audience and may promote itself from obscurity to legitimacy (1971:311).

Nevertheless, B. F. Skinner, an advocate of significant culture designing, warns that even those who wish to revolutionize culture are almost wholly the conventional products of the system which they seek to overthrow. They speak the language, use the logic and science, observe many of the ethical and legal principles, and employ the practical skills and knowledge which their particular society and culture provide them. The designer of the totally new culture is culture-bound, since he or she cannot be entirely free from the predispositions engendered by his or her social environment. To some extent, such cultural revolutionaries must create a world which fits their likes and which will appeal to those who are going to adopt their new culture. These adherents also are necessarily the products of an older culture. Skinner suggests as a definition of culture that "Man is said to differ from the other animals mainly because he is 'aware of his own existence.' He knows what he is doing; he knows that he has had a past and will have a future; he 'reflects on his own nature'; he alone follows the classical injunction 'Know thyself.' Any analysis of human behavior which neglected these facts would be defective indeed" (1971:124,164,190).

While Skinner is a promoter for culture control, he recognizes the futility of attempting to develop a Utopian culture, or a total social design which will become the dominant reason that the members of the culture want it to survive. Basically, Skinner believes that in the real world, the word *Utopian* means *unworkable*. The Utopian culture seeks to remain elitist, small, isolated, and strives for harmonious balance of religion, home, education, work, and government. Eventually, it disintegrates, partly because of its simplicity, smallness, and isolation. Prime examples are the Shakers, a subculture destined to die because a principal value is to remain celibate. Another principle is not to seek converts. Today, the youngest member of the subculture is about sixty years old, and the oldest of less than a dozen remaining members is eighty-five years or more.

Monastic orders of priests and brothers and religious orders of nuns are symbols of Utopian societies. Some flourish, others decay and disintegrate. Their goal is a spiritualized Utopia. In Eastern society, the Buddhist monks are representative. Contrary to the Shakers, such monastic communities do seek to people their monasteries with other followers. Skinner says that the fundamental question in all Utopian designs is, "Would it really work?" He responds that while a traditional culture has been examined and found wanting, and a new version has been set up to be tested and redesigned as circumstances dictate, the utter simplification of the Utopian culture is seldom feasible in the real world; various Utopian designs have been proposed for nearly 2500 years, and most attempts to set them up have been ignominious failures. Still, he believes that the real mistake is to stop trying to build the ideal culture (1971:153-156).

Survival is the key value of culture

Skinner and Nieburg both insist that every culture must seek a balance between stability and change in order to survive. Skinner suggests: "The simple fact is that a culture which *for any reason* induces its members to work for its survival, or for the survival of some of its practices, is more likely to survive. Survival is the only value according to which a culture is eventually to be judged, and any practice that furthers survival has survival value by definition" (1971:36). Nieburg notes that culture represents contradictory functions; as a means of containing chaos and background noise, it maintains arbitrary order. This very order causes it to lose its adaptability, and it becomes vulnerable because of dissidents in the culture or through environmental changes. The very success of a culture helps to initiate fundamental change in the culture itself (1973:81,76).

Nieburg suggests that *the principle of cultural reality lies in the continued legitimacy of any culture in a given population over a period of time.* To constitute socially significant change, the new values must be adopted by a significant number of the population to give it currency and to integrate it into other patterns of culture. Such significant changes in a culture are accomplished by an unheralded process of interaction and exchange of values among individuals and groups. It is seldom possible to recognize the vast cultural changes in customs, traditions, values, and norms until they are already highly ritualized, formal, and open to challenge by others. People wish to change the culture again because, in their judgment as cultural change agents, it has been found wanting (1973:56-57). Nieburg argues that *the natural process of cultural growth is conflict*, that is, relative disorder. Values of the dominant group are always in conflict with those of subjugated groups. While the myth of the culture and its ritual help to hold disorder at bay, new culture forms are always replacing the old ones. Nieburg separates all culture forms into a continuous cycle: passing through alarm, anxiety, interest, exploration, improvisation, ritualization, extinction, and replacement, in turn. This cycle develops because there is a relentless tendency to refresh old culture forms by variation and invention on the one hand, and on the other hand, to work jealously to preserve such old forms (1973:81,76).

Stability and change are in constant conflict

Jules Henry, in his *Culture against Man*, summarizes the essential conflict caused by the need for members of a culture both to struggle for stability and to break free from the bondage which culture offers them: "Creativity is the last thing wanted in any culture because of its potentialities for disruptive thinking; the primordial dilemma of all education derives from the necessity of training the mighty brain of *Homo Sapiens* to be stupid; and . . . creativity, when it is encouraged (as in science in our culture), occurs only after the creative thrust of an idea has been tamed and directed towards socially arrived ends. In this sense then, creativity can become the most obvious conformity" (1963:237). We say to our children—the generation to whom we are attempting to pass down our traditions, customs, norms, and values—that they should be creative. However, total creativity within the cultural setting breeds utter chaos. Henry comments: "Creative cultures have loved the 'beautiful person'—meditative, intellectual, and exalted. As for the creative individual, the history of the great civilizations seems to reveal little about creativity except that it has had an obstinate way of emerging only in gifted individuals, and that it has never appeared in the mass of the people" (261).

In viewing the cultural conflict over stability and change, Henry reasons: " . . . Inherent in the human condition is the fact that we must conserve culture while changing it; that we must always be *more* sure of surviving than of adapting—*as we see it.* Whenever a new idea appears our first concern as *animals* must be that it does not kill us; then, and only then, can we look at it from other points of view. . . ." Henry stresses that in general, early peoples walled off their children from new ideas by educational methods that (largely through fear) narrowed the perceptual sphere so that only traditional ways of viewing the world became thinkable. In this way throughout history, the cultural pattern has been a device for binding the intellect. Henry believes that: "Today, when we think we wish to free the mind so that it will soar, we are still, nevertheless, bound by the ancient paradox, for we must hold our cultures together through clinging to old ideas lest, in adopting new ones, we literally cease to exist" (1963:234).

Three cultural types: postfigurative, cofigurative, and prefigurative

In Culture and Commitment: A Study of the Generation Gap, Margaret Mead observes that the relationship between cultural stability and change can be seen as three cultural types generally present throughout the world in one phase or another: *postfigurative, cofigurative, and prefigurative cultures.* She calls the prototype postfigurative culture the isolated ancient society, the culture in which only the accommodating memories of its members preserve the study of the past: "The voiceless stones, even when they are carved and shaped by the hand of man, can easily be fitted into a revised version of how the world has always been. Genealogists, unembarrassed by documents, condense history, so that the mythological and the recent past flow together." She argues: "To destroy the memory of the past or preserve it in a form that merely reinforces the different present has been a continuous and highly functional adjustment by primitive peoples, even those who have been most historically minded, as they have come to believe that their small group originated in the place where they now live" (1970:16-17).

In essence, Mead suggests that while it is necessary for the continuity of all cultures to depend on the living presence of at least three generations, the postfigurative culture assumes that their culture is unchanging. Members of the older generation express this in their every behavioral act. For such a culture to be perpetuated, the old members were needed to complete the model of what life was:

When the end of life is already known—when the song that will be sung at death, the offerings that will be made, the spot of earth where one's bones will rest are already designated—each person, according to age and sex, intelligence and temperament, embodies the whole culture. . . . Any segment of cultural behavior, when analyzed, will be found to have the same underlying pattern, or the same kind of patterned allowance for the existence of other patterns in that culture. . . . Postfigurative cultures [emphasized] the absence of a realization of change and the successful printing, indelibly, upon each child of the cultural form (1970:2-3).

Mead suggests that the answers to the question "Who am I? What is the nature of my life as a member of my culture; how do I speak and move, eat and sleep, make love, make a living, become a parent, meet my death?" are predetermined for all members of the postfigurative culture. She concludes, "Change there has been, but it has been so completely assimilated that differences between earlier and later acquired customs have vanished in the understanding and the expectations of the people" (1970:4-5). Continuity, cultural identity, changlessness, timelessness, fatalism, a lack of questioning, and a lack of consciousness all seem to be essential characteristics of the postfigurative community. Its effort to survive, whether its members live in isolation or in contact with other changing cultures and communities, depends upon constant real or perceived stability. It is a culture of the past.

In contrast, the "cofigurative society is one in which the prevailing model is the behavior of their contemporaries," rather than the oldest members of the culture. Generally such cultural transmission is not made only from contemporaries to contemporaries without a generation gap, because older members may still be present as role models. Mead suggests that "there is a shared expectation that members of a generation will model their behavior on that of their contemporaries, especially their adolescent age mates." This often occurs in American society when behavior varies from that of parents and grandparents. Each individual successfully embodies a new style, becoming to some extent a model for others of his or her generation. Thus, configuration has its beginnings in breaks from tradition in the postfigurative system. It may be caused by "a catastrophe in which a whole population, but particularly its old members, [become] decimated; or as the result of the development of new" educational and technological methods with which the older members are unacquainted; or as the result of migration to a new location or society where the old members are less valued; in the aftermath of a conquest in which especially the younger members are required to learn the new language and cultural customs of the conqueror; or as a result of religious conversion, where the older members must teach the younger members traditions and values which they never learned themselves as youth; or as a purposeful step in a cultural, social, or political revolution that establishes itself through the introduction of new and different life styles for the young (Mead, 1970:25-26).

The conditions for change in a cofigurative type of culture become more prevalent after the development of high civilization. Access to greater resources makes it possible for members of one society to annex, subjugate, incorporate, enslave, or convert members of other societies, and to control or direct the behavior of the younger generation, sometimes calling for the establishment of a new postfigurative culture within the limits of a few generations (1970:25-26). Specific examples abound in both ancient and modern societies.

Cultural imperialism and dependency both are key elements in the development of cofigurative styles of culture. Mead stresses that in its simplest form, the cofigurative culture is seen in the absence of grandparents: ". . . when there are no grandparents present who remember in the past, shape the experience of the growing child and reinforce, inarticulately, all the unverbalized values of the old culture, . . . the child's experience of his future is shortened by a generation and his links to his past are weakened. . . . The past, once represented by living people, becomes shadowy, easier to abandon and to falsify in retrospect" (1970:34-35).

Cultural conflict is not absent to either the postfigurative or cofigurative culture, but Mead speculatively predicts the emergence of a new cultural form, prefiguration:

As I see it, children today face a future that is so deeply unknown that it cannot be handled, as we are currently attempting to do, as a generation change with cofiguration, within a stable, elder-controlled and parentally modeled culture in which many postfigurative elements are incorporated. . . . For the figure of migration in space (geographical migration), I think we must substitute a new figure, migration in time. . . . Even very recently, the elders could say: "You know, I have been young and you have never been old." But today's young people can reply: "You have never been young in the world I am young in, and you never can be."

Today, suddenly, because all the peoples of the world are part of one electronically based, intercommunicating network, young people everywhere share a kind of experience that none of the elders ever have had or will have. Conversely, the older generation will never see repeated in the lives of young people their own precedented experience of sequentially emerging change. This break between generations is wholly new; it is planetary and universal (1970:48-50).

Calling *communication the true dialogue*, Mead worries that the dialogue between the old postfigurative and even the new cofigurative cultures and the still unknown prefigurative culture, represented by the unborn or newborn child, is seriously endangered before it begins: it has no vocabulary which transcends the old, the new, and the totally unknown. Mead poses what she believes is the key question: What are the new conditions that have brought about the revolt of youth around the world? She posits that it is first the emergence of a world community, where for the first time it is technically possible to be tuned in to any other part of the world through such advances as the transistor radio and thereby to share the common information of modernization and danger:

We cannot say for certain now that at any period in the past there was a single community made up of many small societies whose members were aware of one another in such a way that consciousness of what differentiated one small society from another heightened the self-consciousness of each constituent group. But as far as we know, no such single, interacting community has existed within archaeological time. . . . Most importantly, these changes have taken place almost simultaneously within the lifetime of one generation— and the impact of knowledge of the change is world wide. . . . Men who are carriers of vastly different cultural traditions are entering the present at the same point in time" (1970:54-56).

Mead concludes her speculation thus: "I believe we are on the verge of developing a new kind of culture, one that is as much a departure in style from cofigurative cultures, as the institutionalization of cofiguration in orderly—and disorderly— change was a departure from the postfigurative style. I call this new style *prefigurative*, because in this new culture it will be the child—and not the parent and grandparent—that represents what is to come" (1970:68).

Can excessive stability or excessive change be avoided?

The linkages between communication and culture in a setting such as that described by Mead for today's world have the utmost importance for us as cultural communicators. It would seem that the changeless nature of the postfigurative culture of the past is no longer viable for most of the cultures in the world today. The culture of the past simply cannot cope with today's world. The dangerous, unpredictable world of the prefigurative culture suggests change at an alarming rate. As in the other issues of concern to us, the best goal would seem to be to avoid both excesses. How to achieve a perfect balance between enough stability and change is not easily answered. When we communicate either within our own culture or with members of other cultures, we must take care to remember that as each culture matures, it constantly is in a state of change. We are all caught in this change. We have to be aware of how we serve in our own culture to hold back or promote reasonable change. We must also be aware of how others help to transmit their own cultural values and norms.

Is the communication of culture inherently imperialistic?

In *The Bias of Communication*, Harold Innis postulates that:

It is perhaps a unique characteristic of civilization that each civilization believes in its uniqueness and its superiority to other civilizations. Indeed this may be the meaning of culture—i.e., something which we have that others have not. It is probable for this reason that writings on cultures can be divided into those attempting to weaken other cultures and those attempting to strengthen their own. . . . A brief survey of cultural development in the West may indicate the peculiarity or uniqueness of culture and elements which make for duration or extension. Cultures will reflect their influence in terms of space and in terms of duration (1973:132-133).

The point suggested by Innis is that most cultures seek to extend their culture both geographically and temporally, by forcing others to accept their cultural controls. The very notion of cultural imperialism is an outgrowth of the concept of cultural control. Whether it is a matter of forcing cultural customs, traditions, norms, and values on others with entirely different inclinations directly or indirectly, cultural imperialism appears to be an inherent factor in culture. All of the issues already addressed tie into this concept.

Naturally, if cultures appear imperialistic by nature, their survival seems adversely affected if they cannot spread their culture beyond their own time and space framework. Innis suggests that a major limitation on cultures in terms of time and space is the inability to muster the intellectual resources of a people constantly to the point where stagnation and boredom can be avoided.

The relationship of power to cultural imperialism is very important. Many cultural groups do not have sufficient power or force to make other dominant cultures accept their positions. While they are thereby culturally dependent upon more dominant cultures, they may utilize imperialistic means to force cultural dependency upon others less able to stave off their cultural thrusts. In the urban migrations which have occurred in the United States, one group always seems dependent upon the next most powerful group. Cultural activity as expressed communicatively in architecture, sculpture, city planning, armed forces, weaponry, and modern conveniences is designed to emphasize cultural prestige. It becomes an index of power. Innis argues that Western cultures clearly believe in their dominance and superiority over other civilizations. "In contrast with the civilization dominated by Greek culture with its maxim 'nothing in excess,' modern civilization dominated by machine industry is concerned always with specialization which might be described as 'always in excess'" (1973:139).

Essentially, the concept of cultural imperialism and cultural dependency indicates that subjection of a cultural sort is not so much military, economic, or political superiority (although these elements are extemely important), but a communicational force. This force provides cultural dominance over cultures and countries with values and images either totally extraneous to them or not representative of the need of their majorities. As Elizabeth de Cardona (1975:122-127) suggests: "Cultural dependency means that the people of our countries have to brush their teeth three times a day even if they don't have anything to eat." The meaning of this comment in the crosscultural communication context is that new values are constantly being created, not so much for their propriety, as for the ability to sell toothpaste to persons too poor to have adequate food and clothing.

The transistor radio is perhaps the foremost symbol of cultural imperialism and dependency, as more people in the world are potentially brought under its spell regularly than through any other communications media. Through the radio, members of one culture receive vivid examples of successes of other cultures which they wish to emulate. More propaganda from members of their own dominant cultural groups reaches the culturally dependent members of a population this way than by almost any other means. Literacy is not required, though an ability to understand the language of the medium is important. Still, music needs no linguistic ability for the listener and thus culture spreads from community to community by way of the transistor radio.

Margaret Mead describes the effect of the differences in the Tambunam culture of New Guinea from her visits in the 1930s and a return visit in 1967. The people still did many things the same way over a period of more than thirty years. Earlier, the natives had requested medicine and trade goods such as razor blades, fishhooks, salt, and cloth. However, Mead reports that in 1967: " . . .the first question was: 'Have you got a tape recorder?' 'Yes, why?' 'We have heard other people's singing on the radio and we want other people to hear ours.' A major shift. Through the spread of a world culture of transistor radios and democratic theories about the value of each small culture, the people of Tambunam had heard New Guinea music, which it was now government policy to broadcast and they had come to feel that they could participate, on an equal footing, in this new world of broadcasting" (1970:xviii). Even when they couldn't speak the language of the other culture, Mead remarks that their awareness of what others had was being developed, so that they wanted it. They wanted to share their talents with others. In effect, they were beginning the stages of cultural dependence upon others, and at the same time seeking to transmit their own cultural contributions over space and time to others. Furthermore, the irreversibility of technology indicated that the transistor radio and the tape recorder were but the first communicative symbols of cultural norms and values which they would seek from the outside. Today, a return visit by Mead to New Guinea would probably produce requests for other forms of Western cultural technological advances, so that they could continue to gain that which they did not have, and to be able to expand further their own culture. The transistor radio is a powerful medium of intercultural communication (and also encourages communicative and cultural sameness, conflict, control, assimilation, technological dependence, change, and a simultaneous cultural imperialism and dependency). The same types of developments are even more likely to occur as more members of specific cultures communicate and interact.

Summary

In this chapter, we have seen an additional set of major issues in the discussion relating communication and culture. These issues—the impact of technology upon culture, stability and change, and cultural imperialism and dependency—are of considerable importance in linking communication and culture. These issues and those discussed in Chapter 1 can serve, either directly or indirectly, and individually or collectively, to define most of the relationships which can be developed between communication and culture, for the intercultural communicator, and for the spokespersons of cultural groups in collective contact.

References

Bell, Daniel, 1970. "The Cultural Contradictions of Capitalism." In *The Public Interest*. September.

de Cardona, Elizabeth, 1975. "Multinational Television." In *Journal of Communication* (Spring) XXV, 2, 122-127.

Ellul, Jacques, 1964. *The Technological Society*. Introduction by Robert K. Merton. Translated by John W. Wilkinson. New York: Knopf.

Henry, Jules, 1963. *Culture against Man*. Middlesex, England: Penguin.

Innis, Harold, 1973. *The Bias of Communication*. Toronto: University of Toronto.

Mead, Margaret, 1970. *Culture and Commitment, A Study of the Generation Gap*. Garden City, New York: Doubleday.

Nieburg, Harold L., 1973. *Culture Storm: Politics and the Ritual Order*. New York: St. Martin.

Reich, Charles, March 8, 1971. "Beyond Consciousness." *New York Times*, p. 311.

Skinner, B.F., 1971. *Beyond Freedom and Dignity*. New York: Knopf.

Part Two
The Components of Communication

The components of communication are those factors essential for an effective minimal study of communication in a community or culture. We want to expand our understanding of communication to its relationships with the components of culture. We wish to see how the cultural communicator interrelates these components in various cultural contexts, and how cultural spokespersons manipulate these characteristics in interaction with the cultural spokespersons of other cultural groupings. Part of what we are seeking to accomplish, in the words of Clifford Geertz (1973:19-23), is an understanding of "the said of speaking." Stated more directly, *we are interested in social discourse.* However, while we have indicated that communication and culture are intertwined, and while this linkage involves various forms of social discourse, *our chief aim is to understand social discourse in the cultural context, that is, cultural dialogue.*

The purpose of the ethnographer is to describe the social discourse of a community or culture. Naturally, the total understanding of a community or culture is difficult to achieve. As Geertz suggests, cultural analysis should involve guessing at meaning, assessing the guesses, and drawing explanatory conclusions from the better guesses. Thus, Geertz argues that ethnographic description is interpretative: it is interpretation of the flow of social discourse. The interpretation attempts to rescue the "said" of such discourse from perishing, and to fix it in perusable terms. Much of the perishability of social discourse is attributed to the fact that no matter how advanced the technology aiding us to gain our information, all aspects of social discourse cannot be adequately captured. Geertz adds a key element to his description of ethnographic collection: it is microscopic. It is simply not possible to study an entire culture from all of its potential vantage points (1973:19-21). The mapping of a culture or community may include thick (in depth) ethnographic detail, and thin (relatively superficial) ethnographic detail. Both types of detail aid in understanding the ethnography of a community's social discourse.

Attempting to understand cultures in general, and specific cultures and their members in interaction, is an enormous task. A useful departure point is a consideration of the communicative components present in most communties or cultures. In his essay, "Toward Ethnographies of Communication'" Dell Hymes suggests: "The starting point is the ethnographic analysis of the communicative habits of a community in their totality, determining what count as communicative events, and as their components, and conceiving no communicative behavior as independent of the set framed by some setting or implicit question. The communicative event is thus central" (1973:46). The communicative event may be seen as the total communicative involvement of the community or culture. While communication does not describe all that occurs in culture, it does become highly significant for the later interpretation of other cultural components. Hymes considers the study of communication and its components one of the greatest challenges in the broader study of culture. He argues that the componential elements of communication must be seen as an interacting whole, although one or more of the elements may be isolated for study or emphasis. In this way, Hymes believes that communication makes the closest contacts in culture with its social, political, and moral concerns. This frame of reference leads Hymes to the following questions: What are the communication events and their components in a community? What are the relationships among them? What capabilities and stages do they have, in general and in particular cases? How do they work (1973:58)?

Hymes suggests that the consideration of communication can be initiated with any of the components as long as the communicative event remains the central point of the analysis. As an example, he selects "message" as the first component to be considered:

The concept of message implies the sharing (real or imputed) of (1) a code or codes in terms of which the message is intelligible to (2) participants, minimally an addressor and addressee (who may be the same person), in (3) an event constituted by its transmission and characterized by (4) a channel or channels, (5) a setting or context, (6) a definite form or shape to the message, and (7) a topic and a comment, i.e., it says something about something—in other words that the concept of message implies the array of components previously given (1973:48).

For our purpose we will place the greatest stress on the message, the communication participants, the codes which they utilize, and their channels or media channels as they interact in the communication event. The next several chapters will develop these concepts.

References

Geertz, Clifford, 1973. *The Interpretation of Culture.* New York: Basic Books.

Hymes, Dell, 1973. "Toward Ethnographies of Communication." In *Intercommunication among Nations and Peoples.* Edited by Michael H. Prosser, New York: Harper & Row.

CHAPTER 3

The Message

Without the message, other communication components are irrelevant

John Weakland states that communication "always involves a multiplicity of channels, of context, and of messages. These are never absolutely separable, but interact so that, for example, messages and contexts, verbal message and vocal or facial expression, or related verbal messages are mutually qualifying in ways critical to interpretation and response—and therefore to effective analysis of communication" (1967:2). Hymes would accept Weakland's interactional emphasis that we can use various starting points to view the interrelationships between the components. However, Hymes considers the message of still greater impact because it includes all other components of communication in a balanced ratio: "If the message is taken as subsuming all, or all the immediately relevant, other components, then focus on the message as surrogate of the whole event may be taken as entailing metacommunicative functions [or communication about communication]" (1973:56). The source with no message to send has no need either of channels in which to send it or of a receiver to decode it.

Setting and topic closely relate to the message

Two other communication components which Hymes categorizes are very closely related to the concept of message itself: the setting (or context) and the topics (or comment) of the message. The communication setting or context as a component means that every message is produced by a sender or encoder for a recipient or decoder with the framework of a specific setting or context. The settings or contexts can also be seen as the environmental, physical, or psychological "places" where communication messages are being formulated or received. They may not be the same for message-senders and receivers, especially in the collective framework. Nor must they be the same when the messages cross cultural and national boundaries. Often various "gatekeepers" or interpreters exist between the message-sender and the message-recipient. The message generated and contained in an igloo has certain dimensions different from those formulated and contained in a Western rectangular building, a public bath in Japan, a ghetto, barrio, or Navajo hogan. Without understanding the context or setting in which a message is sent and received, the meaning of the message itself becomes relatively useless.

The setting or context not only emphasizes the places where the messages are sent and received, in terms of their geographical and cultural locations, but also helps to define the likely participants in the communication situation, and the channels which are likely to be used. If the setting or context is a highly urban area for example, Karl Deutsch would suggest that "any metropolis can be thought of as a huge engine of communication, a device to enlarge the range or reduce the cost of individual and social choices," and its power "is thus attested indirectly by its power of attraction over people." Deutsch describes the "attention overload" and the "communication saturated" society as characteristic problems of modern—and thus particularly of urban and metropolitan—culture, and argues that "cities therefore may produce a pervasive condition of communication overload" (1966:386-390).

People who live in metropolitan areas are there either by choice or because of families, resources, or work opportunities which prevent them from leaving. The city's communication overload, along with various other overloads, frustrates them by loneliness and a loss of a sense of identity. Individuals thus find their opportunities for effective interpersonal communication diminished. They become primarily recipients of various forms of collective and relatively impersonal communication messages since friends and relatives may be too far away or too costly to reach on an interpersonal level. Many more channels of communication, and especially mass media channels, are available, but they also may be too expensive or impersonal to be useful. Urban areas everywhere are filled with people who have little interpersonal contact with others, and who are unable to utilize, for one reason or another, the collective channels of communication. At the other end of the spectrum, persons living in a remote village or rural area theoretically have more opportunity for interpersonal communication and almost no opportunity available for any forms of collective communication. In the setting or context of that village, however, there may be stringent restrictions on the type of communication messages which may be exchanged and with whom the villager may communicate.

The subject or topics of messages is another important communication component cited by Hymes. At the simplest level, the message's topic is seen as the "what" of the famous Lasswell paradigm: "Who says what to whom through which channels with what effect." The setting or context may prescribe what subjects are talked about or may characterize the major topics discussed there. In a nursing home, major topics of the residents may include frequent references to their age, their closeness to death, their need for God, their recall of long-ago events, and their families. We might expect the major topics in a Christian church to center around a dependence upon God, the salvation gained for sinners through Jesus Christ, the need to avoid sin and evil, and the desire to strive for a good and moral life. In the Islamic mosque, we can expect messages based on the moral authority of the Koran often with practical applications of contemporary political life, especially because Islamic teachings incorporate both religious and moral themes and the role of the religious beliefs in all other aspects of life. In a legislative assembly, we might hear a dominant number of messages about the need to pass certain laws, while in a judicial court we might hear most messages concentrating on upholding the laws and punishing those who fail to uphold them. Similarly, the reader of an American newspaper may expect certain topics to appear regularly in certain portions of the paper: for example, a sports section, an editorial page, major news stories on front pages, and stock reports on a financial page. In a different societal setting, the topics might be arranged entirely differently in the newspaper. For example, advertisments are placed on the front page of British newspapers.

Messages require focused interaction

Dean Barnlund comments on the intricate nature of what he calls focused interaction. It is the willingness, at least briefly, to supply cues for others to act on, to be reasonably responsive to the cues provided by others, and to be capable of weaving these two coding activities into an acceptable pattern. Barnlund writes: "Coding requires the selection of appropriate verbal and nonverbal signs to express the internal state of the sender of the message. But to be effective, this must be accompanied by an imaginative interpretation of the probable meaning to be assigned by the receiver. Without the capacity to encode *and* the capacity of interpretation from the vantage point of the receiver, the sender would not know what to put into a message" (1968:9). He makes an important distinction between interpersonal and collective communication in relation to the exchange of messages in each communicative situation. On the one hand, in the interpersonal situation, messages are being constantly initiated and exchanged between or among the participants. On the other hand, in the collective situation where persons are only vaguely in contact with each other, Barnlund suggests that messages have a one-way orientation and a single major source of the messages. Attention is focused exclusively on the cues this source provides. In the collective situation, most responses are ritualized and the communicative roles of the paritcipants are polarized in formal settings. The vast majority of the participants are confined more or less permanently to interpreting messages and relatively few, usually a single person, serve to initiate the messages. The cues are planned in advance, are relatively impersonal, and utilize fairly rigid channel systems in contrast to the episodic, impulsive, and fragmentary nature of interpersonal interaction (11).

The status of the communicators affects the messages

It is important to recognize, as Barnlund suggests (361ff), that in almost any communicative system the status of the communicator has a great deal to do with how much he or she initiates, organizes, manipulates, and responds to messages. The communicator's high status, ethos, or credibility typically means that his or her messages will be taken more seriously than those of low-status communicators. His or her response to an initial message will also receive a more serious hearing than that of the low-status individual or group. Barnlund emphasizes that the flow of messages is also greater for persons of high status than for lower-status persons, and that out-of-status communication is directed primarily toward those of higher rather than lower rank. This occurs because the greater power and esteem of persons in high positions generates pressures toward higher and upward mobility (1968:362-363). Status is sometimes achieved by collective coercive action by persons whose messages normally would have low influence. Such instant status caused by a violent or threatening action against those in power is usually short-lived. After awhile, when the collective power dissipates, the influence of such messages tends also to disappear.

Messages function in various ways

Just as communication may or may not be consciously planned to be influential, messages function in various overlapping ways. The language of a culture may help to determine how messages function. The Japanese language requires more sense of modality and ambiguity than does English. English requires more inductive patterns of messages, while European languages stress more deductive patterns. Russian as a language emphasizes a dialectical approach to deductive and inductive patterns of thinking. Thus, messages in two different languages may take on entirely different meanings by the very nature of the languages. Messages may serve to provide relatively neutral information such as weather, time, road signs, or the artificially developed codes of mathematics and geometry. Such messages have considerable crosscultural application because past or present cultures have adapted them as having a widely accepted meaning.

Messages may operate expressively and may refer to emotional attitudes such as anger, astonishment, and romance. The communicator seeking influence over the attitudes or behaviors of others utilizes persuasive messages. Such messages are the central emphasis of studies in rhetoric, and attitudinal and social change. Poetic messages seek to bring together perceptions and abstractions into a united symbolic presentation through poetry, music, and painting. Phatic communication messages serve to open or maintain other channels of communication, and help to unite communicators or to stress an affiliation which individuals may have toward others (Stewart, 1974a:14-16).

The context of a situation may itself function as a message. The message may be metacommunicative, that is, communication about communication. The human metacommunicative function is a chief ingredient in culture, as only people can reflect on the communication in which they engage. Similarly, since only humans can reflect on language, we have the possibility of developing a metalanguage about language. Animals can communicate but cannot think about the communication which they have engaged in. Humans can. Finally, time appears to have at least two aspects in the functioning of communication. The reception of a message is registered in the individual's memory and experience, processes which systematically can be considered as aspects of long-term memory, storage and synthesis of perception, experience and learning. In terms of communicative events, such as the Wounded Knee protest or the Watergate situation in the United States, the Lockheed scandals in Holland or Japan, and the imposition of press censorship in India, time divides one phase from another and projects messages into a temporal frame which is much broader than individual sending-receiving relationships. If we consider that history repeats itself, and messages that are broader than isolated messages on the same subjects recur, we can see culture as an aspect of time and space through the way messages function at the broadest levels (Stewart, 1974a:14-16).

Messages are formed and shaped in various ways

Hymes indicates that when we consider the forms and shapes of messages, it is not possible to define totally any phenomenon in advance as never to be counted as constituting a message. The nature of "message" is based partly on the intention of the message-sender and largely on how the message-recipient has construed the message. He relates an incident about members of the Ojibwa tribe in Africa who construed the clap of thunder as a specific message being given them by the Thunder Birds.

Hymes suggests that "the casualness of the remark and even the trivial character of the anecdote demonstrate the psychological depth of the 'social relations' with other-than-human beings that become explicit in the behavior of the Ojibwa as a consequence of the cognitive 'set' induced by their culture" (1973:49). Such an example implies that the range of message forms or shapes becomes limitless. Certainly, the role of nature speaking to humans or supplications to the deity or other supernatural beings all provide substantial elements of many human communication messages. This range of message forms and shapes exists even before we consider the normal array of message types exchanged in human interaction, both at the linguistic and nonverbal levels of communication.

The forms and shapes of all messages include both overt and covert levels. The relationships between levels may be contrasting or ambiguous as in overt verbal messages which are contradicted by covert nonverbal messages. When the English-speaking person greets a Spanish-speaking person verbally with "amigo" while indicating nonverbally superiority or disdain, the one message gives the lie to the other.

If we follow the suggestions of writers like Hymes and Stewart, most aspects of human life provide us with the forms or shapes of messages in various ways. They may be verbal, nonverbal, or technological. How we build our buildings, what we put in them, how we arrange their interiors, and how we function in them all provide specific forms and shapes of messages which are culturally expressive. Even the fact that Americans wear varying styles of underwear, often brightly colored for both males and females, offers a cultural statement about American values and about our cultural dependency on certain types of communicatively expressive clothing. The irreversible nature of technology itself helps to form and shape messages quite differently in developed countries than in developing societies.

Our messages powerfully affect our intercultural communication

Until recently, with the protests and riots against the Vietnam and Cambodian wars, most American students have considered themselves relatively low-status communicators. Students in other societies, well before the American student involvement in civil rights protests, considered themselves social reformers and cultural change agents. Their messages reflected their acceptance of high-status communicators both in their own societies and on an intercultural level. In the 1950s and 1960s, such students aimed their messages crossculturally at other societies' leaders whom they considered imperialistic. Latin American students so frightened the Eisenhower administration by their real and symbolic attacks against Vice President Nixon in Caracas, Venezuela, that the American government seemed paralyzed for some time in its cooperative efforts with various Latin American states. In 1960, Japanese student protests helped to prevent Eisenhower's planned visit to Japan. Later, the very shape and form of the messages to the American presidents are thought partly to have caused President Johnson to abandon seeking a second full term and to have brought an eventual end to the Vietnam war. When we consider that current students possess— or potentially possess— greater status already than more than two-thirds of the human race presently can expect ever to achieve, student power as communicators both within our society and across cultures is considerable. Student messages are too important to be ignored. The very nature of such messages often causes the most serious communication breakdowns within and between cultures.

Message selection and control become an important aspect of communication and culture

John C. Merrill and Ralph Lowenstein explore the reasons that collective recipients of messages, particularly the audiences of the mass media, select certain messages over others:

The first of these general principles of selection states that the audience member takes the path of least effort, that he naturally tends to read, view, and listen to media and messages that are most accessible. The second of the priniciples of selection assumes that audience members expose themselves to messages that will give them the greatest reward. Of course, it should be said that, in a sense, all messages offer some degree of reward, even if it is a kind of "escapism" or momentary enjoyment. It should also be noted that audience members are seeking—often unconsciously—messages that reinforce their opinions, their preconceptions, and biases. They, in effect, take in those messages compatible with their mental and psychological predispositions. They perceive those messages that cause them no "pain"—that tend to substantiate their beliefs. A person's past experiences and his philosophy of life play important parts in determining which media and messages he will select. This factor in message receiving is usually called *selective perception* (1971:133).

Collective messages recipients can be isolated in several ways

At the mass-communication level and various other collective levels, Merrill and Lowenstein predict two types of message recipients or audiences. The first is a general public audience, which though other writers think it is mythical, offers the truest characteristics of a broad, heterogeneous general or mass group, especially in relation to such advanced media as newspapers, radio, and television. The second is the specialized audience, which consists also of a broad, relatively heterogeneous audience bound together by a more specialized common interest, such as sports news. These audiences may vary in composition from time to time and for different types of messages. Usually the larger the audience, the less homogeneous the group. Additionally, such audiences vary according to the length of time that they remain in contact with the mass medium and its message, as well as in terms of intensity of involvement in the message itself (1971).

Within the more general and specialized types of audiences, Merrill and Lowenstein delineate three basic subgroups: the illiterates, the pragmatists, and the intellectuals. They suggest that the illiterates include both those who genuinely do not read and write and those who read and write at a minimal level or are attitudinally illiterate. They expose themselves essentially to *picture media* for which the least amount of effort is required. They share the messages which they have received from the mass media very sparsely. Fundamentally, they turn their "communication world" inward, except perhaps for sports or sensational types of news. Since such persons often have a low education level, they are also likely to have a relatively lower income level and may be in lower-class blue collar jobs. It is possible that they may have higher paying jobs and have received a reasonably good education but still remain illiterates by the limited range of their interests. Even in a country like the United States where educational and income levels remain among the highest in the world, Merrill and Lowenstein believe that nearly 60 percent of the total population are included among such a grouping (1971).

In North America 30 percent of the total population could be considered pragmatists and are persons who actively involve themselves in their society by participating, working, campaigning, voting, belonging to organizations, traveling, building homes, purchasing the latest appliances and automobiles, watching television, listening to radio, and reading books and magazines. Like Americans, typical urban Russians are considered very hard-working and industrious. Probably many of them would closely fit the role of pragmatists described by Merrill and Lowenstein as recipients of messages. Usually they are upwardly mobile, and exercise social and buying power. They seek to become high-status message senders. As pragmatists, they receive and seek out messages which will help them advance, gain more and better material possessions, help others, and live a more satisfying life. In American society, such persons tend to join service clubs, accept church memberships, take Dale Carnegie-type confidence-building and public-speaking courses, seek higher levels of education, and involve themselves at least somewhat seriously in ideas and issues, mostly because they feel that such activities will help them to advance or may be useful information for them at some later point (1971).

Merrill and Lowenstein suggest that the smallest segment of such an audience consists of the intellectuals, persons who represent about 10 percent of the total population. They are deeply and genuinely interested in issues, aesthetic matters, philosophical problems, and concepts. They tend to be well educated, and are often at medium or higher income levels. They see see themselves as idea-oriented, creative, and concerned with human priorities. Frequently, they are nonsocial in the broad sense because they are more concerned with their own brand of nonconformity. As elitists, they tend to disregard the masses. Often they read sophisticated newspapers and magazines, and are highly selective of what they will view on television or listen to on the radio. Sometimes they refuse to have "the boob tube" in their homes. Some intellectuals, or even pseudo-intellectuals, are actually ideologues, or dedicated crusaders on particular subjects. Most intellectuals are creating and thinking, not solely for their own satisfaction, but also are passionately concerned in a limited range of issues about which they try to convince others, thereby becoming message ideologues (1971:120-133).

It is very likely that most of us do not consider ourselves illiterates. Some of us may consider ourselves genuine intellectuals, and a few of us may grudgingly admit to being ideologues, but for the most part we call ourselves pragmatists, or possibly intellectual pragmatists. If this is correct, while we may be interested in conceptual ideas, there may be practical reasons for these interests. Present goals may be pragmatically related to living "the good life" later, achieving a certain income level, or advancing in other ways. Pragmatically, as well, we may be interested in the next possible interaction with others, including persons from other races or cultures, and we may wish to seek practical measures which will assist us in such effective communication.

We tend to think that we have great selection and control over the messages that we receive and that we are generally immunized to the incursion of unwanted messages. Merrill and Lowenstein indicate that "one research study has shown that the average American is exposed to 1,600 advertising messages each day, but is moved pro or con by not more than 15 of them." Another study by the Batten, Barton, Durstine and Osbourne advertising agency included only those messages disseminated by mass media and outdoor advertising. The findings, released in 1970, show that the average American male is exposed to 285 advertising messages a day—35 television commercials, 38 radio commercials, 15 magazine ads, 185 newspaper ads, and 12 outdoor messages (Merrill and Lowenstein, 1971:137-138). In contrast, in Great Britain, commercials on radio and television are strictly prohibited on the BBC networks and available only on the independent television channel for six minutes an hour. At least twice that amount appears on American television. In such a situation we might predict that the British male's exposure to commercial messages might be greater in the print media than in the broadcast media.

Propaganda functions to control messages within and between cultures

Merrill and Lowenstein's functional definition of propaganda is "the effort or the activity by which an initiating communicator intends to manage the attitudes and actions of others by playing on their preexisting biases with messages designed largely to appeal to their emotions and/or irrationality" (1971:214). We may believe that we are neither message propagandists nor affected by such messages because we are intellectuals or intellectual pragmatists. Even if we are subjected to various forms of propaganda, we are capable of rejecting them. Nevertheless, Jacques Ellul stresses that intellectuals are in fact most prone to the acceptance of propaganda messages because *propaganda basically is a Siamese twin of the technological society*. Ellul argues that two kinds of propaganda exist: *agitation propaganda*, which leads people from resentment to rebellion, and *integration propaganda*, which leads people to adjust to desired patterns. The latter, he argues, is especially needed for the technological society to flourish. Its chief technological communications systems, such as the mass media, help to make intregration propaganda possible. A major aspect of such propaganda according to Ellul is that education is the absolute prerequisite for modern propaganda to work. He calls education a type of pro-propaganda which conditons minds from early childhood especially to accept types of integration propaganda to which they are continuously exposed by living in a culture and society. Ellul believes that people who consider themselves intellectuals or intellectual pragmatists are the most vulnerable to modern propaganda for three major reasons: they absorb the largest amount of second-hand unverifiable information; they feel a compelling need to have an opinion on almost every important question of our time; and they consider themselves capable of judging for themselves (1966).

Ellul argues that *intellectuals need propaganda*, especially since they often have abandoned the simple answers offered them in the past by such institutions as their early family contacts, their church, and their early teachers, in favor of a "deeper meaning of life." We could speculate that the ideologue especially is most prone to the acceptance of the propagandistic messages. In the framework of developing his or her own beliefs and crusading goals it gives a reason for being, accents personal involvement, and provides participation in what he or she considers the important issues of the day. An integrative function, Ellul argues that propaganda tends to tie individuals into the technological society in a way that the technological state and society want them to fit. Often, there is little complaint from individuals who believe that the state's and society's aims are akin to their own aims (1966).

Controlling countercultural propaganda in the 1970 Cambodian invasion

Peter M. Hall and John P. Hewitt indicate that in the spring of 1970 when President Nixon sent troops to Cambodia, the administration's response to campus demonstrations throughout the United States was to cool its own rhetoric, establish lines of communication, appoint a consultant, send aides to meet with groups of protesters for discussion, make a symbolic appearance in the person of the President, and lend verbal support to the right to dissent. The President himself called for communication rather than violence. Hall and Hewitt argue that in fact "there was a preoccupation with communication (its presence or absence, its process, and its style) that deflected and obscured the basic issue of the war, perhaps intentionally, by defining the situation in terms of a quasitheory of communication breakdown, barriers, or failures. This quasi-theory is strongly rooted in our political culture and is at the same time a means or device for cooling controversy and managing discontent" (1973:531-532)

Hall and Hewitt believe that underlying the emphasis upon communication as a tool for conflict resolution is an American myth of common values—a widely shared set of values upon which all Americans finally agree: "Thus, in the political sphere, it is culturally possible to treat conflicting points of view and conflicting goals as merely manifestations of disagreements on how to go about realizing the values (unspecified) that we all share" (1973:531-532). For Nixon, such a theory utilized the systems approach to conflict resolution which Hall and Hewitt feel was built on a cultural myth or, as Ellul would suggest, on the propaganda of a technological society. It was the American societal belief that communication is a major component of all social action, or the pragmatic statement that "the end-product of the communication process is action, action that is affected by the meaning ascribed to the content of the communication." Hall and Hewitt called this American cultural premise a trap which the Nixon administration sought to entice the student and other protestors to enter:

The force of his (Nixon's) action is directed to the transformation of a substantive issue into a technical problem, so that basic conflict comes to be denied and, in its place, communication failure becomes the definition of the situation. The goal is to achieve cooperation of student protest by appearing to link the students into the political order without relinquishing any power or in any way altering the course of events. . . . The possibility of substantive differences, real disagreements, or basic conflicts of interest is denied by this perspective (1973:532-533).

Hall and Hewitt stress further that "American culture fosters a number of widespread assumptions about the nature of social reality and of permissible political behavior:1.) we are all part of the same community; 2.) our leaders represent that community; 3.) we are all rational and reasonable . . .; 4.) our troubles and disagreements are fundamentally caused by misunderstandings or lack of information about values and goals that we, as a community hold in common; 5.) consequently solutions to political and social problems lie in their open discussion" (535). Although the Nixon administration was not entirely successful in diffusing the explosive nature of the dissent, all of the technology at the administration's disposal plus presidential authority was used to seek a solution.

Hall and Hewitt suggest that many Americans, including a reasonable segment of the student dissenters, came to accept Nixon's statements that his administration wanted the same goals as they did; they came to believe that he was making every effort to end the Vietnam War and its side effects; and they agreed that while he and his administration were attempting to halt the war, student protest was not to be allowed to escalate into futher domestic conflicts.

It is obvious that the Nixon administration had the power to control its messages—and even its responses—more effectively than the highly vocal, but relatively powerless, collective movement of dissenters. Whether the administration or the students eventually had the more effective communication strategies and message selection and control is problematical, at least on the issue of the Vietnam War, since as a presidential candidate in 1972 President Nixon received the largest majority of votes in the history of American politics. Many other factors were present, of course, and there is little evidence to suggest that Nixon's resignation in August 1974 negated his administration's attempt to make the dissenters' arguments on

Vietnam in the late 1960s and early 1970s seem to be based on technical rather than real differences.

It is probably true that in the Watergate situation the Nixon administration ultimately lost its ability to select and control the most important messages. The free press in the United States can oppose government policies and expose fraudulent policies, which allowed a greater selection and control of messages from outside the administration to overcome the typical advantage which the incumbent American administration has in utilizing communication strategies. In the United Kingdom, many editors rather smugly have indicated that a Watergate situation could not have happened there. It would seem that their "Official Secrets Act" and the inability of the press to treat court cases after they have been formally initiated could actually allow a Watergate situation to occur there without the advantage of being uncovered by the press.

Summary

In this chapter, we have stressed what Dell Hymes considers to be the most important of the communication components: the message. We have suggested that without the message, all other components are irrelevant. We have noted that other components, such as the setting and the topic, closely relate to the message itself. The setting and topic serve to identify the nature of the message and often determine how effective a particular message will be. All messages require focused interaction, but interpersonal messages develop more focused interaction than do collective messages. Whether the status of the communicator is high or low, it affects the messages. The higher-status communicator both sends and receives more messages, while the low-status communicator tends to receive more messages but responds essentially in a formal and routine manner. The messages function in various ways, just as communication itself functions variously. Messages are also formed and shaped variously, often by the way that they are intended to function. At the intercultural level, we have noted that our messages powerfully affect our communication.

As one of the key issues stressed earlier, we note that message control and selection become significant aspects of communication and culture. Various types of audiences try to select and control messages which they receive. Propaganda serves as a message control within and between cultures. We have offered an example of President Nixon seeking to control the countercultural propaganda against his administration during the 1970 Cambodian invasion by showing that he sought to demonstrate that the division between him and the antiwar protestors was not based on substantive issues, but rather on failures in communication.

References

Barnlund, Dean, 1968. *Interpersonal Communication: Survey and Studies.* Boston: Houghton Mifflin.

Ellul, Jacques, 1966. *Propaganda: The Formation of Men's Attitudes.* Translated by Konrad Kellen and Jean Lerner. Introduction by Konrad Kellen. New York: Random House.

Hall, Peter M., and John P. Hewitt, 1973. "The Quasi-Theory of Communication and the Management of Dissent." In *Intercommunication among Nations and Peoples.* Edited by Michael H. Prosser. New York. Harper & Row.

Hymes, Dell H., 1973. "Toward Ethnographies of Communication." In *Intercommunication among Nations and Peoples,* Edited by Michael H. Prosser. New York: Harper & Row.

Merrill, John C., and Ralph Lowenstein, 1971. *Media, Messages, and Men: New Perspectives in Communication.* New York: McKay.

Stewart, Edward C., 1974a. "An Overview of the Field of Intercultural Communication." Mimeograph released by the Intercultural Communication Network. Pittsburgh: University of Pittsburgh.

Weakland, John, 1967. "Some Formal Aspects of Communication." In *The American Behavioral Scientist,* April 4-8.

CHAPTER 4

Hierarchial Sets of Communication Participants: A Model

Communication can be classified in various ways. For example, the number of participants according to their characteristics and the directionality of the message flow are such classifications. They also assist in identifying the definitive ingredients of communication. A continuum of communication participants can be developed ranging from intrapersonal, to interpersonal, to cultural, to collective, and to what may be described somewhat ambiguously as global communication. Within the hierarchial sets, each system can be thought of as subsumed by the others, especially in terms of numbers of participants, their characteristics, and the directionality of the message flow among participants. As we move along the continuum, more and more participants are involved. Characteristics (such as the utilization of the individual senses in the communication event) change from a highly personal involvement or sense relationship to a highly impersonal, formalized, and less involved relationship by the majority of the participants. The directional flow of the communication is one-way at the intrapersonal level; becomes two-way in interpersonal and cultural communication; and essentially reverts back to one-way in collective and global communication. The greater the number of participants, the more orientative feedback is minimized, delayed, and routinized.

Figure 1 demonstrates the five hierarchial classifications of communication participants: *intrapersonal, interpersonal,*

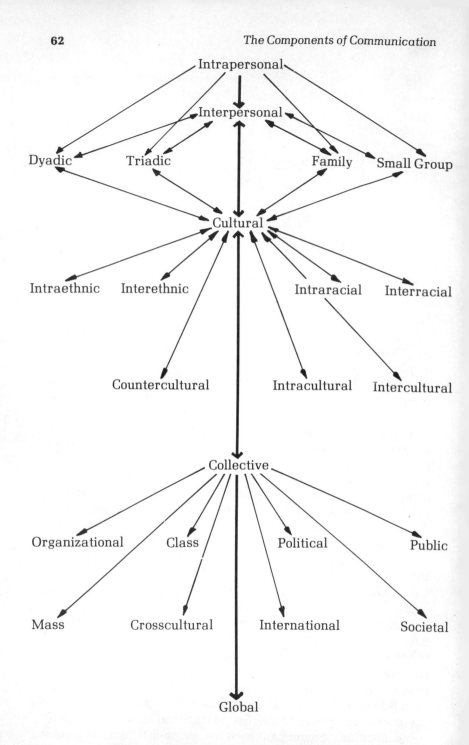

Systems of Participants in Communication

cultural, collective, and global. Subsets are also included. It is assumed that sets in the hierarchy as it progresses from the microscopic to the macroscopic are subsumed; it is not possible to assume that each set is mutually exclusive. Our chief interest lies in emphasizing those aspects of the model which include cultural dimensions. Every set and subset includes such dimensions to some degree, if we accept the early premise that communication and culture are linked in any setting or situation. All of the sets and subsets include both unconscious or unintended communication, and conscious or purposefully influential communication. The highor we move in the hierarchy, the more the planned, purposeful, and influential nature of communication becomes apparent.

Intrapersonal communication involves only one person, is naturally individualistic, includes all of the senses in a balanced ratio, and is of course one-way. *Interpersonal communication* requires two or more persons; typically includes all of the senses in a balanced ratio; is relatively spontaneous, though the larger the group, the more structure is introduced; and is typically two-way, interactional, and externally directed and perceived, with considerable opportunity for direct feedback. *Cultural communication* includes the dimension of interpersonal communication and adds a heightened emphasis on culturally distinguished charactoristics such as linguistic and nonlinguistic codes, perception, attitudes, values, and thought-patternings. *Collective communication* subsumes the earlier sets, but includes large numbers of participants; fewer sense modalities because of greater distances; more structured and planned aspects; much less two-way communication; and less interaction or feedback, except through formalized, delayed, or ritualized responses. *Global communication* is characterized by elements of the other sets, but with goals which transcend cultural, national, and societal boundaries in a world sotting. Each of the five sets and subsets will be explored in more detail.

Intrapersonal communication stresses our cultural uniqueness

Since intrapersonal communication is characterized by the communication taking place in the individual, it is always an unconscious or conscious expression of the person's cultural imprint and response to it. In addition to our human biological communicative capacities, each of us speaks and behaves within the context of a particular cultural setting. While we can generalize about individuals in various settings, there is also the notion of "personal culture" for all individuals. As individuals, we perceive, observe, evaluate, and act upon the cultural data which we receive. We attach meanings to ideas, events, and experiences which have affected us over time and space. As individuals, we cannot entirely unlearn our culture. Certainly technological advances now appear to make it possible completely to forget our cultural past, as in cases of brainwashing. But unless the brain itself is radically altered, we cannot totally erase the influence of our culture to the point that we no longer are able to respond to the cultural events which affect us. We are capable, as we have suggested, of actively influencing culture, rather than simply passively reacting to it. All human communication begins and returns to us as individual participants in culture.

Interpersonal communication is focused interaction

Interpersonal communication is characterized by the presence of two or more individuals who have the capacity to supply cues for others to act upon in a social contact and context. They must also be able to respond to the cues of others. Such participants must be reasonably capable of integrating both the encoding and the decoding functions into an appropriate pattern of meaning. In interpersonal communication, meanings are normally exchanged which require the ability to encode a message on the one hand, and to decode it on the other hand. Communicative codes represent both verbal and nonverbal cues as consciously or unconsciously intended by the communicator and perceived by the message recipient.

Dean Barnlund isolates the characteristics of interpersonal communication succinctly by noting that in the initial contact between two or more individuals, some sort of "perceptual engagement" identified as "unfocused interaction" must take place. Then, as people become aware of each other they may go beyond simple monitoring of their own appearance and the appearance of others. They begin to provide cues that are a direct result of cues supplied by others, and a "focused interaction" begins to occur. The cues which are provided and responded to begin to develop a pattern by which messages and responses can be understood. The complex cognitive process of constructing messages proceeds. Coding the message requires the selection of appropriate verbal and nonverbal signs to express the internal state of the message sender. To be effective, the message must be imaginatively interpreted by the message receiver. Without the communicator's capacity to encode a message and the receiver's capacity to interpret it, the sender would not know what to put into a message. This notion leads Barnlund to emphasize the careful analysis of message forms and effects to fully understand the nature of interpersonal communication (1968).

The communication which occurs provides a rich source of cues, since all of the sense modalities may be exploited, especially the closer the physical proximity of the communicators are able to verify their interpretative assumptions quickly, although less empirically, from the point of view of scientific analysis. The interpersonal setting is largely unstructured. Relatively few rules govern the frequency, form, or content of the messages. They are highly spontaneous. Participants decide to speak when they choose, and to whom they choose. Barnlund suggests: "It is the episodic and elliptical character of interpersonal discourse, with its topical vacillations and alternating strategies, that is its most widely recognized feature" (1968:9-10).

Four subsets are included under interpersonal communication: *dyadic, triadic, family,* and *small group communication.* These subsets are also included as elements of the third set, cultural communication, and less so as parts of collective and global communication. Dyadic communication is that social discourse which occurs when only two persons are present. Triadic communication occurs when three persons, or three groups of persons, interact. Normally, even if three groups exist, the total number in the group is small. Theodore Caplow asserts that while a dyad cannot ordinarily constitute an organization because it has no collective identity apart from its two principals, it takes no more than three members to establish a collective identity capable of surviving the replacement of one member by another. In a structured collective situation, Caplow believes that triads are the building blocks of which all organizations are constructed. Unfortunately, Caplow suggests that whether the triads consist of individuals or organizations or societies, their most significant property is that they are conflict-oriented. The tendency of the triad is to divide into a coalition of two members against the third, no matter what the size of the triad (Caplow, 1968:1-3). At the *intercultural* level, the development of conflict in triads is probably even more frequent than within an *intercultural* setting where the participants might be expected to have more in common.

The *family* includes many of the spontaneous elements of interpersonal communication at its most unstructured levels. At the same time, it tends to have a certain permanency and begins to share the agenda-setting function of the small group. Each family unit, whether nuclear (in the broad American and urbanized sense) or extended (in the sense of the large tightly knit family groups in less urbanized cultures and societies) creates its own patterns of interpersonal interaction and social discourse. Caplow stresses that the primary triad is the father-mother-child (children) group. Since the family is a principal agency of socialization, family communication serves to introduce children to the traditions, values, and chief characteristics of the larger societies, communities, and cultures to which the family belongs. Nevertheless, no matter what style of family communication the culture imposes upon it, Caplow argues that the two-against-one theory takes effect at a very early stage when the interpersonal relations in the family move from the dyadic, husband-wife interaction to the triad. The basic conflict caused by the triad begins to develop even before the child or children consciously manipulate their interaction to influence the parents. The father and mother against the child; one parent and child against the other parent; parents and children against grandparents; or two children against another child are frequent triadic developments in the family, no matter what culture it is found in. Often such alliances are short-lived. They may shift and develop along certain issues, or change as the child grows older, but Caplow feels that such relationships are inherent in the nature of the family (1968:62ff). When the family itself is intercultural, as many families increasingly are, we could presume that the potential for the triadic conflict would be still greater than in families in which all of the members at least share the same culture.

Small group communication still remains essentially interpersonal in nature. Sherif and Sherif define the group as the "structure or organization of interaction among members, defining the statuses and roles of members in various respects, and thereby defining the proper attitudes of the members toward each other and toward members of other groups; a set of values or group norms shared by group members, over and above the sectors of values they have in common with others in their setting and the society of which they are a part"

(1964:249). Their definition of a group almost defines a culture in microcosm.

Despite the fact that Americans generally consider their individualism one of the strongest societal values, we are bound inseparably to various groups. We give groups our loyalties and define our status, role, and prestige with an emphasis on the individual in the group. People from other cultures are often surprised to learn how group-oriented we really are. All through childhood, adolescence, and early adulthood, considerable pressure is felt to join various small groups. A major difference between the small group membership and communication in the United States and countries such as those in the Middle East is that in the Middle East people join fewer small groups, but these are groups with virtually lifelong commitments. In the United States, group membership shifts and people move from group to group without much recognition of those left behind in the earlier groups.

Cultural communication intensifies differences

All intercultural communication is interpersonal as well. While all interpersonal communication has cultural dimensions, differences in linguistic, nonverbal, attitudinal, value, and thought-patterning orientations are not so great among those who share the same culture as among those who are members of contrast cultures. Within the framework of cultural communication, we can include such subsets as *intra-* and *interethnic, intra-* and *interracial, countercultural,* and *intra-* and *intercultural.* The terms are less important in themselves than they are in suggesting added dimensions of communication involving culture. We could assume that the first subsets eventually merge into the final subset intercultural communication, which is the term most often used to describe the subject of this book. Other related terms sometimes include *crosscultural* and *transcultural communication.* These terms can also be used in describing collective communication, stressing comparative studies between collective cultures or the efforts between cultural spokespersons.

Intraethnic communication emphasizes the interaction between members within separate ethnic groups, and *interethnic communication* stresses the interaction between members of different ethnic groups (or with members of the ethnic groups and members of the dominant society). Ethnic groups often remain united because of feelings of superiority or dependency.

The idea of "social Darwinism" is based on the belief of the inherent superiority of some cultural groups and the inferiority of others. The nature of this problem in the United States during the late 1800s and early 1900s was considerable and has had a lasting effect on American life. The nationalistic trend of Germans as the superior race ended in the major conflict of World War II. In *The Vertical Mosaic*, John Porter comments: "There gradually develops a reciprocal relationship between ethnicity and social class. A given ethnic group appropriates particular roles and designates other ethnic groups for the less preferred ones. Often the low-status group accepts its inferior position" (1965:63). All of the issues discussed earlier play a role in communication relating to ethnic groups. When a group of people feels either superior or inferior, biologically or culturally, the group's efforts at cultural stability or change, imperialism or dependency, cultural control and conflict all cause specific difficulties in communication.

Where members of ethnic groups may feel compelled to protect and preserve their cultural heritage, religion, customs, economic base, and their language, members of other groups seek to get the first group to discard their cultural background quickly so that they can assimilate into the main cultural group. Such ethnic problems are considerable, but generally the added feature of distinctive racial and biological characteristics makes the problems and barriers to effective *interracial communication* still more difficult. Although people can more comfortably *interact intraracially*, communication between members of a racial minority and a racial majority are often marked by the same problems affecting ethnic groups, plus the added problems caused by color differences. The terms *interracial communication* describes the difficulties added to normal communication because of differences in language, nonverbal codes, stereotypes, prejudices, perceptions, attitudes, value orientations, and thought-patternings between members of different races. The differences between interracial and intercultural communication would seem to be largely matters of degree rather than of kind, except for the very important difference in color of participants in interracial communication. Color differences do affect stereotypes, prejudices, perceptions, and even value orientations. Language is also affected, not only in the range of linguistic stereotypes, but also in the widely documented notion that "black English" differs substantially in terms of both structure or grammar and in vocabulary.

Countercultural communication is that interaction between members of a subcultural or cultural group whose members largely are alienated from the dominant culture. Members of the group may not only reject the values of the dominant culture or society, but may actively work against these values. Conflict is often the result. Either the members of such a group isolate themselves as much as possible from other members of the dominant culture, or they seek to overcome the dominant culture, often through violence. For example, both the Symbionese National Liberation Army and the Black Panthers in the United States committed themselves to guerilla warfare against the dominant culture and generally were unable to establish a real countercultural revolution because their violence led them to neglect a chief cultural value, survival. Additionally, just as all culture designers are, they were products of the cultures that they were attempting to destroy. They could not articulate their goals precisely enough to maintain a consistent and large set of cultural converts.

At the other end of the spectrum, the Amish and the Hasidic Jews are examples of countercultural groups whose members have attempted to withdraw as far as possible from the modern technological culture. They passively react to the dominant culture, but the irreversibility of technological change makes it increasingly difficult to maintain their old customs and ways, and especially to impose their cultural norms and values on their young. We can make the general assumption that countercultural communication poses even greater problems than in many other cultural situations, especially when active antagonism exists between members of different countercultural groups or between members of a countercultural group and the members of a dominant culture.

The communication patterns between the individuals or groups which must cross considerable cultural boundaries would seem to make their interaction more difficult than in *intracultural* communication where the differences are less pronounced. The situational characteristics for members of an intracultural group include sharing common codes such as similar language, values, and frames of reference. In *intercultural* communication there may be obvious differences in codes such as languages and customs. The differences in experiences, meanings, values, and frames of reference may be even more real but not so apparent. Lorand Szalay contends that in the communication process itself, the intracultural situation provides the illusions of a shared universality of common sense: "What I say can and should be automatically understood by you." The spontaneity of the process seems to indicate that communication functions as a form of spontaneous self-expression. In contrast, however, to the intracultural setting, Szalay argues that in the *intercultural communication* process, cultural relativism and pluralism must supersede the more homogeneous nature of the illusions affecting intracultural communication. In the intercultural setting, effective communication requires a systematic bridging of differences. It requires cultural self-awareness, a knowledge of the alternative culture. Participants must develop a systematic and less spontaneous adaptation to the alternative cultural frame of reference with an understanding or appreciation of its code systems such as language and nonverbal cues (Szalay, 1974:2).

The new kind of multicultural person

Peter Adler argues for the notion of the multicultural person. Such a person is rare and cannot be entirely culture-free. However, such a person can be seen as "a new kind of person, a person who is socially and psychologically a product of the interweaving of cultures in the twentieth century. Communication and cultural exchange are the preeminent conditions of the twentieth century." Adler suggests that the new type of person may be called international, transcultural, or intercultural, but all such terms define someone whose horizons extend significantly beyond his or her own culture. Such persons are intellectually and emotionally committed to the fundamental unity of all human beings. At the same time they recognize, legitimize, accept, and appreciate the fundamental differences that lie between people of different cultures.

These new kinds of people cannot be defined by the languages they speak. Nor are they defined by their professions, their places of residence, or their cognitive sophistication. Instead, multicultural men and women are recognized by the configuration of their outlooks and world views, by the way they incorporate the universe as a dynamically moving process, by the way they reflect the interconnectedness of life in their thoughts and actions, and by the way they remain open to the imminence of experience (Adler, 1974:24).

Adler contends that multicultural persons are both old and new, the individuals described by philosophers throughout the ages. Such a person "approaches, in the attributions we make about him, the classical ideal of a person whose lifestyle is one of knowledge and wisdom, integrity and direction, principle and fulfillment, balance and proportion" (24-25). John Walsh, in *Intercultural Education in the Community of Man,* writes: "To be a universal man means not how much a man knows but what intellectual depth and breadth he has and how he relates it to other central and universally important problems" (1973). Adler suggests that what is universal about multicultural persons is an abiding commitment to essential similarities between people everywhere, while paradoxically maintaining an equally strong commitment to their differences. Adler asserts that multicultural persons are neither totally a part of nor totally apart from their culture. They live, instead, on the boundary. Paul Tillich places such persons in the perspective of tension and movement: "It is in truth not standing still, but rather a crossing and a return, a repetition of return and crossing, back and forth—the aim of which is to create a third area beyond the bounded territories, an area where one can stand for a time without being enclosed in something bounded" (1966).

In a sense, multicultural persons are transitional, standing as they do between the old and new. They may be examples of the radically different person, as Margaret Mead describes members of a prefigurative culture. Adler suggests that three features distinguish multicultural persons from others who deal less successfully with intercultural communication. First, they are *psychoculturally adaptive.* They are situational in their relationships to others and with their connections to culture. As persons on the boundary, they have values and attitudes, a world view, and beliefs that are always in a state of change and reformation. The notion of situational ethics would probably be relevant for such persons. Second, they are *always undergoing personal transitions.* They recognize the grounding in their own cultures, but are always in a state of "becoming" or "unbecoming" something different than they were earlier. Adler proposes that "stated differently, multicultural man is propelled from identity to identity through a process of both cultural learning and cultural unlearnings." Third, such persons *maintain indefinite self-boundaries.* Since they are responsive to change and to tolerance of different cultural forms, the parameters of their identities are neither fixed nor predictable. Their styles are always relational and mobile. However, Adler suggests, they are not able to look at their own original cultures objectively. They are thus always in a state of creative tension. They are dynamic, creative, critical, and passionate, often in the face of totalistic ideologies, systems, and movements which do not accept their psychocultural dimensions as being appropriate to the cultural setting from which they come, or toward which they move (1974:29).

Multicultural persons have existed in other times and places. Nevertheless, they are essentially modern-day products. They combine their expansive world views with the developing sense of a world culture. This occurs because of the opportunities and tensions available through the worldwide communications capacity. Such multicultural people may be astronauts, cosmonauts, politicians, humanitarians, writers, artists, scientists, religious figures, or a host of other types of persons. However, we have noted that they are relatively rare because they are not locked into their own culture, which would prevent them from moving easily into other cultures. Many persons have been successful in becoming bicultural and bilingual; others have not been able to make even this step.

More and more, individuals are being forced to consider a multicultural outlook. Few, however, have really adapted the multicultural dimensions proposed by Adler. While the goals are noble, Condon and Yousef cite the danger of "the myth of the universal communicator" which is the belief that certain people will be liked, respected, understood, and will be effective in any culture or society they visit. Condon and Yousef suggest that such universal communicators may not exist. Their faith and optimism reflect idealistic notions of good will which allows them to overcome all obstacles, despite cultural difficulties. Condon and Yousef reject the notion that what in one culture is effective communication, however defined, will also be effective communication in any other culture. They also reject the idea that persons with serious personality problems in one culture will be less effective elsewhere than people who generally get along well with others at home (1975:252-253).

At this point we recognize that the creative tension of being on the boundary does not always produce effective intercultural communication. It may in fact establish very serious communication breakdowns and conflicts. It then becomes clear that while the universal communicator may not yet exist and multicultural people are rare, our goal should be to move effectively from monocultural settings to bicultural settings and finally to multicultural ones. At the same time, those who seek to move into such multicultural settings should be aware that even partial movement from one cultural setting to another is not always possible without considerable creative tension and possible rejection in all the settings. Easy success is not assured. Still, the risk seems worth it for those who can adapt to a multicultural concept of humanity and who wish to share it.

Collective, communication tends to be continuous, planned, impersonal, and unidirectional

Dean Barnlund distinguishes *interpersonal* and *collective communication* as the contrast between personal interaction on the one hand, and impersonal connection with other participants on the other hand. Collective communication always includes a large number of participants. The participants have relatively little interaction, even with the message-senders, making the communication essentially one-way. The roles of the participants are usually formal and ceremonial. In response to messages which are fairly structured and more planned than in the spontaneous interpersonal setting, their responses are structured and by rote. Barnlund notes: "The continuous, planned nature of discourse in public settings contrasts sharply with the episodic, impulsive, and fragmentary character of interpersonal interaction. The impersonality of collective settings, the rigid control of channels, the calculated use of message cues, and the restrictions on communicative roles contribute to a highly structured social situation in which there is the expectation of unidirectional influence" (Barnlund, 1968:11). Subsets which may be included in collective communication are: *organizational, class, political, public, mass, crosscultural, international, and societal*. As in the consideration of other subsets, these overlap considerably and are not mutually exclusive. In viewing collective communication, our chief interest lies in the cultural dimensions involved and in the role that cultural spokespersons serve in the collective setting.

Organizational communication exerts internal controls and responds to external controls

Although organizations may be small or large, the usual implication of *organizational communication* suggests a large group of people directed in a hierarchical fashion by a small group of persons who set the goals and aims of the larger group. It may be seen as (1) the primary means by which organizations select, control, and coordinate the activities of human and material resources *internally*; and (2) the primary means by which organizations respond and adapt to the *external* environment within which they function. The larger the organization, the less horizontal communication takes place interpersonally, and the more vertical communication takes place, generally downward from the organizational managers to the lower members of the collective group. Additionally, the larger the organization, the more formalized are the messages among the participants.

Just as institutional culture such as a church, labor, education, or government seeks to impose its own codes, customs, traditions, and values on its members, so too do organizations attempt a measure of control over their participants. Both institutional culture and organizations act upon their environment as well as react to it. When organizations are essentially cultural in nature, as many are, all of the cultural dimensions already noted also come into play. Within one society, many cultural organizations are operating and many cultural factors are operating on organizations. In the international sphere, more than 3,000 organizations exist with the stated goals of international cooperation of one kind or another. Such organizations naturally also emphasize different cultural dimensions. In such organizations, there is little interpersonal communication between the general members of the various organizations. Cultural spokespersons for such organizations take on added significance. The spokespersons may become puppet speakers for shadow audiences. The interpersonal interaction between the spokespersons may be so circumscribed that very little of it is spontaneous and unplanned. When these spokespersons report to the members of their own organizations, they also typically do it in a collective and unidirectional manner.

Class distinctions remain one of the most critical influences on communication

Thelma McCormack contends that: "Class society is what we have been. Mass society is what we are becoming. . . . Older forms of stratification—regional, ethnic, social—become less important in the conduct of political life. Economic stratification, the keystone of class society, similarly declines as public measures close the gap between rich and poor, insuring the worker against unemployment, the family against illness, and children against educational discrimination" (1973:352). It is true in the North American societal setting and perhaps in the Western urbanized setting as well, that class distinctions are now less important. However, it is also true, as such writers as Michael Harrington and Oscar Lewis argue, that there is a real culture of poverty even in the most sophisticated societies. It may be difficult to delineate so clearly between middle and upper classes, but the differences between the genuinely poor and the other classes are still clear. Mass media, especially radio and television, make it seem that all the members of a highly technological society share the same opportunities, but as John Porter claims, "In a highly developed society, individuals and families could be considered underprivileged if they were denied a reasonable share of the cultural values which have resulted from technology, science, and the modern complex society. Education, high standards of health services, family privacy, and leisure activities of recreation and holidays would be placed high among these cultural values, for the real middle class places greater emphasis on them than on those durable consumer goods, such as cars, refrigerators, electrical appliances and so forth, which are so often taken to mean a high standard of living" (1965: 125-126). Porter points out, as do Harrington and Lewis, that more and more members of the lower classes in the highly developed society do have the consumer goods, but are denied those intrinsic and more-difficult-to-obtain characteristics which sharply distinguish them from middle and upper classes.

The number of those denied communication opportunities among the lower and poor classes in such societies remains alarmingly large. While much interpersonal communication can take place between the members of the lower and upper classes, part of their problem is that the lower classes do not have the same measure of communicative skills that the more educated middle and upper classes have. Thus, they are apt to communicate less interpersonally between classes, and become more the subject of collective communication where they are depersonalized. The messages provided then are more structured and routinized in either direction. Statistics demonstrate that far fewer members of the poor and lower classes than their middle-class counterparts have contact personally with the spokespersons of the middle and upper classes regularly. These are the teachers, government officials, attorneys, clergy, physicians, and employers. When they do have contact, they are much more likely to be treated differently and less individually than are their counterparts. The poorer they are, the less they are protected against unemployment, illness, and educational discrimination. Generally, they do not have articulate spokespersons and they thereby receive more downward messages from the spokespersons of the middle and upper classes than they send upward. Since their class status may correlate with their ethnic, racial, or cultural customs, beliefs, and values, the cultural dimensions for interclass communication problems are considerable.

Political communication helps to shape a society's political and cultural system

Political philosophers before and since Plato and Aristotle have concerned themselves with the communication which takes place in defining and supporting a state. Much of the persuasive discourse in the Greek city-state of Plato and Aristotle's day was engaged in influencing others to take action for or against the interests of the state. In defining the role of political communication, Richard Fagen states: "Most simply, that communicatory activity is considered political by virtue of the consequences, actual and potential, that is had for the functioning of the political system. . . . No matter what the source, message, channel, or audience, it is to the political consequences of the communicatory activity that we must look as the final basis for judgment in those instances when the structure and content of communication may mislead us" (1966:19-20). To understand the political life of a nation, Fagen recommends that we understand the operation of the political system. We must first isolate the communication processes crucial to understanding the system's functioning, and then search for the sources, messages, meanings, channels, audiences, and their relationships. Taken together, these are necessary for an understanding of the communication process in the political situation. For whatever political system under consideration, Fagen would ask: How are the leaders chosen and changed? Who defines political problems and alternatives? Who participates in the making of public policy? What is the scope of allowable criticism? How do citizens become informed about the politically relevant world? Who may choose to isolate himself from politics (1966:17-33)?

Fagen suggests that control is very important in understanding a political system. Accordingly, he would attribute the same element of control to the cultural values which the political systems require or allow for its members. The nature of control in the specific society is revealed by the control over programs of political and national communication media outlets, education, communication rights; the availability of channels, the operation of organizations and institutions; the topics not considered fit for public discussion and advocacy; limits imposed on demands and dissents; what rights are supported or curtailed. Fagen argues that in systems where there can be no room for difference or division among the citizens in its most extreme form, the suspension of communication rights takes the shape of a theory of permanent conflict and crisis. Such a theory states that freedom of political or cultural expression is subversive of national survival in the socio-cultural-political environment in which certain states must exist (1966:136-156).

Political communication does have a bearing on a national cultural value—that of survival—and this value is often used to control the communication of the state's citizens. The political interaction is effected by a smaller number of leaders in a collective and one-way direction. We are all aware of the tremendous power which governments have over political messages and over the mass media. In the United States, governmental cover-ups of events surrounding the Pentagon papers and the Watergate situation give ample evidence of the overwhelming power of government control of communication. The range of controls over political and national values, norms, and patriotism is accomplished in the North American societies through generous transmittal by the media, schools, and in almost every other facet of communication with the citizens and participants in the system.

Public communication Incorporates all phases of a culture and a nation's life

Public communication tends to include leaders (who are small in number), and followers, potential followers, or antagonists (who are generally large in number). Like political communication, public communication tends to remain collective because the leaders often seek to control the actions and attitudes of their followers. It is difficult to say whether political or public

communication is more far-reaching. Often they are considered synonymously. The constraints of the society itself may
dictate who may engage publicly in such communication, who
may oppose it, and what types of messages may be provided.

In the late Roman Empire, the constraints on public and
political communication were such that only ceremonial
speeches were tolerated. The great strength of the Catholic
Church during the Middle Ages and early Renaissance was
demonstrated by the restrictions which it placed on communications which displeased it. *The Index of Forbidden Books,*
the Inquisition, and later attacks against what was considered
heretical protest, are examples of the nature of constraints
against public communication not acceptable to the ruling
leaders. Public communication by priests, ministers, and rab-
bis would differ dramatically in a system where a specific state
religion prohibits other religious beliefs or advocacy, just as
certain political sentiments could not be expressed by public
communicators within the context of societies or nations which
prohibit the expression of such beliefs. In a society or political
system which tolerates a wide range of opinion, as generally is
believed to occur in Canada and the United States, restrictions
on various forms of public expression remain fairly limited. In
the totalitarian society, such freedoms are more seriously
limited. However, even if the political system does not restrict
certain topics, often the cultural system does, and we need only
recall that such topics as birth control, abortion, free love, and
premarital sexual relations as topics were generally considered by the majority of our public leaders as unfit for public
discussion only twenty years ago. Many cultural groups still do
not allow the discussion of such topics openly.

Mass communication implies media manipulators providing messages to the awaiting "masses"

Mass communication can be seen not only as a significant communication channel, but also in relation to participants, involving essentially a one-way form of communication initiated by
the media manipulators and providing messages to the
awaiting masses. Herbert Blumer defines the "mass" as those
people who participate in mass behavior, and identifies four
distinguishable features of its membership: they may come
from all ways of life, and from all distinguishable social strata;
they may include people of different class and cultural posi-

tions, of different vocations, and of different wealth. The mass is an anonymous group, or more exactly, is composed of anonymous individuals. There exists little interaction or change of experience between members of the mass who are usually separated from each other, and, being anonymous, do not have the opportunity to mill as do members of a crowd. Finally, the mass is loosely organized and is not able to act with the concertedness or unity that marks the crowd (1950:43).

More recently, however, researchers have begun to isolate the interpersonal networks which do exist among members of mass audiences. Elihu Katz contends that members of mass audiences do talk to each other, in contrast to the earlier belief that they had no connection beyond collective identification (1966:551-556). Colin Cherry worries about the term: he suggests that at best, communication generally does not take place with the masses but only with individuals in massive numbers. "The term *the masses* is meaningless, unless it is qualified: 'the mass of people who do so-and-so.' It has degenerated into an emotional term which may conveniently be used in a contemptuous or pejorative way. . . .The masses are never you nor me, only 'the others'" (1971:42). Still, communication to the individuals who make up the masses is often considered the best example of collective communication where the messages and channels are controlled by a small group of people. This small group attempts to dictate tastes, morals, and values among the large numbers who utilize their messages. The issues considered earlier and such cultural components as linguistic and nonverbal codes, attitudes, beliefs, values, and thought-patternings all have cultural implications for the study of mass communication as a very important aspect of collective communication. Much cultural assimilation is the result of mass communication, while the very potential of communicating with individuals in massive numbers also allows for a greater range of cultural diversity.

Crosscultural communication represents the cultural spokesperson

In contrast to the individualized and personalized intercultural communicator, the *crosscultural* communicator can best be seen as the cultural spokesperson for an individual culture or members of cultures. The interaction takes place in the large, collective, and impersonal setting. The communication of cultural representatives is horizontal among other cultural spokespersons and vertical with members of their own cultures. When whole cultures are in contact, most of the messages are formal and heavily procedural. The mass concept is apparent, and much of the culturally biased propaganda directed against or toward a particular cultural group suggests the aspect of crosscultural communication. Crosscultural communication tends to be one-way, large group-oriented, official, and formal, with planned and systematically organized messages, and with a hierarchial structure to the communication setting.

Often crosscultural communication research and study emphasize cultural variables which can be present in two or more cultures. Such study may seek to demonstrate or locate evidence of a comparative cultural basis, or to build out of such related data sets of potential universals which may be seen operating in many or all cultures. D. Price-Williams suggests:

In the same way that the study of individual differences shows to what degree a particular person is similar to or different from others, so crosscultural studies focus on the similarities and differences of whole societies. . . . Apart from the advantage of utilizing the differences between cultures as a buffer against generalizing from a comparatively small sample of the earth's population, crosscultural work has the further asset of seeking out situations and influences which are either difficult to find in our own culture or are just nonexistent (1972:36).

Price-Williams suggests areas worthy of investigation related to crosscultural communication are perception, cognition (including language and thought-patterning), socialization, and personality (1972:35-48). We might add the importance of studying comparative mass media systems as key areas of crosscultural concern. Additionally, study is needed about the crosscultural implications of nonverbal patterns, cues, and codes, as well as the long-term study of verbal codes to further demonstrate how people from different cultural groupings utilize and respond to various nonverbal signs and symbols.

International communication stresses political interaction between nations

International communication is often used interchangeably with intercultural and crosscultural communication, but it more properly characterizes the interaction which takes place across national political boundaries. James Markham defines international communication in its simplest forms as "peoples speaking to peoples," and "governments speaking to governments." He refers to the legitimate national governments of individual states whose spokespersons are engaged in various actions and transactions on a binational and multinational basis. By "peoples" he means collectively the nations—but usually the elites—of a given country. They are not necessarily members of the government, but they may be speaking across national boundaries in private, public, or political fashions about issues which transcend individual state concerns. Markham distinguishes comparative communication from international communication in that the former is generally concerned with the study, by a comparative method of analysis, of internal communication systems of two or more states or cultures (1972:172).

The best-known international organization based on international cooperation is the United Nations, which has a multitude of subsidiary organizations. Despite weaknesses in keeping international peace and the resolution of international conflict, the United Nations does serve as a legitimizer of states, and becomes the forum both for heads of state and heads of government and their appointed representatives. It serves also for members of certain elites who might not otherwise have a wide international forum from which to speak. Often the diplomats accredited there have more in common with other diplomats than with the local national and cultural populaces they represent. Similar to other forms of collective communication, international communication tends to be directed from small groups to large audiences; its messages tend to be formalized and ritualized; and the communicators fill the role of serving as puppet speakers for shadow audiences.

Societal communication provides the pattern for social interaction

Emile Durkheim argues that what keeps a society together, what offers it solidarity and a sense of identity, is some kind of collective conscience or set of values and ideas created in the process of living together. He labels these ideas, embodying both values and instrumental knowledge, currents of opinion. He points out that the society's cohesiveness is formed by collective sentiments and ideas which in turn are affected by population densities and mobilities. Durkheim notes that when a society is undergoing rapid economic development, it is caught in a period of cultural and societal instability, just as is the society which is caught up in a "revolution of rising expectations, especially when the societal goals and norms do not match its ability to properly reach these goals" (1951, 1950).

Since the goals and norms of a society are collective, most of its communication is also collective. Often it is difficult to separate the goals and norms of a nation, a culture, and a society as well as the collective communication which is generated to promote these goals and norms. William Rivers explains that in every society, from the most primitive to the most modern, the communication system serves as watcher, forum, and teacher, and perhaps also as societal entertainer. As watcher, the communication system provides other members of the society with information and an interpretation of events as they affect the environment encircling the society. As a forum, it helps societal members to agree on how to handle threats to the society, in terms of its norms and goals. When change is needed or should be prevented, the community can reach a consensus on the society's best decisions. As a teacher, the communication system passes on the society's social heritage and cultural traditions from one generation to the next, through such institutions as home, church, and school. Finally, as entertainment, a society's communication system allows members, in the words of Charles Wright, to "provide respite for the individual which, perhaps, permits him to continue to be exposed to the mass-communicated news, interpretation and prescriptions so necessary for his survival in the modern world" (quoted in Rivers, Peterson and Jensen, 1971:28-29). In effect, the same uses of communication could be applied to a culture as well. Generally speaking, however, the concept of society is considered much broader than a single cultural group, and is thought to include a multitude of cultures and subcultures as parts of the whole. The emphasis of communication in the societal level is typically collective. Even while interpersonal communication is used to help foster the society's goals, much of it is directed by a smaller group of individuals who prepare messages for the broader society as a whole. The messages are predominantly one-way and remain more formal than spontaneous.

Global communication cuts across cultural, national, and societal boundaries

Global communication is an ambiguous term applied generally to collective communication that supersedes cultural, national, and societal boundaries. Such groupings as churches, international societies, or multicultural and international organizations often are separated by linguistic and nonverbal codes, attitudes, values, and thought-patternings. However, generally some common belief unites them, or at least some minimal joint goal (such as Jesus Christ as a unifying force in history for Christians wherever they may live, or Islamic beliefs and traditions for Arabs wherever they may live).

That dialogue, communication, and communications systems do link virtually all parts of the world in some way or another, is as Colin Cherry suggests, "a triumph of common sense." Such systems include the mail, telephones, telegraphs, airways, monetary systems, and satellites, all of which are essential for the beginning of a global communication system. Behind such technology, individual cultures, governments, and societies must agree to the minimum requirements and goals which allow such a global communications system to operate. Additionally, Cherry stresses a common-sense fact that both ends of a communications link of any kind must have some degree of benefit, even if the benefit is greater to one than to the other, for the system to work at all. Cherry denies McLuhan's "global village" notion by arguing that the world is not his village, which would imply interpersonal rather than collective communication. Still, he does stress that global communication planning is a fundamental requirement if any collective cooperation is to occur at all. Such planning needs to take place at the global, regional, and national levels (1971: 126-127). Such agencies of the United Nations as the Universal Postal Union, the International Telecommunication Union, and the International Civil Aviation Organization do function to organize global or world communication, particularly in the development of telecommunication, without which none of the other systems could operate on a truly global scale.

Cherry suggests that the first benefits which global communication brings are practical and economic, by providing the means for the first time for rapid and effective multilateral exchanges of many kinds. They provide the "mechanics of living" for international organizations to operate. The value of global communication lies in the contribution which the various systems can make toward removing the frustrations caused by not being able to communicate on a global scale. He proposes that the value of global communications "lies not in their unlikely power for persuading everybody else to be like us, but rather in putting our various distinct characteristics, arising from our different histories, geographies and peoples, to positive value. That is, to work *through* these differences, not *upon* them, and to use these differences, which may seem to be dissent or even heresy, as a creative source of change of our own institutions" (1971:203-204).

To balance the communicative needs on a collective global scale of interacting groups, cultures, nations, and societies is indeed a considerable task. As often as not, attempts to bring various groups into an effective communicative exchange on the global scale are as likely to fail as succeed. As Colin Cherry argues: "The greatest powers for preventing the realization of these possibilities [for better international cooperation] are still non-technical; they are the emotional blocks in people's minds, values, national parochialisms and other human factors. Whether our new-found powers will become used for mutual benefit, or not, cannot depend upon technical criteria alone. They may bring us closer together in some ways, but equally well drive us farther apart in others" (1971:167-169).

In Chapter 4, we have concluded our dicussion of hierarchial sets of communication components by concentrating on the collective and global sets of participants. We suggested that collective communication tends to be continuous, planned, impersonal, and unidirectional. Usually it involves a smaller group attempting to control and manipulate the messages going to a larger group whose members respond in a relatively formalized and ritualized manner. In this set, we have included organizational, class, political, public, mass, crosscultural, international, and societal participants. Our focus has emphasized the cultural aspects of the collective set, and the role of cultural spokespersons for the various subsets. Finally we have noted that global communication cuts across cultural, national, and societal boundaries. Seen in the sense of the global village, it suggests the ideal of interpersonal communication to a much greater degree. Viewed more realistically from the perspective of collective communicators consistently crossing such boundaries, global communication does provide many more opportunities for world interaction through various cultural spokespersons and offers greater problems because of continuing difficulties between peoples and nations.

Summary

An organizing principle of Chapter 4 has been first to consider such sets as *intrapersonal, interpersonal,* and *cultural communication* participants, with an emphasis on the number of participants in each set, their characteristics, and their directionality. We have characterized intrapersonal communication as unitary, individualistic, and unidirectional. Intrapersonal communication stresses our cultural uniqueness and our "personal culture." Interpersonal communication participants include such subsets as dyadic, triadic, family, and small group communicators. The interaction remains focused with relatively few participants; is characterized by a greater personal use of sense modalities; and is often multidirectional. Such communication emphasizes the spontaneous, unplanned nature of communication among the participants.

Cultural communication has been demonstrated to include such subsets as intraethnic and interethnic communication, intra- and interracial communication, countercultural communication, and intra- and intercultural communication. The last term is frequently used to subsume all of the others. We have suggested that cultural communication intensifies the differences in linguistic, nonverbal, attitudinal, value, and thought-patterning orientations.

We have suggested that the new type of person is multicultural. Such people are on the boundary between the rules and constraints of their own cultures and those of other cultures. The multicultural man or woman is transitional, standing between the old and the new. Such a person is rare but may be seen as one goal to work toward in the study and effective practice of intercultural communication. Moving toward such a state provides rich challenges and critical problems.

References

Adler, Peter S., 1974. "Beyond Cultural Identity: Reflections on Cultural and Multicultural Man." In *Topics in Learning* (August), 23-40.

Barnlund, Dean, 1968. *Interpersonal Communication: Survey and Studies.* Boston: Houghton Mifflin.

Caplow, Theodore, 1968. *Two Against One: Coalitions in Triads.* Englewood Cliffs, New Jersey: Prentice-Hall.

Cherry, Colin, 1971. *World Communication: Threat or Promise.* New York.

Condon, John C., and Fathi Yousef, 1975. *An Introduction to Intercultural Communication.* Indianapolis: Bobbs-Merrill.

Durkheim, Emile, 1951. *The Division of Labour in Society.* Translated G. Simpson. Glenview, Illinois: Scott Foresman.

Fagen, Richard, 1966. *Politics and Communication.* Boston: Little, Brown.

Katz, Elihu, 1966. "Communication Research and the Image of Society: Convergence of Two Traditions." In *Communication and Culture: Readings in the Codes of Human Behavior.* Edited by Alfred Smith. New York: Holt.

McCormack, Thelma, 1971. "Social Change and the Mass Media." In *Intercommunication among Nations and Peoples.* Edited by Michael H. Prosser. New York: Harper & Row.

Markham, James W., ed., 1970. *International Communication as a Field of Study.* Iowa City: University of Iowa.

Porter, John, 1965. *The Vertical Mosaic: An Analysis of Social Class and Power in Canada.* Toronto: University of Toronto.

Price-Williams, D., 1972. "Cross-Cultural Studies." In *Intercultural Communication: A Reader.* Edited by Larry Samovar and Richard Porter. Belmont, California: Wadsworth.

Rivers, William L., Theodore Peterson, and Jay W. Jenson, 1971. *The Mass Media and Modern Society.* San Francisco: Rinehart Press.

Sherif, Muzager, and Carolyn Sherif, 1964. *Social Settings and Reference Groups: A Reader.* Dubuque: William C. Brown.

Szalay, Lorand B., 1974. "Adapting Communication Research to the Needs of International and Intercultural Communication." In *International and Intercultural Communication Annual,* I, 1-16.

Walsh, John E., 1973. *Intercultural Education in the Community of Man.* Honolulu: East-West Center Press.

CHAPTER 5

Communicative Codes: Linguistic Aspects

A code may be referred to as a system of laws or rules intended to augment or guide certain aspects of human interaction. Legal systems such as the Twelve Tables of the Romans, English common law, the United States Constitution, and international law represent specific codes of justice. Religious rules in the Ten Commandments, the Torah, the Christian Bible, Roman Catholic or Episcopal canon law, and the Koran are codes for moral living. The language systems of the Indo-European family, with their similar patterns of grammar and syntax, provide a general code for the languages within that family. Each specific language in the family differs enough from the others that it is supplemented by its own specific code of rules.

Culture itself is a code which we learn and share with others. The socializing process in every culture for the young involves both written and unwritten codes of rules and laws. Likewise, within and between societies and cultures, communication proceeds by certain prescribed and inferred codes of behavior. Albert E. Scheflen argues that people are socially organized to perform and interpret repertoires of coded behavior. They have learned multichanneled, highly-patterned communicative behavior for multiple social roles and multiple occasions. The social organization for their interaction is not a simple alteration of speaker and listener, but involves kinship and other affiliational systems, dominance hierarchies, territorial arrangements, and other abstractable dimensions (1967:8).

George Gerbner defines communication as "social interaction through symbols and message systems. The production and perception of message systems cultivating stable structures of generalized images—rather than any tactic calculated to result in 'desirable' (or any other response)—is at the heart of the communications transaction" (1966:102-103). David Berlo isolates the role of code as an aspect of the total communicative situation:

A code can be defined as any group of symbols that can be structured in a way that is meaningful to some person. . . . Anything is a code which has a group of elements (a vocabulary) and a set of procedures for combining those elements meaningfully (a syntax). If we want to know whether a set of symbols is a code, we have to isolate its vocabulary, and check to see if there are systematic ways (structures) for combining the elements.

In the same way, if we want to learn a code, to "break a code," we look for the elements that appear, and we look for consistent ways in which the elements are structured. . . . Whenever we encode a message, we must make certain decisions about the code we will use. We must decide (a) which code, (b) what elements of the code, and (c) what method of structuring the elements of the code we will select. Second, when we analyze communication behavior, messages, we need to include the source's decisions about the code in our analysis. It is for these reasons that we include code as part of our analysis of structure (1960:57-59).

Berlo emphasizes that in linking *messages* and *codes*, we must also be aware of the content of the message, which like the code, has both elements and structure. We must also recognize the best ways to present our messages or how to select and arrange both our codes and message content. As message recipients we need to understand and accept messages. We must have the ability to interpret the codes as well as to perceive the intention of the messages. Berlo comments: "When we decode messages, we make inferences as to the source's purpose, his communication skills, his attitudes toward us, his knowledge, his status. We try to estimate what kind of person would have produced this kind of message. We often decide what the source's purpose was, what kind of 'personality' he has, what objects he values or believes in, what he thinks is worthless" (1960:59-61).

Verbal linguistic codes provide the link for cultural communication

Both the verbal linguistic and the nonverbal codes which we use in human communication are of considerable interest to the intercultural communicator and crosscultural researcher. They add significantly to the ethnographic study of a community or mapping of a culture which Hymes recommends. As symbol-builders and -manipulators, we can encode and decode a nearly limitless variety of verbal and nonverbal messages, depending upon our own capacities. Colin Cherry writes: "This great variety of roles which humans are able to adopt seems to be mediated by their phenomenal powers of a sign-usage, above all by those of language. It is their powers of language which set them apart from the creatures of a gulf, a gulf which Susanne Langer has seen as 'one whole day of Creation'—a whole chapter of evolution. All races of man, all nations, all tribes everywhere have language" (1971:2). Nonetheless, our capacity to use sign-systems such as language and conscious nonverbal codes serves both to unite and to divide us from each other. As Cherry stresses, the very fact that language forms a major part of our identity, of our view of ourselves and in relation to our friends, our fellow citizens, and foreigners, helps to make us inseparable from our social groups. Thus, we accept certain groups and reject others. Cherry insists, however, that: "Man has endless uses of language, signs and ritual, significant of the fact that he is a member of a nation, or a class, or a tribe, or a race, of this or that group; but he has no common language, few signs, and virtually no universal ritual significant of the fact that he is a member of the human race" (1971:3-7).

By its nature, language is the key link between our ability to communicate and to pass on our cultural traditions to our children. Joseph H. Greenberg emphasizes that:

Among all the aspects of the cultural inheritance, anthropologists are virtually unanimous in pointing to two, tools and speech, as the most fundamental, in that they provide the indispensable prerequisites for the remainder. . . .

The two basic human traits of toolmaking and speech are more similar to each other than might appear at first glance. They have in common indirectness of action on the environment: the natural environment, for tools, the social environment, in the case of speech. . . .

When we find, in the archeological record, specific types of such purposefully fashioned tools persisting over time in the form of a definite toolmaking tradition, we see a cultural trait that, we assume, could not have come into existence without language. From its transmission we infer the operation of a fundamental function of language: the communication of already acquired knowledge. . .(1971:271-273).

Speech is the basic coding procedure followed by language

In relating communication and codes, George A. Miller suggests: "Our analysis of communication begins with the most important encoding procedure of all—human vocalization. Other ways of encoding information could be studied instead, but certainly speech is the first learned and most widely used. In many respects speech is the basic encoding procedure. Some linguists reserve the term 'language' exclusively for the code of vocal symbols; writing, gestures, Braille, etc., are also codes that can be used for communication but are not dignified by the title of languages" (1951:10). Most writers on language recognize that speech and language are not precisely the same. Language is seen as an abstract system which is realized through vocalized utterances. A person unable to speak may understand speech, but still has the innate ability to utilize language. Joseph DeVito observes: "Language is the *potential* vehicle whereas speech is the *actual* activity of communication. There is also an important distinction between speech and writing. Speech is clearly the primary form of communication; writing is a secondary and derived system—a system developed in imitation of the spoken language. Speech is not spoken writing, nor is writing simply written speech" (1970:9). The notion of speech as having among its partial origins the behavioral aspects of vocal behavior or oral gesture is widely held, as Miller observes: "To think of speech as audible movement and comparable to movements of the arms and legs is to think of speech as vocal behavior. Viewed in this way, speech is not essentially different from acts of other types. Its apparent uniqueness rests upon its importance to man, the talking animal. Speech accomplishes the same sort of result that other behaviors could, only more expeditiously" (1951:3).

A major concern for the study of speech is the patterning

ability which allows us to make many different combinations of sounds. Without patterning its individual sounds, Miller suggests that there would be very few things such a language could talk about, as we can make and distinguish less than 100 different speech sounds. In the English language, there are about forty different sounds. We could produce fifty different sounds to discuss millions of different things, which is a feature of human speech sound combinations. Miller stresses that if "we use all the possible pairs of fifty sounds, we can make 2,500 different statements. If 2,500 statements are not enough, we can go on to use patterns of three or four or even a thousand sounds. There are many more patterns than there are individual sounds. The ability to use such patterns, however, is uniquely human" (1951:5-6). This patterning which occurs in English speech includes recognizable units called *phonemes* (the smallest meaningful elements of sound) *words,* and *sentences.* The patterning, often carefully prescribed by rules, becomes a *grammar,* which helps to structure the coding of a language. Miller suggests: "The grammar of any language has two main parts: (1) *morphology* deals with the structure of words, and (2) *syntax* deals with the combination of words in phrases and sentences. To define what a word is in any given language is to describe the morphology of that language. To define what a sentence is describes the syntax" (1951:82).

Language symbolizes and catalogs our perceived reality

As a code, language may be seen both as a component of communication and of culture. The noted sociolinguist Joseph Greenberg summarizes his view of language:

Language is unique to man. No other species possesses a truly symbolic means of communication and no human society, however simple its material culture, lacks the basic human heritage of a well developed language. Language is the prerequisite for the accumulation and transmission of other cultural traits. Such fundamental aspects of human society as organized political life, legal systems, religion and science are inconceivable without that most basic and human of tools, a linguistic system of communication. Language is not only a necessary condition for culture, it is itself a part of culture. It, like other shared behavioral norms, is acquired by the individual as a member of a particular social group through a complex process of learning. Like other aspects of human culture, it characteristically varies from group to group and undergoes significant modification in the course of its transmission through time within the same society (1971:156).

DeVito defines language as "a potentially self-reflective, structured system of symbols which catalog the objects, events, and relations in the world." He argues that symbols are arbitrary "stand-ins" for the actual things. For example the word *rain* is not the actual rain but serves as a symbol of rain. Signs, however, do bear real relationships to the things for which they stand. For example, high fever is a sign of sickness. Here there is a real, rather than arbitrary, relationship between the thing (sickness) and the sign (fever).

DeVito notes that symbols are arbitrary according to certain rules, and may be made of any substance. He offers varied examples, such as pyramids, purple cloth for the royalty, black cloth for mourning, or vocal symbols as representative of speech. The symbols of language are words.

DeVito contends that because language is potentially *self-reflexive* it is capable of being used on at least two different levels. It must permit symbolic reference to the real or object world, and it also must allow reference to itself or to talk about language. Language is language only if it can be used for language analysis that is, metalanguage (DeVito, 1970:7-9).

While it is possible for the "language" of bees to duplicate certain features of human language, it is a very limited duplication. Despite the work with certain members of the family of ape, researchers so far have not been able to develop any nonhuman being which can either systematically produce all of the human sounds in a meaningful way, or utilize the distinctively human features of language as the human can. David McNeil speaks of the centrality of the sentence to the development of language because virtually everything that occurs in language acquisition depends on prior knowledge of the basic aspects of sentence structure. He suggests that through the two-step alarm call produced by baboons, accepted at face value, they might be said to show sentence structure. However, "it is a structure sharply limited in use. If baboons have a language, it is a language with only one sentence. In contrast, sentences are obligatory in human language. Whatever favored sentence structure in the evolution of human language must have operated at an early point to have had such a wide scope" (McNeil, 1970:2, 52).

Language universals serve as a primary link between language and cultures

Cultural universals are properties of all human cultures found in all groups, such as speech, material traits, art, knowledge, religion, society, organized social institutions, belief systems, property, government, and war in the abstract. While cultural universals represent only the minimum patterns of similarities in cultures across time and space, their study has led to crosscultural research to determine systematically what other more detailed universal statements can be made about human societies. In a similar way, a primary concern in linking language and culture is the concept of language universals. In an early attempt to distinguish the concept, Western linguists assumed that the Western descriptions of parts of speech were universally accepted, and that all sentences could properly be divided into *subjects* and *predicates* as bare minimums, without regard for the entirely different logical and thought-patterning prevalent among the other cultures and societies. Such statements have been unfounded crossculturally. As a simple example, while the English sentence does proceed in a subject-verb-object pattern (John ate a sandwich), the Japanese sentence proceeds instead in a subject-object-verb pattern. Such crosscultural differences obviously cause problems in intercultural communication.

Language universals are summary statements about all human speakers

A major contribution to the study of language universals has been their central place in the theoretical framework of the generative transformational school of linguistics, now the dominant trend in American language studies. Greenberg suggests: "Language universals are by their very nature summary statements about characteristics or tendencies shared by all human speakers. As such they constitute the most general laws of a science of linguistics." Further, he argues that since language is both an aspect of individual behavior and human culture, its universals provide both the major point of contact with underlying psychological principles and the major source of implications for human culture in general. He stresses, however, that a major stumbling block for the proper development of a system of detailed language universals is first, the

difficulty caused by making unwarranted assumptions based
on the Greco-Roman grammatical and linguistic patterns and
logic. A second important problem is the lack of a central
source of data, or a crosscultural file for a large and representative sample of the world's 3,000 to 5,000 living languages
(1971:297-298, 143-144).

Recognizing the principle of differences in studying
culture, we become aware that the diversity of languages, even
those within the same language families, is far greater than
even most linguists have been willing to admit. As Clifford
Geertz challenges the viability of the concept of cultural
universals as being too simple, Greenberg argues that it is not
enough to establish language universals by simply accepting
statements that all languages have vowels; all languages have
phonemes; and all language sound systems may be resolved into distinctive features. He believes that the concept of
language universals must be expanded to include generalizations which hold true in more than a chance number of comparisons (1971:297-298, 143-144).

Language universals may be distinguished by logical structure and substantive content

Greenberg recommends viewing language universals as differentiated both in their *logical structure* and their *substantive
content*. The *logical structures* of universals incorporate the
ability to define universals as any statements which include all
languages in their scope. Examples are characteristics
possessed by all languages, the relationships between two
characteristics in all languages, or the case of mutual implications between characteristics in specific languages or
language families that are not universal in all languages. The
logical structure of universals also includes a certain
characteristic which has a greater probability than some other
characteristic. It includes "near universals" in some extreme
cases. Additional considerations include the relation of several
characteristics in terms of probability, and instances in which
a certain measurement—for example, redundancy in information theory—may be applied to any language to demonstrate
characteristic means and standard deviations from other
languages (1971:146-149).

Substantive classes of universals cut across the *logical
structure* of languages, and include *phonological, grammatical,*

semantic, and *symbolic* types. In this classification, Greenberg suggests that the first three involve either form without meaning or meaning without form. The last classification, which is concerned with sound symbolism, involves the connection between the two. For example, the near universality of nasals such as *m* and *n* is a phonological universal which is not concerned with semantic meaning of forms; and the semantic universal that all languages have some metaphorically transferred meaning is not concerned with the particular sounds of the forms as they occur. On the other hand, a statistical symbolic universal such as "there is a high probability that a word designating the female parent will have a nasal consonant" as in English *"mother,"* French *"mere,"* and the Latin *"mater,"* involves both sound and meaning and is therefore of the symbolic type (Greenberg, 1071:150).

We are interested in the symbolic uses of social discourse in and between cultures. Thus, language universals relating to the ability for communicators to encode and decode messages symbolically through channels in time and space become more relevant and interesting to us than others. On a practical level, if we understand that we can begin to decode certain messages in various languages because language universals always or normally apply to certain aspects of these languages, our intercultural communication begins to become somewhat easier than if we had no methods at all for decoding. In the simplest way, if we are aware that the English word "me" has essentially the same basic form and meaning in dozens of languages, and if the paralinguistic pointing of a person points at himself or herself with approximately the same meaning, the initial step has been made in understanding a verbal and nonverbal cue offered in a different linguistic framework by a member of another culture. If a frantic vocal tension is added, some notion is provided to help decode a message of some urgency involving oneself. Naturally, a far more systematic probing into language universals is needed to assist in understanding the real or apparent connections even between very similar languages.

In a much more systematic and empirical way, the Cross-Cultural Universals of Affective Meaning Project which has been headed for the past several years by Charles E. Osgood at the University of Illinois is an example of an application of cultural and language universals theories in twenty-five cultures. It is designed to test the hypothesis that regardless of language or culture, human beings use the same qualifying and descriptive framework in allocating the affective meanings of concepts which involve values, stereotypes, attitudes, and feelings. Osgood and his colleagues, many of whom come from the cultures under consideration, maintain that the hypothesis has proven valid, and that as the project continues it may be possible to isolate truly reliable cultural and linguistic universals (Osgood et al., 1975).

Stability and change play a role in the understanding of language universals

Language universals can be stated by observing universally discoverable regularities of how languages remain the same. They can also be stated by emphasizing how languages change by various intracultural and intercultural influences over time and space.

The interrelationship of these approaches to language universals is important because one cannot be viewed systematically without understanding the other. The observer cannot develop universal rules for language without knowing how the language functions in a static position, relatively free of immediate change, and vice versa, especially in the context of the wide diversity of languages and language families. Such a study is of greater interest to the trained linguist than to us as regular intercultural communicators, but it is useful for us to know that there are universals which do powerfully affect and assist us as we try to communicate with persons from different language backgrounds.

Generative grammar argues that all natural languages have universally similar grammatical systems

In contrast to the Sapir-Whorf hypothesis that every language designates the culture and the cultural communicator's individual thought-patterning, David McNeil proposes that "the description of linguistic universals is included in the theory of universal grammar. As opposed to the grammar of a single language, the theory of a grammar is a description of the general form of human language. . . . The purpose is to state the universal conditions that the grammars describing individual languages must meet" (1970:71). Noam Chomsky, a chief proponent of the theory of generative or transformational grammar, states that two central problems are present in the descriptive study of a language: the primary concern to discover simple and "revealing" grammars for natural languages, and to arrive at a general theory of language structure crossculturally (1966:140-141).

In many languages, there are certain cases of correct grammar and certain cases of incorrect grammar, for example in English, "John ate a sandwich," and "Sandwich a ate John." In this case, Chomsky says that we can test the adequacy of a proposed linguistic theory by determining in each language whether or not clear cases are handled properly by the grammars in accordance with this theory. Chomsky calls the first step in the linguistic analysis of a language the provision of a limited system of representation for its sentences: "No matter how we ultimately decide to construct linguistic theory, we shall surely require that the grammar of any language must be finite. It follows that only a countable set of grammars is made available by any linguistic theory; hence that uncountably many languages, in our general sense, are literally not describable in terms of the conception of linguistic structure." Chomsky asks: Are there interesting languages that are simply beyond the range of description of the proposed type? Can we construct reasonably simple grammars for all interesting languages? Are such grammars revealing in the sense that the syntactic structure that they exhibit can support semantic analysis, can provide insight into the use and understanding of language (1966:141-142)?

Several basic assumptions underlie generative grammar

Joseph DeVito demonstrates that several basic assumptions underlie generative grammar in terms of the distinctions made between concepts and processes, that is, between *static* and *process descriptions*, between *competence* and *performance*, between *descriptive* and *prescriptive grammars*, and between *deep* and *surface structures*. In the distinctions between *static* and *process descriptions*, DeVito points out that earlier linguists attempted to describe language change as *process* over time. More recently, especially in the twentieth century, the emphasis developed so that they began describing the sound and structure of languages in a *static* or unchanging situation. Then, still later, the emphasis was placed on the description of the *process* of language with an emphasis on generative grammar and grammatical transformations—

processes or operations by which strings of elements are altered or changed by addition, deletion, substitution, or permutation (1970:44-45). Chomsky provides an example of such a string with no general relation between the component parts and its grammaticalness: "colorless green ideas sleep furiously." The string does have grammatical sense, even if it has no semantically correct meaning. Another example, this time of a string which has no grammatical correctness, is "furiously sleep ideas green colorless." Both sentences can be improved syntactically or semantically by additions and deletions (Chomsky, 1966:144).

To delineate between *competence* and *performance*, DeVito utilizes the distinction offered by the generative grammarians which says that *competence*, similar to language, refers to the rules of grammar which the native speaker "knows," that is, can apply with a conscious understanding of them. *Performance*, similar to speech, is the actual vocal noise uttered and heard, and may have no relation to a conscious understanding of the rules behind it. DeVito asserts that the study of language is primarily concerned with *competence* and the generative grammarian will seek to discover the grammar which in turn *generates* grammatical sentences and offers no ungrammatical sentences. Such a grammar provides that while there are a limited number of linguistic elements and rules, there are an infinite number of possible sentences in any human language. Normal human adults can offer thousands and thousands of different sentences. This is an important factor for the intercultural communicator because once we know the basic rules and a substantial vocabulary in a second language, we become able to encode and decode a nearly limitless number of sentences or message components in that language as well as in our own. The generative or transformational grammar theory would lead us to believe that the same features can be duplicated over and over again to the extent that an individual's capacity for learning sets of rules and vocabularies is possible. This would seem a reasonable assumption, given the warning that the diversity of grammatical rules and vocabularies still makes it unusual for individuals to master more than several highly contrasting languages in terms of their structure and semantic range of meaning. This defines language (as opposed to language in general) as an infinite set of grammatical sentences, and defines grammar as the device for specifying or describing this infinite set of sentences (DeVito, 1970:45-46). Chomsky has stimulated linguists to describe a universal grammar as a correlate of language universals (1967).

Most contemporary linguists prefer *descriptive* grammar over *prescriptive* grammar because they wish to describe the competence of speakers rather than prescribe rules for instruction in proper language usage. Such linguists do not concern themselves with the nature and background of the specific user of the language nor with concepts such as "right" and "wrong" in language. They are less concerned about a speaker's use of "ain't" than whether it fits correctly in a sentence or a grammatical structural basis. Such language specialists would consider "black" English on this basis rather than on the basis that some of its usage and vocabulary seem incorrect to users of standard English. Chomsky distinguishes between *deep* and *surface* structure of a sentence universally by emphasizing that in addition to the surface or superficial structure of a sentence, there is also a deep structure and that sentences are understood on the basis of their deep rather than their surface structure (1968). DeVito exemplifies a sentence whose surface structure is: "The criticisms of the student were negative," which has two confusing deep structures: "The student has given negative criticisms" and "Someone gives the student negative criticisms." DeVito suggests that another way in which the distinction between deep and surface structure becomes apparent is seen in sentences which are different on the surface but which have only one deep structure as in: "The boy hit the girl," and "The girl was hit by the boy." These sentences are understood in essentially the same way, not because their surface structure reveals this similarity, but because their deep or underlying structure is the same (1971:46-47). Interrogatives also form part of the deep structure and are generated semantically in any language, e.g., "Did the boy hit the girl?" "Why did the boy hit the girl?" "The boy hit the girl, did he?" "How did the boy hit the girl?"

DeVito acknowledges that generative grammar is only one possible way of approaching language, but he argues: "It seems to me, however, that generative grammar is at present the only workable candidate for a theory of language simply because it is the only grammar which provides a convincing account of the speaker's linguistic competence. . . . The influence of generative grammar on the study of psycholinguistics has far surpassed the influence exerted by any other approach" (1970:56). Comparing the argument between those who accept the linguistic relativity hypothesis of Sapir-Whorf, which makes each culture dependent upon its language, and the argument of Chomsky and others that generative grammars provide a sort of universal grammar, Condon and Yousef suggest: "If we expect to find great diversity in languages, it is only a matter of time until—as the transformational grammarians seemed to find—we discover how remarkably similar languages are at heart. That is, from the transformationalist point of view, the apparent differences in the ways languages code 'reality' are mostly superficial (if not exactly above the surface then at least not below the surface). If we go to a deeper structure on a level that ordinary speakers are not aware of, we can find remarkable consistency across languages" (Condon and Yousef, 1975:175).

A counterargument to the underlying universality of language

A major counterdevelopment in the Western world to the problems caused by the application of essentially a Greco-Roman grammatical tradition was structuralism. This emphasized linguistic structural differences rather than the uniformities of language. In structuralism, every language is perceived as an organized structural system which must be described in its own terms without the imposition of the observers' ethnocentrically derived categories (Greenberg, 1971:296). In this sense, the principle of differences was recognized as the basis for crosscultural linguistic research.

When we consider contemporary theories of language and culture which stress linguistic differences from culture to culture in contrast to the notion that language universals serve as a primary link between language and culture, the "linguistic relativity theory," associated primarily with Edward Sapir and Benjamin Lee Whorf and variously called the "Sapir-Whorf hypothesis" or "the Whorf hypothesis," is a dominant one. However, it is considered by many writers as out-of-date. It is not the sort of hypothesis that can be proven or disproven, and it is not even clear whether Sapir and Whorf meant what is considered as the focus of their theory today. Still, its staying power is the chief reason why it is of considerable interest to the student of intercultural and crosscultural communication.

Sapir's statement of his hypothesis can be summarized as follows: "Language is a self-contained, creative, symbolic organization, which not only refers to experience largely acquired without its help but actually defines experience for us both by its structure and by our unconscious acceptance of the language's ability to influence all of our experience by shaping symbolic meanings for us." The argument is that meanings are not so much discovered in experience as imposed upon it, because of the tyrannical hold that linguistic form has upon our orientation of the world. Language is a guide to "social reality." According to this hypothesis, we are at the mercy of the particular language which has become the medium of expression for our society. Our reality is determined by our own language. No two languages are ever sufficiently similar to be considered as representing the same social reality. The worlds in which different societies live are distinct, not merely the same world with different labels attached (Sapir in Mandelbaum, 1949:162). Sapir's student, Whorf, proposed essentially the same thesis several years later. Whorf argues that in the "constant ways of arranging data and its most ordinary every-day analysis of phenomena that we need to recognize the influence; . . . [language] has no other activities, cultural and personal" (Whorf, 1952:27). He emphasizes both its structural and semantic aspects, including a self-contained system of meanings. It is of course easier to study language structure than its meaning, since meanings reside in the individual. It is still more difficult to link the structural aspects with its symbolic aspects.

In "A Systemization of the Whorfian Hypothesis," Joshua Fishman stresses that Whorf was not deeply concerned with "Which was first, the language patterns or the cultural norms?" but was content to conclude that "in the main they have grown up together, constantly influencing each other." Nevertheless, Fishman indicates that it was Whorf's feeling that if the two streams were separated from each other for the purpose of analysis, language is by far the more impervious, systematic, and rigid of the two, thus causing cultural innovations to have less influence on language than the other way around. Fishman suggests that Whorf apparently "considered language structure not only as interactingly reflective of 'cultural thought' but as directly formative of 'individual thought.'" Fishman schematizes the Whorfian hypothesis at four levels: 1.) languages differ "in the same ways" as the general cultures or surrounding environments of their speakers differ; 2.) attempts at this level are made to codify some correspondence at the cultural level between language behaviors and nonlanguage behaviors; 3.) the structure of language, for example, its grammar, shapes ideas in the particular culture; and 4.) the actual prediction of individual and cultural behavior based on linguistic structure (1966:505-512).

Fishman contends that while levels 1 and 3 could be seen as *large group* or *collective phenomena*, and levels 2 and 3 are concerned with *individual interpersonal behavior*, few studies have demonstrated the actual linkages between culture and language, which Sapir and Whorf seemed to feel possible. Fishman stresses that each level becomes progressively more debatable in terms of offering real proof. If the hypothesis were entirely valid, Fishman feels that its implications would be counterproductive to intercultural relations: "All of us in most walks of life and most of us in all walks of life are helplessly trapped by the language we speak; we cannot escape from it—and, even if we could flee, where would we turn but to some other language with its own blinders and its own vice-like embrace on what we think, what we perceive, and what we say? . . . What hope can there be for mankind?; what hope that one nation will ever fully communicate with the other?" (1966:514). In his critique of the linguistic relativity hypothesis, Fishman indicates that while evidence favoring it exists at each level, "It seems likely that linguistic relativity, though affecting some of our cognitive behavior, is nevertheless only a moderately powerful factor and a counteractable one at that" (1966:514,516).

To summarize, Fishman's critique of the Whorfian hypothesis seems reasonable. Obviously, language does have great power as a distinctive influence in culture and individual thought-patterning. Nevertheless, language may simply be one of many important influences on culture and thus on intercultural communication. Actually, though the individual language and culture are tightly linked, and therefore do cause important barriers for intercultural communication and for cultural spokespersons, the language problems may be less severe than other cultural barriers; for example, perceptions, attitudes, stereotypes, prejudices, beliefs, values, and thought-patterning itself. Additionally, the initial issues discussed earlier also may serve as even more formidable barriers for intercultural communication than the pervasive influence that language is likely to hold over culture and individual thinking. Based on my understanding of the inability to prove or disprove the linguistic relativity hypothesis, I believe that it is a less viable way of offering the primary link between language and culture than are the theories of language universals and generative grammar.

The notion of cultural pluralism vs. assimilation is relevant in an understanding of these two opposing theories. The Sapir-Whorf hypothesis, which stresses that language pervasively shapes each specific culture and the individual thought-patterns contained within the culture, may be seen as an expression of cultural pluralism. The generative grammar theory insists that all or most languages are governed by similar structural systems. While their surface structure may be vastly different, at the level below the surface, remarkable similarities appear. This theory attempts to assimilate all languages into a common type at the "deep structure" level. The principle of similarities and differences also comes sharply into focus in considering these theories with the principle of similarities being favored by the generative grammar theory, and the principle of differences being favored by the Sapir-Whorf hypothesis. We must assume, then, that both theories do offer a degree of merit and that there are important cultural observations about linguistic and nonverbal coding which can be drawn from both theories. Taken together, without either theory being considered absolutely mutually exclusive, both do add to our understanding, especially of language as a chief component both of communication and culture, and of the problems and opportunities facing the intercultural communicator and cultural spokesperson.

The focus of language contact is the bilingual or polylingual individual

Joseph Greenberg suggests that if the United States had the same linguistic diversity as Nigeria, more than 500 languages would be spoken within the American borders. He speculates *that areas of high-linguistic diversity are those in which communication is poor and that the increase of communication which goes with greater economic productivity and more extensive political organization will lead typically to the spread of a* lingua franca, *whether indigenous or imported*. Such a condition results in widespread bilingualism and the ultimate disappearance of all except a single dominant language as the principal means of exchange between diverse peoples (1971:70). In Africa, Greenberg indicates that tribal life and its extensive associations both with the living and their ancestors for formulating codes of social behavior is still a persistent mode of life, despite the increasing sense of national identity and urbanization. Since language is a social phenomenon whose fundamental role is to make possible "that accumulation of learned behavior which we call culture and which is the distinctively human mode of adjustment," the focus of language contact is the bilingual or polylingual individual. It is not the languages which are in contact so much as it is the individual in contact with his or her own culture and other cultural groupings (1971:119).

Africa offers a prime example of the need for bilingualism and polylingualism

Though rural life in Africa tends to be defined in large measure by the first language, many Africans not only are forced to be bilingual but also polylingual, particularly in light of the linguistic diversity within tight geographical settings in Africa. Typical Africans may normally learn two or more African languages or dialects, often quite different in character and structure, simply to cope within the context of ethnic interaction. Their intercultural communication would be impossible without bilingualism and polylingualism. They are more likely to give allegiance to one language than the others, and may be required to think differently in each language. Additionally, the vast colonization of Africa, especially by France and Great Britain, has increasingly led to the imposition of a European *lingua franca*. Such a *lingua franca* can be used in urban African centers, in the schools, in political contacts with the government, in trade, in the ability to read printed materials, and in developing general literacy. In some parts of Africa, it remains predominantly French, while in still more parts it remains English.

Greenberg suggests that it is not enough simply to consider language from the utilitarian point of view, that is, as a chief means of communication but perhaps the most important single criterion of group identification, at least among groups sufficiently large to play a political role. He argues that if a common language did not have this important first "language" function, people who had learned a foreign *lingua franca* of wider usefulness than their native language would be likely to abandon their first language, or at least not insist that their children learn it. However, Greenberg states:

In interviews I conducted in the Plateau Province of the Northern Region of Nigeria, a highly multilingual area in which Hausa is the undisputed *lingua*, practically all informants with children said that they taught them their tribal language as their first language, and Hausa somewhat later. In the words of one informant, "If we abandoned our own language, we would become Hausa just like the rest." Pagans said that their ancestors would be greatly angered by the abandonment of their language. Several illiterate informants ventured the opinion that the language itself had a positive aesthetic aspect. There was, however, no hostility to the learning of Hausa. In fact, my informants expressed a unanimous desire for their children to learn Hausa because it was the medium for instruction in the lower grades and because ignorance of Hausa condemned a man to a restricted and economically marginal traditional agricultural existence (1971:205).

Since most Africans speak tonal, nonstress native languages, they are likely to identify stress with high pitch and thus do not reduce unstressed vowels as native speakers of English would. Many Africans first encounter European languages through educated African speakers, causing them to use African renditions as a model. This helps to develop reasonably uniform "dialects" of English and French which may have a greater state of purity than in Great Britain and France. Even if such a European *lingua franca* is practically no one's first language, its purity is similar to that found among nonnative speakers of English in the Asian subcontinent. Such languages are relatively free of the linguistic inference often imposed by first languages in other situations and the rival allegiances which are developed toward various native languages. In any case, a European *lingua franca* such as English or French may serve more neutrally for interaction than either the first or second usual languages of potentially rival tribes. Thus, its power interculturally is markedly increased (Greenberg, 1971:186-187, 194-195).

"Bilingual" is a euphemism for "linguistically handicapped"

Einar Haugen relates that as a bilingual from childhood he was unaware of the stigmata of bilingualism placed on him: "Without knowing it, I had been exposed to untold dangers of retardation, intellectual impoverishment, schizophrenia, anomie, and alienation, most of which I had apparently escaped, if only by a hair's breath. If my parents knew about these dangers, they firmly dismissed them and made me bilingual willy-nilly. They took the position that I would learn all the English I needed from my playmates and my teachers, and that only by learning and using Norwegian in the home could I maintain a fruitful contact with them and their friends and their culture" (1972:307). Sadly enough, Haugen believes, instead of properly defining bilingualism in terms of its positive relations to the learning of two languages, "for many people 'bilingual' is a euphemism for 'linguistically handicapped.' It is a nice way of referring to children whose parents have handicapped them in the race for success by teaching them their mother tongue, which happens not to be the dominant language in the country they now inhabit. The term has enjoyed a semantic development not unlike that of 'minority group' " (308). In many countries and in many earlier societies bilingualism means to be educated. Haugen provides many more examples of countries in which bilinguaism means to be uneducated, usually where a dependent and dominated social group has refused to submit to the imposition of the language of the culturally imperialistic and dominant group:

The power relationship of victor over vanquished, of native over immigrant, of upper class over lower class; these have bred bilingualism as it is commonly understood. The fact that it is unilaterally imposed by a dominant group is a major source of the pejorative connotations where these exist. It is part of what keeps the underprivileged groups underprivileged, and it is taken up for general discussion only when it forms part of a syndrome of segregation. Our neighbor Canada offers a charming example of the ambiguities of the situation. The English-speaking Canadians are heartily in favor of bilingualism, so long as it means that the French will learn English; the French, however, think of it as requiring that all the English learn French. But in the meanwhile the French are doing what they can to ensure that Quebec at least will remain all French—and no more bilingual than is absolutely necessary (308-309).

Both Haugen and Wallace Lambert note that many studies have been completed to demonstrate that bilingualism has a detrimental effect on intellectual functioning; very few indicate that there are favorable effects; and some indicate that bilingualism has no effect on intelligence. Lambert feels that the wide diversity of contradictory studies fails to establish any sort of generalized norm. He indicates that some recent studies have emphasized the importance for second-language learning of an individual's attitude toward the second-language community.

Using a language involves persons, participation in a second culture. . . . A bilingual person belongs to two different communities and possesses two personalities which may be in conflict if the two language communities are in social conflict. Changes in the bilingual's attitude toward a language community may account for the variation in his efficiency on intelligence tests. . . . The fact that an individual becomes bilingual in a bicultural community may be attributable to a favorable disposition toward both the linguistic communities, whereas the monolingual may be retarded in his acquisition of a second language because of his unfavorable attitudes toward both the other culture and its language (122).

Lambert draws several conclusions from a study on the developmental aspects of second-language acquisition in Montreal between French and English native speakers who were either bilingual or were studying a second language. He feels that they may be generalizable in this one study from the hypotheses which were confirmed or not confirmed, based on the tested data. First, the acquisition of a second language entails a series of barriers to overcome, with the vocabulary barrier being easier to overcome as experience with the language progresses. However, the cultural barrier is more resistant, and to overcome this barrier, one must assimilate those aspects of a different culture which influence language behavior. Second, bilinguality needs to be tested at various stages of experience with a language, as individuals recently acquiring a second language might differ on the measures falling within a vocabulary cluster. The individuals who are more advanced in second-language acquisition might do equally well in terms of vocabulary, but might differ importantly with respect to measures falling within a cultural cluster. This would require testing from both clusters to assure success at various states of language acquisition. Third, one could speculate that when the adults acquire a second language, they develop in relatively the same way as small children when they learn their first language—that is, the task of amassing vocabulary is the first problem for both and can be done with relative ease. Incorporating the cultural aspects of the linguistic community seems to be at the more advanced state of development for both children and adults. Finally, the process of linguistic enculturation takes the most time both for the children learning their own first language and for adults learning a second language (Lambert, 1972:9-31).

The true bilingual masters both languages at an early age and has facility with both as means of communication: O'Doherty states that there can be no question that genuine bilingualism is an intellectual advantage. Pseudobilinguals are the real problem, as they know a second language only superficially. Very often they fail to master either language. (O'Doherty, 1958:285; Lambert, 1972:120). Genuine bilinguals may also be multicultured persons. In a parallel fashion, we might speculate that the same condition might exist between pseudocultural communicators and genuinely effective cultural communicators. The first know the second culture marginally, and may not even know their own culture well; the latter understand well both cultures and can function equally well in both.

Canada's decision to become bilingual and bicultural and the impact of language planning

The Canadian government's decision in 1969 to make Canada officially bilingual and bicultural has had profound effects on Canadian life. The October 1970 riots in Montreal essentially resulted from conflict which grew out of the implementation of the Bilingual and Bicultural Act. In this case, the language planning which had been initiated earlier pointed to the social, political, and cultural need in Canada to recognize a factual situation and to help nurture an ecological linguistic balance already existing somewhat precariously between French and English-speaking Canada. The language planning was hastened by the acute fear that Quebec would secede from Canada, in part because of the language problem. The planning for a genuinely bilingual and bicultural country required not only the federal passage of extensive legislation, but also the involvement of social agencies, the media, labor, the schools and various other forms of Canadian cultural maximizers and elites.

The problems encountered simply at the business and labor level in such planning can be seen in microcosm in the decisions of the jointly owned Stromberg Corporation and Miracle Mart grocery chain. Since the company had considerable holdings both in Quebec and Ontario, and was based in Montreal with essentially an English-speaking management, frequent protests and boycotts and potential lawsuits were aimed at the chain in the early 1970s by the French-speaking population of Montreal and Quebec. The decision to become bilingual and bicultural from the top management down to store managers and clerks was not easily reached; nor was it simply a decision made in support of the country's official bilingualism and biculturalism. The company's economic base was the major consideration. Very real decisions had to be made about hiring and firing to achieve a linguistic balance at every level in the company. Decisions had to be made about whether the discussions themselves about the decisions had to be bilingual, about whether language classes in French and English must be offered by the company for those employees who were monolingual, about whether all printed messages for employees and customers would have to be offered in both French and English, and about whether all the merchandise must be labeled in French and English. Decisions were needed for whether all store employees would be required to respond to customers either in French or English, and whether all new employees should be required to pass written and spoken tests in both languages. The turmoil in the company, especially in top and middle management, was very real, but realistic long-term goals were set. Gradually a genuine ecological bilingual and bicultural balance is beginning to be reached in the company.

The company is starting to be known as a leader in the movement at the business and labor level for genuine adoption of bilingualism and biculturalism in Canada. Problems are continuing and much more time is needed to claim success for such a far-reaching organizational effort at intercultural communication. Even the most important goal to move toward a bilingual and bicultural status for the entire company was extremely courageous for the top management, especially since nearly all of them were monolingually English-speaking. Other companies based in Montreal with English-speaking managements simply made the decision to move out of Quebec or to maintain absolute linguistic stability, rather than change in the face of hostile reactions from the French population.

we can see that key issues affecting intercultural com-
ation are of very great practical importance in im-
nting a country's official decision to become bilingual
and bicultural. The opportunities and problems for intercultural communicators and the cultural spokespersons in
such a situation are very real and are not easily solved.

Summary

A primary way to understand the linkages between
language and culture is through language universals. These
are linguistic characteristics which may be found in most or all
cultures as an aspect of culture itself. The logical structure of
such universals and their substantive content give important
clues both to their nature and their importance. While logical
structure suggests the need for consistent characteristics
throughout various languages, the substantive content of the
universals includes such aspects as phonology, grammar,
semantics, and symbols. We note that language universals are
very closely connected to the concept of generative grammar,
which suggests that beneath the surface, all natural languages
share certain similarities. In contrast to the theory of
generative grammar, we have seen that the Sapir-Whorf
hypothesis holds that every language is unique in its capacity
to shape its culture and the individual thought-patterns of the
culture, and that language has an even more pervasive influence than culture itself.

In this chapter, we have noted several linguistic aspects of
communicative codes as components of communication. We
have stressed that culture makes codes of human interaction
possible.

We have seen that verbal linguistic codes provide the key
link for cultural communication and for the passing on of
cultural traditions. This is possible because of our ability to encode and decode a virtually limitless number of messages.
Speech becomes the basic coding procedure, while written
language is a secondary coding procedure. Language, whether
spoken or written, serves to symbolize and catalog our perceived reality.

Both the Sapir-Whorf and generative grammar theories
have come under attack, though the generative grammar
theory appears to have the most adherents today. Both theories

would appear to have distinct merits. Both are so important to the study of language and culture that they cannot be ignored.

In this chapter, we also stressed that the focus of language contact is the bilingual or polylingual individual. Africa offers a prime example of the need for bilingualism and poly- lingualism. Unfortunately, for many persons, bilingualism seems to suggest a linguistic handicap. However, we have at- tempted to demonstrate that when bilingualism is encouraged and positively reinforced in the bicultural community, it becomes an asset rather than a liability. The important distinc- tion between interest and competence in the second language is marginal for the pseudo-bilingual while it is crucial for the genuine bilingual or polylingual.

The Canadian decision to become officially bilingual and bicultural had many effects on language planning and an ecological linguistic basis in Canada. It serves as a useful example of the opportunities and problems which arise inter- culturally and crossculturally in such a setting. The decision of one good chain in Canada to become bilingual highlights the intercultural opportunities and conflicts possible in such a situation.

References

Berlo, David K., 1960. *The Process of Communication*. New York: Holt.

Cherry, Colin, 1971. *World Communication: Threat or Promise*. New York.

Chomsky, Noam, 1966. "Three Models for the Description of Language." In *Communication and Culture: Readings*. Edited by Alfred Smith. New York: Holt.

Chomsky, Noam. 1967. "The Formal Nature of Language." In *Biological Foundations of Language*. Edited by Eric H. Len- nenberg. New York: Wiley.

Condon, John C., and Fathi Yousef, 1975. *An Introduction to In- tercultural Communication*. Indianapolis: Bobbs-Merrill.

DeVito, Joseph, 1970. *The Psychology of Speech and Language: An Introduction to Psycholinguistics*. New York: Random House.

Fishman, Joshua A., 1966. "A Systematization of the Whorfian Hypothesis." In *Communication and Culture: Readings*. Edited by Alfred Smith. New York: Holt.

Gerbner, George, 1966. "On Defining Communication: Still Another View." *Journal of Communication*, 16, 99-103.

Greenberg, Joseph H., 1971. *Language, Culture, and Communication: Essays*. Selected and introduced by Anwar S. Dill. Stanford: Stanford University.

Haugen, Einar, 1972. *The Ecology of Language: Essays*. Selected and introduced by Anwar S. Dill. Stanford: Stanford University.

Lambert, Wallace E., 1972. *Language, Psychology and Culture: Essays*. Selected and introduced by Anwar S. Dill. Stanford: Stanford University.

McNeil, David, 1970. *The Acquisition of Language: The Study of Developmental Psycholinguistics*. New York: Harper & Row.

Miller, George A., 1951. *Language and Communication: A Scientific and Psychological Introduction*. New York: McGraw-Hill.

O'Doherty, E.F., 1958. "Bilingualism: Educational Aspects." In *Advances in Science*. 56, 282-286.

Osgood, Charles E., William H. May, and Murray S. Miron, 1975. *Cross-cultural Universals of Affective Meaning*. Urbana, Illinois: University of Illinois.

Sapir, Edward, 1949. *Selected Writings of Edward Sapir in Language, Culture, and Personality*. Edited by David G. Mandelbaum. Berkeley: University of California.

Scheflen, Albert E., 1967. "On the Structuring of Human Communication." In *Communication and Culture: Readings*. Edited by Alfred S. Smith. New York: Holt.

Whorf, Benjamin, 1952. *Collected Papers on Metalinguistics*. Washington, D.C.

CHAPTER 6

Communicative Codes: Nonverbal Aspects

All normal children in the world develop toward adulthood with the social contact both of language usage and the very precise language usage of their cultural milieu. They also possess the paralinguistic and nonverbal characteristics which complement the use of language. Exceptions include such children who are retarded, deaf-mutes, mentally or physically handicapped in such a way as to affect their powers of speech, and those few children who have been totally devoid of normal human contact from birth. As humans we have the innate ability to learn the major language or languages within our own cultural context. Children learn many of their language patterns by imitation, long before they begin to learn specific reasons for the patterns. In a similar way, they learn paralinguistic and nonverbal cues, often without any consciousness of learning them or why they are learning them. The adults teaching them such cues may also be unconscious that they are doing so. Children imitate certain nonverbal cues or are taught them deliberately simply because "that's the way we do it." Nonverbal communication cannot be seen out of the context of its primary linkages with language.

Nonverbal communication can be learned for manipulative purposes

Unfortunately, many of the recent coffee table books on nonverbal communication give the impression that one can

master its art for the purposes of manipulation of others in
most communicative situations. Julius Fast's *Body Language*,
Maude Poiret's *Body Talk*, Gerald I. Nierenberg and Henry H.
Calero's *How to Read a Person Like a Book*, Flora Davis's *Inside
Intuition*, and Leonard Zunin's *Contact: The First Four Minutes*
provide a popular and generally misleading genre of literature
on "body language," a catch-all phrase that includes facial expressions, body gestures, tone of voice, touch, interpersonal
space, and dress (Koivumaki, 1975:26). Koivumaki stresses that
the appeal for the study or pseudostudy of the subject stems
from the fact that almost anyone can consider himself or
herself an expert by informally testing hunches. Koivumaki
criticizes the popular nonverbal communication manuals
because of the lack of accuracy of the research represented
therein. Findings are oversimplified; hypotheses and truisms
are stated as facts; and the reader is often uninformed as to
whose research is being reported. She notes: "These books
exploit our curiosity—indeed, our ignorance—about why relationships succeed and fail, and they feed our apparently in-
satiable desires to improve our social status, to make it with
the opposite sex, and to succeed in business—in short, to exercise social control. These books encourage, quite literally, the
exploitation of one person by another" (28). Koivumaki notes a
key assumption made by the popular authors that people's unconscious nonverbal cues are "truer" than their conscious or
intended cues (such as what they say). She suggests that the
authors of the popular books base their cases on the assumption that people's "real" feelings are reflected in their nonverbal behavior. However, she contends that "these books are, in
essence, manuals of body language fakery, the very thing
assumed to be impossible or at least very difficult to do!"
(1975:28-29)

Fortunately, sound research is being done as well to explore the various paralinguistic and nonverbal codes which
generally accompany linguistic codes. Even those nonverbal
codes which influence human social interaction, such as
geography and climate, landscape and architecture, personal
space and position, appearance and poised expression, personal apparel, physique and posture, manual and facial expression, and physical behavior are seen as nonverbal codes
precisely because they do involve us both as a symbol and tool-
builders and users. By such involvement, these nonverbal

codes must be intimately connected to individuals and their social relations as communicators with other human beings. Just as language is inherently tied to culture in general and with individual cultures specifically, so too is nonverbal communication. Its study for the student of intercultural communication bears close scrutiny.

Definitions of nonverbal communication are difficult to establish

Recent respected writers on nonverbal communication agree that the use of the term "nonverbal" is misleading, especially since the word attempts to distinguish all that which is verbal against all that which is not. Another way to speak of communicative codes is "verbal communication and everything else." The difficulties inherent in defining nonverbal communication properly are considerable. Eisenberg and Smith distinguish verbal communication as the system by which action is organized with verbal behavior through the use of language, and nonverbal behavior is organized in a different way. They suggest that verbal expressions are self-reflexive, meaning that lanuage can be used to analyze language, or what we call metalanguage, but that nonverbal acts, lacking self-reflexiveness, are thereby different from verbal acts (1971:21). The early classification system of Ruesch and Kees serves as a central starting point for the consideration of nonverbal communication as codes:

In broad terms, nonverbal forms of codification fall into three distinct categories:

Sign language includes all those forms of codification in which words, numbers, and punctuation signs have been supplanted by gestures; these vary from the "monosyllabic" gesture of the hitch-hiker to such complex systems as the language of the deaf.

Action language embraces all movements that are not used exclusively as signals. Such acts as walking and drinking, for example, have a dual function: they serve personal needs, and they also constitute statements to those who may perceive them.

Object language comprises all intentional and nonintentional display of material things, such as implements, machines, art objects, architectural structures, and—last but not least—the human body and whatever clothes or covers it. The embodiment of letters as they occur in books and on signs has a material substance, and this aspect of words also has to be considered as object language (1956:189).

Expanding upon the broadly inclusive classification of

Ruesch and Kees, Knapp further identifies the nonverbal dimensions of human communication as: 1.) _body motion_ or _kinesic behavior_, which includes gestures; movements of the body, limbs, hands, head, feet and legs; facial expressions such as smiles; eye behavior such as blinking, direction, and length of gaze, and pupil dilation; and posture; 2.) Knapp incudes as significant to nonverbal communication _physical character-istics_ including physique, body shape, general attractiveness, body or breath odors, height, weight, hair, and skin color or tone. Leonard Doob summarizes such similar characteristics as _basic media_ (1961:3). Knapp tentatively includes touching behavior, though he stresses that not all writers on nonverbal communication would include this aspect. Subcategories of touching behavior include stroking, hitting, greetings and farewells, holding, and guiding another's movements. Montagu calls touching and tactile behavior the most important cultural aspect of nonverbal communication (1971:4). Knapp defines _paralanguage_ as dealing with how something is said and not what is said, and thereby includes the range of nonverbal vocal cues surrounding common speech behavior; 5.) The study of _proxemics,_ or the relation of people's use and perception of social and personal space, plays an important part in the consideration of nonverbal codes of communication. Edward Hall's _The Hidden Dimension_ (1966) focuses entirely on this important aspect of nonverbal communication; 6.) Knapp relates _artifacts_, such as perfume, clothes, lipstick, eyeglasses, wigs and other hairpieces, false eyelashes, eyeliners, and so on, as another aspect of the nonverbal codes; 7.) Finally, Knapp includes as nonverbal codes the various _environmental factors_ like architecture, variations in arrangements, materials, shapes, or surfaces of objects and other related factors, which may affect any communicative interaction (Knapp, 1972:5-8).

In _An Introduction to Intercultural Communication_, Condon and Yousef provide a most interesting chapter, "Out of House and Home," which is devoted precisely to the environmental aspects of the home as a prime factor in teaching the child both effective verbal and nonverbal patterns of communication. Condon and Yousef offer interesting comparisons of the American authority-centered home versus the American social-centered home, plus comparisons with other cultures: the Swahili home in which several families live and have social contact largely outside the home and at the rear where food is prepared and cooked; the Middle Eastern home with its formal "salon," or living room, and its kitchen with exclusive use by members of the family; the Japanese home with its highly flexible movement of walls and furnishings; the relatively rigid German home setting; and the Mexican home with its still different Latin style of living. The different living styles and home settings provide different cultural norms for encouraging or discouraging verbal and nonverbal communication patterns to develop within the socially accepted provisions of the individual culture (1975).

A key writer on nonverbal kinesics, Ray Birdwhistell, seeks an integration of verbal and nonverbal communication as a total unit: "My own research has led me to the point that I am no longer willing to call either linguistic or kinesic systems *communication* systems. All of the emerging data seem to me to support the contention that linguistics and kinesics are infra-communicational systems. Only in their interrelationship with each other and with comparable systems from other sensory modalities is the emergent communication system achieved" (1967:71). Whatever else can be said, it is certainly obvious that nonverbal communication codes are inseparable from the verbal ones, and that together they make up a very important component of the entire communication system which serves as the primary focus for an individual, culture, or society.

The ratio of the senses almost defines the culture in its entirety

Walter J. Ong develops a specific linkage between culture and the interrelationship of the senses:

Man's sensory perceptions are abundant and overwhelming. He cannot attend to them all at once. In great part a given culture teaches him one or another way of productive specialization. It brings him to organize his sensorium [or sense ratio] by attending to some types of perception more than others, by making an issue of certain ones while relatively neglecting other ones. The sensorium is a fascinating focus for cultural studies. Given sufficient knowledge of the sensorium exploited within a specific culture, one could probably define the culture as a whole in virtually all its aspects (1967:6).

The inherent meaning of Ong's statement bears directly on the relation of nonverbal communication to culture because the sense-ratio is the way that each culture combines its attitudes and usages of nonverbal cues in connection with verbal communicative codes. If the preliterate society or culture essentially promotes the oral-aural nature of sound, while the script-oriented society or culture stresses visual aspects of communication, each society provides its own definitions of its cultural attributes. The electronic society combines visual aspects with oral-aural aspects of communication, especially in such modern areas as television, cinema, and new copying processes by which printed materials can be precisely reproduced through telephone cables and videotelephones. Since the senses are rarely isolated one from another, the concept of the sense-ratio as communicative is that the senses operate on each other to communicate within or between cultures. Ong calls *touch* a bridge between *sight* and *sound*, since it tends to annex itself to both. For example, texture can be seen and touched, but the perception of texture comes not from sight but from touch. Sight does not convey sound, smell, or taste with any of the directness with which it conveys touch. Touch is associated with sound, as for example when musical rhythm or even oral discourse sets off in the auditor a feeling of movement, clapping, snapping the fingers, or stamping the foot (165-166). The eating of food particularly involves several of the senses in an overlapping function. Food is seen, smelled, tasted, and touched and sometimes heard, as in the sizzling of a steak. If we take seriously the statement of Watzlawick and Beavin (1967:4-8) that in the presence of another, all behavior is communicative, then to eat in the presence of another, as a basic example, is clearly communicative in that all the aspects of the sensorium are interacting as signs to the perceptive observer.

As the senses actively interact within all human cultures and between communicators from these cultures, it is also clear that the concept of a sense-ratio or sensorium is itself a minimum cultural universal. However, while there are many similarities in the way that particular cultures exploit or manipulate these ratios, there are also many differences, which add to a more careful understanding of the total ethnographic study of a cultural community. Some of these similarities and differences relate more to cultural or societal groupings than to specific cultures. For example, heavily dependent societies or cultures which may not have advanced far in the development of literacy, urbanized industrialization, and technological communications media are more likely culturally to emphasize the oral-aural nature of sound over the aspects of sight. They generally seem to be more tactually oriented than are highly urbanized, technologically oriented individuals and cultures. Ashley Montagu notes that human beings in general develop their senses in a definite sequence, moving from tactile, to auditory, to visual developments, but as they approach adolescence, the order of precedence becomes reversed, with emphasis on visual, then auditory, and then tactile sensory relationships. Nevertheless, even when the normal reversal takes place, vision becomes meaningful only on the basis of what the individual has felt and heard (1971:236). Thus the society or culture which emphasizes the auditory and tactile senses incorporates the visual within the context of the former senses, while the society or culture which emphasizes vision would tend to subsume the others under the domination of visual development.

Certain nonverbal communicative codes are learned perceptually

The simple notion of being able to wink, blink one eye, or shut an eye for the purpose of looking in a microscope or focusing a camera is actually a perceptual concept which must be learned. The child in an urbanized and technological society learns such a concept from about the age of five to eight, but the adult in the preliterate society may never have learned it. Edmund Carpenter's delightful *Oh What a Blow That Phantom Gave Me* describes the excitement of native New Guineans, unfamiliar with most of the technology of Western society, when they try to learn to wink and close one eye without putting a finger over it to close it, and the intensive nonverbal encouragement given them by their other adult friends (1972). We also tend to forget that just as the child in the modern society must learn to recognize writing when it is right-side up and must learn visual images as images, adult members of preliterate oral-aural societies must learn to focus their vision so that either script, printing, or even pictures themselves can be perceived as real instead of a meaningless object in front of them. Otherwise, they may live their entire lives without ever having recognized their own reflection or that of the environment in a still, clear pool.

One very interesting play by African playwright Joseph Mukasa-Bilikuddembe titled "The Mirror" (1968) describes the preliterate native African woman whose husband has returned from a nearby city with a gift for her. She enters her hut to find to her astonishment a strange woman there. The more she shouts and gestures for the stranger to leave her home, the more the stranger silently taunts her by mimicking her every action. The woman is driven into a frenzy at the stranger's actions and finds herself enraged that her husband has brought home this menacing "hussy" to replace her. Finally, the play ends when the husband returns and eventually convinces his wife that she is in fact the stranger, as he has brought her a mirror as his gift from the city. As a member of a nonvisually oriented culture, his wife did not recognize her own image or reflection, and thereby had no understanding of what she looked like to another person or to herself.

Touch and tactility play a varying role in different cultures

Montagu proposes that there are many families in which a great deal of tactile contact occurs, not only between mother and child but also between all of the members of the family, while other families within the same culture have a minimal amount of tactile contact on any level. He suggests that the differences in the quality, frequency, and timing of the tactile experience which the newborn, infant, child, adolescent, and adult undergo in different cultures demonstrates the whole range of possible variations: "National and cultural differences in tactility run the full gamut from absolute nontouchability, as among upper-class Englishmen, to what amounts to almost full expression among peoples speaking Latin-derived languages, Russians, and many nonliterate peoples. Those who speak Anglo-Saxon-derived languages stand at the opposite pole in the continuum of tactility to the Latin peoples. In this continuum Scandinavians appear to occupy an intermediate position" (1971). He suggests that there exists not only cultural and national differences in tactile behavior, but also class differences. In general, it seems possible to say that the higher the class, the less there is of tactility, and the lower the class, the more there is. There is one exception in the American sample: upper-class mothers seemed to be more at ease with tactility than lower-class mothers. Montagu speculates that it is possible that this finding could be generalized for the American population as a whole, with exceptions represented by blacks and other minority groups who would be more tactile. Where the European and English upper classes are likely to be hereditary and long-entrenched in their nontactile ways, in America, social mobility is so great that one can move from lower to upper-class status in a single generation (1971).

Montagu notes that among the English upper classes relationships between parents and children were, and continue to be, distant from birth till death. At birth the child was usually given over to a nurse who either wet-nursed or bottle-fed it. Children were generally brought up by governesses and then at an early age sent away to school. They received a minimum amount of tactile experience. (Winston Churchill often remarked on this impersonal and nontactile influence in his own life.) Montagu concludes that it is not surprising under such conditions that nontouchability could easily become institutionalized as part of the way of life. The conditioning in nontactility received by so many English of the upper classes seems to have produced a virtual negative sanction on tactility in English culture.

Even more nontactile than the English, Montagu suggests, are the Germans: "The emphasis upon the warrior virtues, the supremacy of the hardheaded martinet father, and the complete subordination of the mother in the German family made for a rigidified, unbending character which renders the average German, among other things, a not very tactile being." At the opposite end of the spectrum, Montagu characterizes the Jews, as a tribe, culture, or people, by a high degree of tactility. "The Jewish mother" has become a cliché for deep and unremitting care for her children. This meant that until recent times the children were breast-fed on demand, and that there was a great deal of fondling of children by mother, father and siblings. Hence, Jews tend to be tactually very demonstrative. Canadians of Anglo-Saxon origins perhaps even outdo the English in their nontactuality. On the other hand, French-Canadians are as tactually demonstrative as their counterparts are in their land of origin (1971:260-268).

A major premise offered by Montagu is that the early tactile relationships, often complemented by sound as in the oral-aural preliterate society, determine to a large extent how open, warm, and loving individuals will be when they reach adulthood. Obviously, too, from Montagu's perspective, the way in which a culture encourages tactility at different stages (of life determines whether adult members of that culture generally are able to seem contact-oriented or not. Those cultures which are characterized by a "noli me tangere" (do not touch me) emphasis in life seem distant, aloof, and cold, while others have tactility so ingrained in their entire life style that there is so much fondling and kissing that it appears strange and embarrassing, if not immoral, to nontactile peoples (1971:221ff). Such differences in behavior in terms of nonverbal cues cause the most serious communication breakdowns at the intercultural or interracial levels. At the same time, we should note the possibility that such examples as those offered by Montagu and other authors who have been quoted here have their own potential for crosscultural stereotyping and should be viewed critically by those interested in avoiding crosscultural problems.)

Culture determines tactile relations

Montagu demonstrates both that the culture dictates largely the tactile relations between members within the culture and with members of the other cultures, and that early tactile experiences are very important in developing the individual, Montagu offers an extended illustration of the Netsilik Eskimo of the Canadian Artic, based on the close work of Richard James de Boor, who lived in a snowhouse among them during the winter of 1966-67. De Boor's chief interest was the maternal-infant caretaking relationships among these Eskimos. Montagu suggests that the Netsilik mother, even though she lives under the most difficult conditions, still remains "an unruffled personality who bestows warmth and loving care upon her children." Almost from birth, the child is snuggled naked against the naked back of the mother, and both she and the baby are completely encased in fur to protect them from the fierce Artic cold. Not until the infant achieves locomotor ability and later receives what the Netsilik Eskimo calls cognitive sense is the child long separated from the mother. The "Netsilik mother and child communicate with each other through their skins. When hungry the Netsilik infant roots and sucks on the skin of its mother's back, alerting her to its need. Then it is brought round to the breast and suckled. . . . The rocking movements and contact with the mother's skin promote the sleep the infant so much enjoys. Bowel and bladder elimination occur on the mother's back. . . .The infant's needs are anticipated by the mother tactually" (1971:234-235).

Based on their interaction through the skin, the infant's responses are invariably pleasant, and thereby become the key to the Netsilik Eskimo's stress-coping and conflict-resolution abilities. By the age of three, the Netsilik child has acquired "the only two motivational characteristics necessary to his or her functioning as a self-regulated human being," namely pleasant or altruistic responses to interpersonal relationships, and the power of symbolic manipulative ability. A balance of harmony between the Netsilik and his or her society is thus achieved because of helpful early tactile experiences. Montagu states that from the earliest orientations and essentially throughout their lives, the Netsilik Eskimos rely virtually upon a sense of touch, and by responding to sensations of touch or contact, learn to find their way in the environment created for the child by the mother. Later, the Eskimo male especially knows instinctively by combinations of touch how to discover a seal hidden beneath a frozen patch of ice, or how to find his way home after a long hunt in a blinding snowstorm.

Montagu stresses that the Netsilik Eskimos show their friendliness toward those they have never seen before by touching and stroking them. They invite guests to share their tightly encompassed igloos, and their beds which they all occupy in the nude in close proximity. Eskimo men in some settings still offer their wives for the night as special hospitality for guests. Combined with the Eskimos' special tactile enjoyment and use for defining their interpersonal and spatial relationships are the mixtures of the sense of smell from their body odors, burning blubber oil, and partly uncured sealskin clothing. The sense of sound with the mother's voice humming and singing, and an igloo filled with the sound of other voices accompany many of the aspects of Eskimo life. Visual perception almost certainly follows upon the development of auditory perception among the Eskimos. In a similar way, Edmund Carpenter illustrates the interrelationships of the various senses as they interact on the proxemic aspects of their space for the Aivilik Eskimos:

They define space more by sound than by sight. Where we might say, "Let's see what we can hear," they would say, "Let's hear what we can see. . . ." To them, the occularly visible apparition is not nearly as important as the purely auditory one. The essential feature of sound is not its location, but that it be, that it fill space. We say "the night shall be filled with music," just as the air is filled with fragrance; locality is irrelevant. The concert-goer closes his eyes.

I know of no example of an Aivilik describing space primarily in visual terms. They don't regard space as static, and therefore measurable; hence they have no formal units of spatial measurement, just as they have no uniform divisions of time. The carver is indifferent to the demands of the optical eye; he lets each piece fill its own space, create its own world, without reference to background or anything external to it. Each carving lives in spatial independence. Size and shape, proportions and selection, these are set by the object itself, not forced from without. Like sound, each carving creates its own space, its own identity; it imposes its own assumptions (1959:32).

The relationships between the senses within the specific Eskimo culture suggest that the Eskimo view of reality is bound with the oral-aural nature of the Eskimo culture in which the culture itself is tied together, especially by the interaction of sound and touch, somewhat less so by taste and smell, and only minimally by sight. Quite the reverse would be true in a modern technological culture and society. Montagu would agree that the Eskimo's early tactile, auditory, and spatial experiences, and the continuous reinforcement of the culture itself does support the statement provided earlier by Ong that "Given sufficient knowledge of the sensorium exploited within a specific culture, one could probably define the culture as a whole in virtually all its aspects" (1967:6). (Eskimo illustration by Montagu based in part on De Boor, 1969:8-15, and Montagu, 1971:225-235).

Nonverbal codes play a significant role in culture

Drawing from the definitions and parameters already suggested for understanding nonverbal communication as aspects of communicative code, and the examples provided above, it is possible to generalize that every culture develops its own sign-action and object-language, and corresponding uses of body motion or kinesic behavior, physical characteristics, touching behavior, paralanguage, proxemics, artifacts, and environmental factors which help to set that culture off from others. In some cases the differences between that culture and others in its nonverbal codes are considerable. These differences also accompany verbal communicative codes, and may follow from the culture's perceptions, attitudes, thought-patterning, values, and role system, which in large part help to locate the culture in space and time. The proximity and interaction of the members of that culture with other cultures affect a change relationship upon the bases of the culture and upon the subsequent verbal and nonverbal codes and cues which its members exhibit. Obviously, too, there are similarities between the nonverbal communicative codes, just as there are between the verbal communicative codes of various cultures. These similarities provide the distinguishing qualities of humanness. Taken with the differences, they provide the richness of the many manifestations of human culture.

Edward Hall's *The Hidden Dimension* ably links people as the shapers of culture, and culture as shapers of people, particularly in social settings with their concomitant verbal and nonverbal communicative codes:

No matter how hard man tries it is impossible for him to divest himself of his own culture, for it has penetrated to the roots of his nervous system and determines how he perceives the world. Most of culture lies hidden and is outside voluntary control, making up the warp and weft of human existence. Even when small fragments of culture are elevated to awareness, they are difficult to change, not only because they are so personally experienced but also *because people cannot act or interact at all in any meaningful way except through the medium of culture.*

Man and his extensions constitute one interrelated system. It is a mistake of the greatest magnitude to act as though man were one thing and his house or his cities, his technology or his language were something else. Because of the interrelationship between man and his extensions, it behooves us to pay much more attention to what kinds of extensions we create, not only for ourselves but for others for whom they may be ill-suited. The relationship of man to his extensions is simply a continuation and a specialized form of the relationship of organisms in general to their environment. . . .

The ethnic crisis, the urban crisis, and the education crisis are interrelated. If viewed comprehensively all three can be seen as different facets of a larger crisis, a natural outgrowth of man's having developed a new dimension—*the cultural dimension*—most of which is hidden from view. The question is, How long can man afford to consciously ignore his own dimension? (1966:188-189).

Summary

In this chapter, we have seen that nonverbal communication codes are very often linked with language as a code, and can scarcely be separated from language. While many popular writers have argued that nonverbal body language can be learned easily and can be used for manipulative purposes, the opposite is more often true. Their findings are oversimplified. Their hypotheses and truisms are stated as facts, and the research often has no firm data basis or does not give proper credit to actual studies.

It is of course hard to define and set boundaries for nonverbal communication because it seems to include everything except language itself. As codes, nonverbal communication can be seen as sign-language, action-language, or object-language. Within a culture, it is almost possible to say that the culture itself it defined by the importance placed on individual senses, often of a nonverbal quality, and the ratio of emphasis toward particular senses within a society. Many nonverbal codes are learned perceptually, that is, on the basis of previously learned individual experiences, reflected by such learned aspects of communication as the wink. Blinking is natural, but winking has to be learned by every child. The individual from a simple culture may never have learned to wink, or even to understand a self-image in the water or a mirror, as this is also a perceptually learned experience.

Touch and tactility play a varying role in different cultures, with some cultures appearing to be "no-touch cultures," while others are heavily "touch" oriented. The Eskimo is an example of a heavily tactile culture. Based on the examples which were offered, we see that nonverbal codes do play a significant role in culture.

References

Birdwhistell, Ray L., 1967. "Some Body Motion Elements Accompanying Spoken American English." In *Communication: Concepts and Perspectives*. Edited by L. Thayer. Washington, D.C.: Hayden.

Carpenter, Edmund, 1973. *Oh What a Blow That Phantom Gave Me*. New York: Holt.

Condon, John C., and Fathi Yousef, 1975. *An Introduction to Intercultural Communication*. Indianapolis: Bobbs-Merrill.

deBoer, Richard James, 1967. "The Netsilik Eskimo and the Origin of Human Behavior." MSS, 1969,8.

Eisenberg, Ralph, and Ralph Smith, 1971. *Nonverbal Communication*. Indianapolis: Bobbs-Merrill.

Hall, Edward, 1966. *The Hidden Dimension.* Garden City, New York: Doubleday.

Knapp, Mark, 1972. *Nonverbal Communication in Human Interaction.* New York: Holt.

Koivumaki, Judith Hall, 1975. "Body Language Taught Here." In *Journal of Communication,* 25,1 (Winter), 26-30.

Montagu, Ashley, 1971. *Touching: The Human Significance of the Skin.* New York: Columbia University.

Mukasa-Bilikuddembe, Joseph, 1968. "The Mirror." *Short East-African Plays in English.* Edited by David Cook and Miles Lee. London: Heinemann.

Ong, Walter J., S.J., 1967. *The Presence of the Word: Some Prolegomena for Cultural and Religious History.* New Haven: Yale University.

Ruesch, Jurgen, and Weldon Kees, 1956, 1970. *Nonverbal Communication: Notes on Visual Perception of Human Relations.* Berkeley: University of California.

Watzlawick, Paul, and Janet Beavin, 1967. "Some Formal Aspects of Communication." In *The American Behavioral Scientist,* April, 4-8.

CHAPTER 7

Channels and Media of Communication

Cultural dialogue almost literally cannot take place without channels and media, whether traditional or technological. Channels and media are typically organized into networks.

Some writers have assumed that most cultural dialogue takes place at the interpersonal communication level. They have subsequently ignored the technological channels for such dialogue. Technology, however, has the most profound effects on all communication and cannot be ignored in considering intercultural communication or the crosscultural communication between cultural spokespersons. Much interpersonal communication occurs in a limited space where the communicators often relate to each other within close earshot, are visually in contact with each other, are possibly in literal touch with each other, and are affected by the sensation of pleasant or unpleasant smells. The organization of the channel through air molocules and light waves has the disadvantage both of considerable noise and the limitation of capacity and transmission speed. The same channels, however, of sound and light have nearly infinite capacities in different situations where they are aided by the most advanced technology.

Communication networks link many senders and receivers of messages

Hiroshi Inose calls a channel with many sources and many destinations a network. He suggests that for networks to be effective, good switching and resourceful design are required to minimize the number of branches and to maximize their capacity (1972:77). The human body effectively provides such a network and maximizes the capacity of its branches. When illness strikes, the total network sometimes malfunctions and requires considerable medical assistance to regain its proper balance and function. Other networks of a technological nature function in somewhat the same way.

Modern society is developed and supported by transport, power, and communication networks

Inose contends that the complex social and economic activities of a modern society are organized, developed, and supported by three major networks: the transportation network, the power network, and the communication network. He argues that the flow of passengers and freight, the flow of energy in the form of electricity, and the flow of information provided by these networks combine the actions of individuals in diverse locations into an integrated whole. Inose calls "the communication network probably the most vital of the three. It clearly plays an indispensable role in almost all aspects of social and economic activity, including the regulation of the transportation and power networks" (1972:77).

Inose suggests that by means of telephone, radio, television, and satellite networks, the world is closely covered with an enormous invisible net by which each citizen is constantly exposed to information. He proposes that if the present annual growth of 30 percent in communication networks continues, intercontinental networks could double in a three-year period and quadruple in six years. The networks are expanding not only at a vast rate quantitatively but also qualitatively through constant technological innovations. Although the establishment, maintenance, and expansion of communication networks are highly technical and expensive, such networks have important cultural and social implications. Inose comments: "As a communication network evolves and integrates human activities ever more tightly, its social role gains ever more weight.

Society can ill afford unreliable communication networks, so that now and in the future there must be much emphasis on reliability" (1972:88).

Communication networks include organizations, groups, mass media, and special channels

In the context of societal structure, Richard Fagen lists a four-fold classification of communication networks: organizations, groups, the mass media, and special channels to articulate their own interests. He notes that while the primary function of the mass media is always communication, serving as communication networks may be a secondary function of organizations, groups, and specialized channels. Fagen's chief interest lies in the area of political orientation, but it can be applied equally as well to other forms of communication networks, including cultural and societal ones. He stresses that organizational channels of political consequence are not necessarily part of the political system in the structural sense; for example, schools and unions may have important political functions. However, in most societal and governmental systems they do not have such functions as a primary goal. As an example, the fully developed Soviet system's penetration and control of unions and other institutions was so complete that those organizations *were* structurally within the political system and network. Fagen indicates that the political use of organizational channels is intermittent or partial in many instances. Sometimes the labor union serves a political function and at other times it serves an economic function in training new workers as apprentices. At still other times, it serves a health function in assuring proper safety and health standards for all workers. Organizational channels differ widely in the political communication uses which they serve. On a comparative basis between societies and political systems, more democratic states place less political connotations on organizations, while in more authoritarian countries the greater emphasis is placed on the tight functioning of all organizations within the political system (1966:39).

Communication in groups and in networks of groups is far less formal than in organizations and organizational networks. Evidence demonstrates, nevertheless, that political communication flows not only from the mass media directly to the individual, but also on an interpersonal level in the face-to-face groups to which the individual belongs. Most attitude change occurs in the context of interpersonal group interaction. Groups perform critical communication functions in almost any process of decision-making. In a modified format, the same characteristics which apply to organizational networks also apply to group networks, but in a less formal way. Fagen insists, however, that "in comparing entire systems the distinction becomes important, because, as we move from the more open to the more absolutist political format, we find fewer and fewer koy political communication activities performed by groups, except at the very highest levels of decision. . . . The elite prefer organizational or mass media channels in which control and predictability are increased. . ." (39-42).

Fagen acknowledges that the content of the media cannot always be said to shape political behavior in a direct and predictable manner. Still, their relationship "changes in a basic way a system's potential for political communication. . . .Thus, all varieties of political systems that are serviced by well-developed mass media networks also enjoy communication potentialities, for both control and coverage that are not shared by their media-poor relations no matter how extensive the latter's organizational and group channels might be" (43-44). In relating communication networks to the concept of mass media linkages, Fagen offers two of special note: the media as lateral channels in which people of different cultures, societies, and political systems interact with each other through the mass media; and the media as links in other network chains (43-48). In North Africa, for example, where the marketplace has functioned for centuries as the spot to disseminate and receive news, rumors, and information very rapidly, today this process is called "radio medina" because of the combination of the interpersonal grapevine and the news blaring from radios in market stalls and from the transistor radios which the individuals carry throughout the market.

Fagen utilizes two examples to illustrate the importance of the media as lateral channels and as links in the chains in broader communication networks. Social scientists believe that the 1960 Nixon-Kennedy television debates were the greatest single campaign episode serving to overcome Nixon's early lead in voter support. Fagen also offers the example of the Israeli who says that he likes to listen to the radio because it makes him feel like a real citizen by knowing what is occurring in his country. In the first case, immediate effects of 70 million people listening and watching the debates could be determined. In the second case, Fagen states that the individual transformations sparked by this type of communication might develop for years before they affect the national political system in any discernible way. Finally, since there are many media channels and networks functioning at the same time in most societies, it is very difficult to determine which medium has specific political consequences (42-48).

The crosscultural implications of the 1960 Nixon-Kennedy debates were not as great, for example, as the 1960 coverage by the international media of the presence at the United Nations by Chairman Khrushchev of the USSR and twenty-one other heads of state and government for the "World Summit Conference" called by Khrushchev. At that time communication satellites had not yet been perfected for instant replay throughout the world. However, more electronic media and press correspondents covered the debates and lengthy speeches of such leaders as Khrushchev, Castro, Eisenhower, Tito, Nasser, Sukarno, Macmillan, Nkrumah, and Nehru for worldwide coverage and replay than any other United Nations events in its first fifteen years. More recently, the media networks through the communication satellites were able to provide full and instant coverage for the 1976 presidential debates for 100 million Americans, and for television viewers in 105 countries scattered throughout the world. In such a case, the potential impact of the communications networks crossnationally and crossculturally was truly remarkable.

Communication networks play a significant role in cultural, societal, and international political communication

Whether we are discussing the 250 million telephones currently in use in the world, or such international news media networks as UPI, AP, Reuters, Agence France Presse, or Tass, it is also obvious that such communication networks play a significant role in cultural, societal, and international political communication. Although many writers believe that such worldwide linkages can only lead to a better world, Colin Cherry challenges this belief: "All these communication media basically do one thing: they remove certain constraints which hitherto existed upon the possibilities for better international co-operation. But the greatest powers for preventing the realization of these possibilities are still non-technical; they are the emotional blocks in people's minds, values, national parochialisms and other human factors. Whether our new-found powers will become used for mutual benefit, or not, cannot depend upon technical criteria alone" (1971:169-170). Cherry stresses: "Our whole world communication network, which has expanded so rapidly within one generation, and continues to do so, may drive us apart emotionally just as well as it may draw us together economically and institutionally, at least at the present time. . ." (175).

Channels and media may be traditional and/or technological

Harold Innis in the *Bias of Communication* (1973), Walter Ong in *The Presence of the Word* (1967), and Marshall McLuhan in *The Gutenberg Galaxy* (1962) suggest that most human societies have developed in approximately three communicative stages: an oral-aural, a script, and an electronic stage. We can add a fourth stage: that of space and satellite communication. The oral-aural stage was a period in which the dominant sense of sound served as the chief channel for transmitting, storing, and retrieving information between communicators. There are still various less technological societies and cultures which have not yet passed from the initial stage. Some have moved from the first to the third and fourth stages without passing through the second, and are only now involving themselves in language planning for the development of a written alphabet and script. An oral-aural society which has only recently had an electronic age thrust upon it suffers an intensive compression of time and space in its evolving cultural development. Often it loses a sense of cultural identity as it is confronted with modern technology in the face of its time and space-bound traditions.

The initial development of the oral-aural stage for Western civilizations was supplanted gradually by the development of an alphabetic script, and later in the 1400s by the invention of movable type with the Gutenberg press. Literacy became a goal not only for members of the church and court, but also for the commoner. The Protestant Reformation used the rapid dissemination of printed information to help break the hold which the Catholic Church earlier held over an essentially oral-aural society.

The stage dominated by visual script was transformed first by the industrial revolution, and later in the 1800s by such electrical discoveries as the use of Morse code in dot-dash messages over a single wire strung on poles between Baltimore and Washington, with the earth serving as the return conductor in 1844; the completion of the first transatlantic telegraph cable in 1858; Alexander Graham Bell's demonstration in 1876 that the human voice could be electrically transmitted over wires; and the first radiotelegraph message which was sent across the Atlantic ocean in 1901. While the oral-aural stage relied on memory to pass on information and cultural traditions, the script stage allowed the transmission, storage, and retrieval of information and tradition essentially in a visual medium. The electronic stage permitted information first to be preserved and then retrieved through the channels of sound, and later through the channels of both sound and sight, as in the development of computers and television.

The drum and radio serve as links between the oral-aural and contemporary society

In his *Muffled Drums: The News Media in Africa*, William Hachten offers a striking African comparison between the most traditional and the more advanced media forms introduced by the former colonial powers and, since independence, by the African nations themselves:

The news in Hausa on Radio Nigeria is always preceded by a brief recording of a Hausa drummer. This is appropriate, for over much of Africa the drum has long been an important traditional means of communication and is still widely used today. In Africa's expanding modern sector, the news media—newspapers, radio, television, magazines—may be regarded as the new drums of Africa. But the news media are as yet "muffled drums"—they are too few and inadequate for the great tasks expected of them and they are often harassed and controlled by self-serving interests. The new drums reverberating printed and electronic messages are still too weak technologically, economically, or politically to carry very far. Their messages often are distorted, garbled, and muted. The new "talking drums" do not yet speak clearly and effectively to the millions of new Africans. Yet in both the colonial period and the years since independence, the press and broadcasting have played an increasingly significant role in the dissemination of news and public information. (1971: viii-xiv)

As a form of traditional media, essentially for the oral-aural society or culture, drums represent an important channel of communication, not only for much of Africa, but in many other ancient societies as well. The drummer has been an influential figure in early societies throughout history. A substantial amount of the world's art, music, literature, healing ceremonies, and calls to worship and to war of a large number of the world's cultures have involved the drummer and his craft. Its importance is especially strong in the oral aural society.

The Eskimo's Shaman has beaten the time of the drum dance for the Eskimo dancers for thousands of years. The American Indian smoke signals complemented the drum as a major means of providing information. Most of the Plains Indians overcame their inability to speak each other's language by utilizing common nonverbal signs and drum language simple enough to be understood by vastly different groups. In reference to drums as extending African media in the early twentieth century, Leonard Doob comments that the important subjects for which drummers and audience have stereotyped drum messages were: 1.) the calling up of any particular chief by name; 2.) notice of danger, an enemy, fire, etc.; 3.) death of a noted individual; 4.) approach of Europeans; 5.) summons to take up arms or a declaration of war; 6.) pieces drummed at . . . festivals . . . which constitutes a complete drum-history of the particular clan (1961:102). According to Leonard Doob, writing in his *Communication in Africa* in 1961, it is likely that the same characteristics still existed in more contemporary times in heavily traditional African settings (1961:102). Lord Hailey states that "In the African village singing, clapping, dancing, and drumming are not separate entities, but may be said to constitute one homogeneous art form" (1957:67).

A very early medium, sometimes also in connection with the drummer or the player of other early stringed musical instruments, was the bard, or story-teller. The eschatological doomsday prophets of the Old Testament represent the important figure of the bard in the Hebraic tradition, and men like the wandering Homer of ancient Greece who spun the epic tales of Odysseus provide the same force in the Greek tradition.

In the nature of the oral-aural tradition of most earlier peoples, the bard with his patterned memory and trite story lines served as a major means of offering news and entertainment to people throughout scattered rural areas. He served as a cultural unifier. Other traditional channels and media have included the medieval morality and mystery plays, pulpit preaching in the Christian West and the Arab East, the wall poster in ancient Rome and ancient and modern China, the informal and interpersonal grapevine aspect of the marketplace whose people once or still utilize the open market as a major economic and news exchange medium, the Mammy wagons of West Africa, and the dance. The church bell has served as a major medium of communication in traditional and rural Christian societies. Many other such traditional forms can be cited.

William Hachten suggests that the only way to understand the dominance of radio over almost all other technologically modern media in most of Africa is to recognize that the radio captures the oral-aural nature of its people. He suggests that the "advantages of radio in the African milieu are, perhaps, obvious: it easily overcomes great distance; it is, thanks to transistors, cheaply and easily received; listeners need not be literate; and, it is said since Africans cling to their oral traditions, the spoken word offers the best results. Unquestionably, there is evidence of widespread use of radio in the rural and still-traditional areas" (1971:19-20). Hachten argues that radio broadcasting, unlike the press, has surpassed markedly the position it held in colonial time. In fact, there is currently a debate about whether Africa will go through a newspaper age at all enroute to the electronic age of radio, television, and movies, as did Europe and the United States. Some writers believe that African societies will proceed directly and fully into widespread adoption of the electronic media before newspaper and literacy are well established. Others reject such a McLuhanesque future for African media and argue that the printed word and literacy are essential to the modernization process and cannot be bypassed (1971:19-20).

Tom Hopkinson, writing on Africa and its press, suggests: "In the western world, the pattern has been newspaper, radio, television. In Africa and much of Asia, the first contact the ordinary man has with any means of mass communication is the radio. It is the transistor which is bringing the people of remote villages and lonely settlements into contact with the flow of modern life. For the tribesman entering the money economy the transistor now ranks as his second most coveted possession, ousting the bicycle—a wrist watch still being the first priority" (1967,18). Studies from various Latin American countries also demonstrate the major importance of the transistor radio as an extension of the oral-aural traditions prevalent among many of the illiterate or semiliterate campesinos. Margaret Mead's belief that the radio, particularly the transistor, as the dominant medium of an emerging world culture, has already been cited. *It is probably safe to say that the radio serves as the most significant modern technological medium of information and entertainment for most of the world's developing peoples.*

Space and satellite communication is the fourth stage in communicative development

Henri Busignies argues that "in developing technical means of communication inventors and engineers have naturally sought to exploit channels that carry messages at the highest possible speed. The most widely used channels are twisted pairs of wires, coaxial cables (metal tubes about 3/8 inches in diameter surrounding a thin central conductor and the free space between two antennas), one for transmitting a signal and one—or millions—for receiving it" (1972:63). It is probably not unfair to add to the stages of communicative development of human societies a fourth, the *space and satellite stage*. It was initiated directly by the 1957 launching of Sputnik, and the 1962 relaying of live television pictures between the United States and Europe through the communication satellite Telstar. In 1965, Early Bird satellite made available 240 telephone circuits for transatlantic service, and since that time several more communication satellites have been placed in orbit over the Atlantic, Pacific, and Indian oceans, expanding international voice channels from 1,000 in 1957 to more than 25,000, with predictions that the number will reach ten times that in the not too distant future (Busignies, 1972:63-64). Based on present capabilities and discoveries, Busignies predicts:

The decisions to be made as we move into a new era of high speed, high volume information traffic will be difficult and require much thought and care. . . . There will be no shortage of communication channels as far ahead as anyone can see. . . . From now on radio will be reserved mostly for satellites, mobile services (particularly air-traffic control), navigation and radar systems, space and military needs, and radio and television broadcasting, in short, for those applications where radio is indispensable. There will be unlimited capacity for communication through coaxial cables, waveguides and optical fibers. Their expanded use will require negligible amounts of energy, create no problems of pollution and place few, if any, strains on the environment. . . ." (73).

From the biological communications networks in the animal and human bodies to the communications network involved in linking Soviet and American space ships in outer space, the fast movement of information remains a crucial element. As James W. Carey expresses it:

The delay in space exploration did not derive from deficiencies of rocket thrust. The real delay was the development of a system of communication that would allow space travel to be controlled by earth. As printing went with sea-going navigation and the telegraph with the railway, electronic and computer-based communication goes with the space ship. In the absence of communication that matches the speed of light and exceeds the speed of the brain, some hardy pioneer might have tried to thrust himself off to the moon, although capital costs alone, as in the age of navigation, make that unlikely. The availability of electronic communication with its capacity to increase control by reducing signalling time has turned space into the next area of expansion. The meaning of electronic communication is not in the news that informs us or the entertainment that distracts us but in the possibility to turn space into a domain of geographical and political competition for the most electronically advanced nation. All space is now in the potential control of Houston (1975:49-50).

The media serve us as cultural transmitters

In our own lives, contemporary media have a major influence in passing down cultural traditions, beliefs, and attitudes, and in the instantaneous transmittal of new ones. Former Federal Communications Commissioner Nicholas Johnson maintains:

Most Americans tell pollsters that television constitutes their principal source of information. Many of our senior citizens are tied to their television sets for intellectual stimulation. And children now spend more time learning from television than from church and school combined. By the time they enter first grade they will have received more hours of instruction from television networks than they will later receive from college professors while earning a bachelor's degree. Whether they like it or not, the television networks are playing the roles of teacher, preacher, public official, doctor, psychiatrist, family counselor, and friend for tens of millions of Americans each day of their lives (1973:294).

During the 1967 *New York Times* strike which lasted three months, the loss of the only major American daily newspaper with its own comprehensive indexing system was a stunning loss to the archival preservation of day-by-day history in the United States during that period. Many Latin American diplomats and scholars considered the loss very significant in limiting their understanding of American development in the period. Fortunately, other newspapers in the United States were functioning even without comprehensive indexing, which meant that the historical loss was not complete, but only somewhat more complicated for historians, government officials, and diplomats. Outside of the range of New York City and its external subscribers, few other Americans knew or perhaps cared about this historical loss. Still, if we could imagine a three-month period when all print and electronic media were halted, the loss of the cultural transmission affected by the media would be truly incalculable. The crosscultural transmission of news and opinion would be a still greater loss, if it were so curtailed. Such an event does occur in less stable countries when they undergo severe revolutions or civil wars.

Frederick C. Whitney suggests that a true perspective of mass communication as a cultural transmitter is both historical and immediate. As pervasive as modern television has been, with its ability to attract an audience of 100 million persons, are the historical influences on our culture as the Mona Lisa, the Sistine Chapel, Venus de Milo, the Colosseum, and the Great Pyramid. All of these have been seen directly by millions of persons, and indirectly in history books by many more millions, and thereby serve as important mass media for passing down the traditions of Western civilization. Whitney offers the notion that: "Basic to mass communications as a carrier of the culture is man's unique time-binding ability, whereby he can store and sort experience for transmission to future generations, thus assuring that he will progress as a species rather than simply survive." He believes that: "Cultural transmission in contemporary mass media is almost overpowering. In one sense it is a homogenizing influence on society; regional accents and distinctive dress tend to disappear. On the other hand, the very diversity of contemporary media leads to a broader expression of individuality and interests than ever before. This is another of the paradoxes of mass communications: it can be both homogenizing and individualizing at the same time" (1975:406-407).

To deny or ignore the role of the media and its networks—whether traditional or modern, basic or extending—in a discussion of cultural dialogue is to fail to understand the focal point which all of the media play in a people's culture and in its transmission. If all technological media were banished for a year in the American setting, for example, traditional media would still impart a large part of the cultural tradition, but its evolution would be slowed immeasurably. Since most modern societies now move at such a rapid pace, a year's hiatus in the availability of all technological communications media could bring modern society either to a virtual standstill or to the threshold of a revolution of major proportions. The traditional society in such a situation might remain static or return to its oral-aural state. In either case, the cultural loss would be tremendous. Finally, the role of the communication channels and media in transmitting intercultural dialogue and the interacting between cultural spokespersons is extraordinary. The channels for the exchange of information between Rome and London once required one month for the reception of the message. Today, sound and light aided by technology permit the same message to be transmitted in seconds, and satellite and space communication, the fourth stage in the development of societies and cultures, permits simultaneous transfer of information instantly around the globe. As we suggested earlier, technology is the metaphysics of the twentieth century, and communications channels and media are the instrument of proclaiming that metaphysics.

The control of channels and media offers a collective monopolistic advantage

We have already seen that control of communication as a process certainly is one of the most powerful assets open to an individual, institution, society, or state. We have suggested that one definition of culture is that it is controlled by the culturally powerful members over those who are culturally weak. It follows, too, that control of channels, media, and networks provides a singular monopolistic advantage to those who collectively possess it within and between cultures. The entire problem of cultural imperialism and cultural dependency is sharply focused in the management of communications. The ability to define perceptual reality often lies in the hands of the controllers.

When the Roman Empire, the medieval church, and the British Empire all had attempted to exert influence by controlling communications channels, media, and networks, their behavior was symbolic of the closely knit relationships of communications with culture itself. In *The Bias of Communication*, Harold Innis postulates that: "Writings on culture can be divided into those attempting to weaken other cultures and those attempting to strengthen their own. . . . Cultures will reflect their influence in terms of space and in terms of duration. How large an area did they cover and how long did they last? The limitations of culture, in point of duration, are in part a result of the inability to muster the intellectual resources of a people to the point where stagnation can be avoided and where boredom can be evaded. . . . Intense cultural activity is followed by fatigue." Innis argues that cultural activity, evident in architecture and sculpture, and armed military force become capable of impressing peoples over a wide area. It is designed to emphasize prestige. It becomes an index of power (1973:132-133, 139).

Within the context of cultural expansion and control, satellites have become a dominant mode of exerting influence. James Carey comments: "Through satellite communication there is a thrusting out of cultures into new regions of space. This movement is part of a system of national and regional rivalries, which find expression in United Nations debates on international regulation of satellite broadcasting. If in a few years television images can be transmitted over national boundaries to home receivers, the United States and the Soviet Union as the two largest electronic powers can enlarge the region and particularity of their influence" (Carey, 1975:48-49). He suggests that naturally, there are disagreements over international satellite regulations, but the direction of United States policy is clear. At a recent United Nations debate, the United States representative argued that his government, while amenable to international satellite regulation, opposed restrictions on direct telecasting over national boundaries. He declared that the new technology could be used in an "effective and constructive way" without inhibiting the potential for great contributions to education and communication. The American delegate objected to the concept of "prior consent" that the advocates of strict regulation were proposing, because such a principle could rule out direct broadcasting for entire regions. Because a satellite beam would usually cover many states, one country's objection to international broadcasts could prohibit many others from receiving such broadcasts even if they specifically desired to receive them (Carey, 1975:48-49).

In the modern system of states, the ability to control the channels and media which deliver propaganda from one state to another is very strong on the part of the sender but strictly limited on the part of the receiver. Since World War II, jamming the Western-oriented Voice of America and Radio Free Europe has no doubt been nearly as expensive for socialist bloc countries as setting up and maintaining their own media networks. Recently jamming efforts have decreased, perhaps partly because of the futility of policing the information which crosses international borders in this way.

Until very recently, the Republic of South Africa refused to develop any television capacity potentiality in order to prevent powerful messages from outside the country from penetrating the minds of its citizens. When television becomes an important medium there, it will depend upon a large proportion of British and American programming, unless its own industry becomes a very expensive project through government subsidization. To preserve their own cultural identity, the latter alternative is likely to be adopted.

Canadian media is culturally dominated by American content

Even Canada's attempt to place strict limits on Canadian content and foreign programming has led Canadian governmental leaders in control of regulating communications to a variety of curious decisions. They have excluded non-Canadian composers from some musical broadcasts, which limits considerably the range of music to be broadcasted. They have also decided that the American Super Bowl or an important address by the American president actually is Canadian content. Eighty percent of all Canadians live within 200 miles of the American border. Because of this factor and the very high enrollment in cable television reaching about 30 percent of the Canadian homes, many Canadians can watch 100 percent of American content, despite the official Canadian attempts to regulate such viewing. Generally speaking, the major population centers of Canada are so affected. The Today Show, the CBS Evening News with Walter Cronkite, and a twenty-hour continuous Democratic National Telethon Fund Appeal have all been standard fare for many Canadians.

Recent Canadian laws have been established to prevent the extensive tax breaks for American print media which have been available to Canadian advertisers. Also, the utilization of French in much of Quebec has led its people to maintain their own cultural identity better than English-speaking Canada, which always seems to be searching for its cultural roots in North America.

Australia seeks to exert greater control over its own media

In similar fashion to Canada, Australia is attempting to exert a greater control over its own media. USIA representative Wilson Dizard stated in 1964 that "the greatest no-holds-barred market for U.S. telefilm distribution is Australia. The daily schedule of a typical Australian television station is, particularly in prime listening hours, virtually indistinguishable from that of a station in Iowa or New Jersey" (1964:63). Myles P. Breen adds that during this period, American and British film producers and distributors had essentially cornered the market on film distribution in Australia. In 1972 with the election of a Labor government, a Department of the Media was established. The Department appointed a Tariff Board to recommend government measures to establish Australia's own film industry and to lessen the foreign dominance and control over Australian media content. The Board's recommendations, including an Australian content requirement established in 1972, have been initiated, and between July 1973 and July 1976, Australian radio was required to increase its Australian coverage to 30 percent. A television and film school was organized, and various other efforts are in the process of changing the almost total control of the media and their messages from American and British domination to Australian controlled media. Breen concludes his comments on the new developments there: "Whether or not all this activity will provide Australia with the media independence that many nationalistic Australians so passionately desire is, of course, yet to be seen. In the view of government officials, Australia is hooked on American TV programming at the moment, but they are determined that their country is going to 'kick the habit' " (Breen, 1975:186).

Military and media control by the leader in developing countries

We might speculate that *in the context of the developing coun-tries, where a greater degree of instability is typical than in more technologically developed countries, the leader who con-trols the military, and thereby also essentially controls the citizenry, and who also effectively controls the channels and media of communication, also controls the country.* He or she also controls the cultural and societal setting. When that con-trol is lost, titular leadership will continue briefly, or it will shift through a coup. Whether it is bloody or bloodless depends on how difficult it is to wrest these controls away from the present leader. Many bloodless coups in Asia or Africa have resulted while the country's official head of government was absent from the country and was thereby prevented from exer-cising control over the military and the media.

William Hachten supports the notion that control over the communications channels and media is essential in the developing countries.

Radio in Africa is virtually always a function of government. At in-dependence, the new African governments quickly brought radio fully under the official umbrella if it was not there already. . . . The im-portance of radio is underlined by the role it often plays in political crises. In almost all coups d'etat—successful and unsuccessful—seizure of the radio transmitters is one of, if not the, primary goal. . . . In visits to Radio Ghana in Accra and Radio Nigeria in Lagos, I was struck by the fact that both broadcasting installations, fenced with barbed wire, were heavily guarded by armed soldiers behind sand-bagged barricades. This is indeed a tribute to the political importance of radio (1971:19,23).

It seems obvious, with even the limited examples offered, that media and channel control is an extraordinarily important question as it relates to political or cultural power or the absence of power.

Communication media helps to aggravate and contain cultural conflict

Conflict and its resolution have already been cited as major factors in the study and practice of cultural dialogue and most other forms of communication. As Fred Jandt suggests: "Social conflict is a term we assign to particular human com-municative behaviors. Two assumptions are implicit in this statement. First, social conflict is communicative behavior.

There can be no conflict without verbal and nonverbal communication. ... Second, ... conflict exists when the parties involved agree in some way that the behaviors associated with their relationship are labeled as conflict behaviors." Jandt suggests that perhaps the attitude that conflict represents failure is culturally learned. The possible alternatives to conflict are in general: 1.) separation of the parties; 2.) one party winning all, the other party losing all; and 3.) a new creative relationship—sometimes labeled as compromise. Jandt stresses that: "Rather than being undesirable, conflict is desirable from at least two standpoints. It has been demonstrated that through conflict man is creative. Further, a relationship in conflict *is* a relationship—not the absence of one. Such a relationship may result in creativity because of its intensity" (1973:2-3).

Domestically, the cultural implications of the media in aggravating or controlling conflict can be documented again and again. During the 1967 civil rights riots, the 1968 riots at the Demoractic National Convention in Chicago, the second Wounded Knee episode, and later in the massive protests against the Viet Nam War, the mass media of the United States and abroad played a substantial role in expanding the limits of each crisis by the widespread publicity given to the actual events. Sometimes events were especially restaged for the television cameras. At other times, the information provided by the media was simply inaccurate.

The "media coup" seeks to "bring the establishment to its knees"

The cultural implications of these riots and their media coverage, as they actually happened or were made to seem to have happened were considerable. In the case of the American civil rights riots of the late 1960s, the events usually indicated some sort of intense interracial conflict. However, the 1968 Chicago riots at the Democratic National Convention and the Viet Nam protests seemed to attract mostly young white Americans. They felt alienated from the system and considered themselves in countercultural conflict with the hostile law enforcement officers who believed they were protecting American values against a frenzied and radical mob. Considerable evidence demonstrates that young blacks were drawn into these later situations far less intensely than the white participants. In a sense, it seems that the young whites in the United States may have gained an appreciation of the power and exposure which the media coverage brought to the earlier civil rights protesters. Perhaps the protesters were attempting "media coups" against the establishment. Even though much danger is created in such a "coup," participants can seek a moment of public glory or martyrdom. Many were convinced that they were seeking to restore America's lost ideals.

Potential assassins of widely known leaders may be motivated more by the instant media coverage than by specific hatred against the individual whom they seek to kill. Two assassination attempts against President Ford in the autumn of 1975 both seemed geared more toward publicity for the individuals involved than as genuine attempts against his life. Front page and magazine cover spreads provide more fame (or infamy) for an individual through such an effort than a lifetime of efforts normally could offer even to the most gifted person. In the American cultural setting, individual success is of such critical importance that even such a bizarre success makes one feel important enough perhaps to risk death or life imprisonment. The person who has relatively minimum success in life is suddenly, through the media coverage, recognized by millions of persons as a unique individual.

When genuine cultural conflict is involved, the press has the right, within the Western context, to detail the reasons for the conflict, including the cultural ones. However, freedom of the press itself is a Western cultural concept and certainly is not considered a given right in many other cultural settings. If cultural conflict is further aggravated by the vastly excessive coverage given it, then even the creativity which Jandt sees in conflict may approach diminishing returns. At the same time, it is also clear that serious cultural conflicts sometimes cannot be solved favorably for an aggrieved minority cultural group without creating a "media coup" against the dominant cultural majority. Thus, tensions are created by the need for the nourishment of the Western freedoms of information, speech, and the press, and the simultaneous needs for culturally deprived or dependent groups to be able to demonstrate their efforts to overcome cultural imperialism. Additionally, society in general has a certain right to protect its dominant values and to maintain an orderly community. The alternatives are clearly not simple. Still, many of the Western cultural and societal norms are based on the democratic right of the majority to prevail after the minority has received a fair hearing. The minority's fair hearing is possible only with a medium which is free to give full coverage to their grievances and to prevent the dominant cultural group from imperialistically controlling the dependent cultural minority. In this sense, the media's contributions to the solution of conflict do remain inherently creative.

Even assuming that conflict has a creative capacity and must be a desirable occurrence at times, and acknowledging that the media itself may serve to worsen a conflict or crisis, we are left to wonder whether the media also have the capacity to help solve or alleviate conflicts and crises, either at the interpersonal, cultural, or collective levels of communication. Thelma McCormack contends that mass communication can and must act as a counterforce to the totalitarian tendencies of mass society. Judgments about the media are based on the indices of its content, influence, and power, in relation to its protest against the alienation of the individual. It is also gauged as an agency which restores identifies activities that check or break up concentrations of political power. These two elements serve as a model, which includes "two dichotomous pairs of independent variables: social change and social stability; class society and mass society. The intervening variables are the relationships between communication and political institutions, [and] between communication and political roles." Though totalitarian control of the mass media is common and therefore self-perpetuating, the mass media's best service is to keep its critical capabilities without allowing them to become totally subverted to mass society (1973:345-347).

Summary

In this chapter we have begun with the notion that cultural dialogue depends on channels and media, often more important than on interpersonal levels of communication. Networks, such as those affecting power, transport, and communication, have a powerful effect in and between cultures. Communication networks are perhaps the most important as they influence all the other networks. Communication networks include organizations, groups, mass media, and specialized channels. These components are naturally affected by various political ideologies, ranging from the relatively libertarian to the relatively authoritarian ones. Thus, communication networks do play an important role in cultural, societal, and international political networks.

Channels and media may be either traditional, as represented by the drum, or technological, which is illustrated by the transistor radio. The transistor radio may be the dominant mode of crosscultural transmission of information and persuasive messages because it is one of the easiest and cheapest electronic communication channels to be introduced, especially in rural areas. We can describe cultures and societies as progressing through several communication stages, such as 1.) oral-aural, 2.) script or visual, 3.) electronic, and 4.) space or communication satellite. The fourth stage presently envelops cultures and peoples on a worldwide basis and makes it possible for less developed societies to leapfrog from an oral-aural stage into an instant interaction and social discourse with other more developed cultures. Media of all sorts constantly serve as cultural transmitters, whether of historical nature or of immediate consequence. Because of this cultural transmission, media and channels play an increasingly important part in all of our social discourse within and between cultures.

Finally, in this chapter we have considered the relationships between the media and culture as seen in the issues of control and conflict. We have seen that cultural control over the media and channels of communication provides advantage over those who control them, both within and between cultures. Crosscultural control has been cited in the examples of the American influence on Canadian and Australian media. Control within a society is seen as particularly strong in the context of developing countries where the leader who controls both the military and the media often is able to control the country. The communications media can be seen to help aggravate and control cultural conflict as well. "Media coups" seek to bring the establishment to its knees. Often, however, such power is shortlived, for there is usually greater power available to the political leaders of a society. While the media may be totalitarian and reactionary, they also have the power to help solve, as much as to aggravate, cultural and societal conflict. This power is considerable and makes the media and communications channels an important force to be dealt with when we consider intercultural and crosscultural communication and its potential breakdown.

References

Breen, Myles, 1975. "Severing the American Connection: Down Under." In *Journal of Communication*, XXV, 2 (Spring), 183-186.

Busignies, Henri, 1972. "Communication Channels. In *Communication: A Scientific American Book*. San Francisco: Freeman.

Carey, James W., 1975. "Canadian Communication Theory: Extensions and Interpretations of Harold Innis." Paper presented at the Association for Education in Journalism Annual Meeting. Ottawa.

Cherry, Colin, 1971. *World Communication: Threat or Promise.* New York.

Dizard, Wilson P., 1964. "American Television's Foreign Markets." In *Television Quarterly*, 3 (3).

Doob, Leonard, 1961. *Communication in Africa: A Search for Boundaries.* New Haven: Yale University.

Fagen, Richard, 1966. *Politics and Communication.* Boston: Little, Brown.

Hachten, William, 1971. *Muffled Drums: The News Media in Africa.* Iowa City: University of Iowa.

Hopkinson, Tom, 1967. "Newspapers Must Wait in Priority Queue." *IPI Report.*

Innis, Harold, 1973. *The Bias of Communication.* Toronto: University of Toronto.

Inose, Hiroshi, 1972. "Communication Networks." In *Communication: A Scientific American Book*. San Francisco: Freeman.

Jandt, Fred E., 1973. *Conflict Resolution through Communication.* New York: Harper.

Johnson, Nicholas, 1973. "What Can We Do about Television?" In *Mass Media: The Invisible Environment.* Edited by Robert J.

Glessing and William P. White. Chicago: Sciences Research Associates.

McCormack, Thelma, 1973. "Social Change and the Mass Media." In *Intercommunication among Nations and Peoples.* Edited by Michael H. Prosser. New York: Harper & Row.

McLuhan, Marshall, 1962. *The Gutenberg Galaxy: The Making of Typographic Man.* New York: New American Library.

Ong, Walter, J.S.J., 1967. *The Presence of the Word: Some Prolegomena for Cultural and Religious History.* New Haven: Yale University.

Whitney, Frederick C., 1975: *Mass Media and Mass Communication in Society.* Dubuque: Iowa University.

Part Three
Cultural Components and Cultural Communication

In Part 3, we will emphasize the components of culture and will seek some linkages between communication and culture. We will offer cultural definitions and theoretical orientations in Chapter 8. Among the important cultural orientations which assist us in determining the dimensions of cultural dialogue are cultural evolutionism, cultural functionalism, cultural history, and cultural ecology. All of these orientations have individual strengths and weaknesses as theories. Taken together, they allow us to distinguish collective cultural units, such as cultural maximizers, the quantum of culture, cultural universals, the cultural placenta (which surrounds a cultural interchange), the cultural quantum of communication (which a culture or society has developed), and the bias toward specific types of communication which each culture develops.

The most cultural of cultural components, values, and value orientations will be considered in Chapter 9. As the patterns in individuals and groups which are structured primarily by cultural communication, values are generally the most hidden but powerful aspects of culture. As in the case of language, relativistic versus deterministic concepts have dominated the study of values and value orientations both for religious and moral thinkers, and for anthropological studies of peoples and cultures. Value orientations are generalized, organized, and existentially judgmental and can be classified as the crucial orientations common to all human groups. Basing our understanding of values and value orientations on the work of Clyde and Florence Kluckhohn, especially in their studies of five communities in the American Southwest, we will also draw upon Edward Stewart's parallels between North American and Filipino value orientations on such subjects as the relationship of humans to the supernatural and to nature, humans' relationships toward time and space, and their relations with others.

In Chapter 10, we shall emphasize the individual processes of culture which can be called *subjective culture*. As the study of human cognitive processes, subjective culture plays a dominant role in all cultural communication. Since a key aspect of subjective culture is individual perception, the chapter will focus upon this element as it relates to other cognitive processes. We will again relate perception to such concepts as language, art, belief, personality, thought-patterning, and intelligence. We will also return to the principle of similarities and differences in the consideration of uniqueness attributes as perceptually developed in individuals and groups. We will suggest that contributing to the notion of uniqueness in perception are such aspects as naming; scarcity, whether of information, or experiences, or material goods; beliefs as unique; and performance as perceptually motivated in a positive or negative sense because of the feeling of uniqueness. We will argue that for human behavior there exists only subjective reality, which is the universe as perceived by individuals, and thus all cultural communication is affected by individual perceptions.

CHAPTER 8

Cultural Definitions and Theoretical Orientations

Numerous definitions of culture exist. A number of them have been cited in preceding chapters. We have emphasized that culture includes the passing on of language patterns, values, attitudes, beliefs, customs, and thought-patterning. We have also stressed the importance of culture as a feature of control both for members within the social group as well as for outsiders whom the group wishes to bring under its influence. Essentially, as Nieburg suggests, all cultural phenomena are made of socially shared activities and must be considered the properties of the group rather than of the individual alone (1973:38). Bertrand Russell defines culture as "a collection of events connected with each other by memory-chain backwards and forwards. We know about one such collection of events— namely, that constituting ourself—more intimately and directly than we may know about anything else in the world" (1959:26-27). William James's definition of culture emphasizes: "the selection, the rearrangement, the tracing of patterns upon, and the stylizing of the random irradiations and reset- tlements of our ideas" (1950:638). Finally, central to a defini- tion of culture is the view that the social discourse of humans is based on their ability as symbol- and tool-builders, -users and -manipulators.

Four theoretical orientations on the current theories of culture

In *Culture Theory*, David Kaplan and Robert A. Manners (1972) propose that culture theory concerns itself not just with what has happened in culture, but why it happened. They identify four key theoretical orientations which have helped lead to the present theories and study of culture: *cultural evolutionism, cultural functionalism, cultural history,* and *cultural ecology.*

Cultural evolutionism refers to the cumulative, collective experience of humankind: *Culture Writ Large*

Leslie White's view of culture implies that since the behavior of the higher infrahuman animal species is nonsymbolic in nature, such a species is limited to a world of its own sensory experiences. Even though such a species may be capable of a high degree of learning, and may exhibit certain nonbiogenetic characteristics which are passed down from generation to generation, White stresses that over time these learned and transmitted behavior patterns among infrahumans seem to be nonprogressive and noncumulative in nature. However, tool-using is progressive and cumulative among humans in the sense that technology is irreversible. Symbol-building and -using is also progressive and cumulative among humans. White denies the term *protoculture* to describe such nonhuman species; a culture either exists among a species or it does not. To speak of the culture of animals is to misuse the term. On the other hand, because we humans can symbolically represent, and misrepresent, the world to ourselves, we are capable of transcending our own immediate sensory experiences. We can talk about places we have never seen and events in which we have never participated. We can speculate about the past, dream about the future, and even invent entities which do not exist and could not exist. Gilbert Keith Chesterton's enthusiasm for the zoo was expressed in the notion that there he could see animals which should never have existed. After visiting the zoo, he could then dream and create more animals that in fact never did exist. White claims that symboling enables us to husband and to represent our experiences in such a form that they become a part of a cumulative and progressive cultural tradition (1959).

Thus, when White uses the term culture, he and his

nineteenth-century predecessors consider the word to refer to the cumulative, collective experiences of human life, rather than to the history of this or that particular group culture. When he is considering stages of development, he is referring to universal stages which can be said to characterize these collective experiences. White is concerned with *Culture Writ Large—Culture.* The entire concept of *cultural evolutionism* is embodied in the term "Culture." Additionally, while culture is the adaptive device by which we humans accommodate ourselves to nature and nature to us, basically humans-in-culture perform these functions by harnessing free energy and putting it to work for the species. In our energy-harnessing process, White sees all major institutional orders of culture—technology, social and political organization, and ideology—as contributing to the effectiveness with which the cultural system appropriates and utilizes the energy available to it. He agrees with various other writers that the primary role in culture is played by the technological system. Within this concept of cultural evolutionism, White sees all parts of culture as related; each reacts upon the others and is affected by them in turn (1959). Other writers who have followed White have modified his cultural evolutionism to emphasize *cultures* or *groups of cultures* rather than *Culture Writ Large* as White does.

Cultural functionalism emphasizes the society or culture as a working system

Cultural functionalism is the dominant recent emphasis in anthropological research, especially in relation to *ethnographic research*. Kingsley Davis's argument is that functionalism is synonymous with sociological and anthropological analysis. The functionalist seeks to look for the ways that institutions and structures of a society interconnect to form a system. In addition to Davis's interpretation of functionalism as the methodology of exploring interdependence, there is a stronger phrasing of functionalism as a theory about cultural processes, about how societies work. Beyond an interest in seeing how the patterns of a society fit together, the functionalist seeks to explain why these elements relate in the way they do, and more importantly, why certain cultural patterns exist, or why they continue to persist (Davis, 1959:752-722).

Basic to any functional explanation is the assumption, open or implied, that all cultural systems have certain functional requisites, or necessary conditions of existence, or needs—all of which must be somehow met if the system is to continue as an ongoing concern. Presumably if the functional systemic needs are not met, the system will disintegrate and die, or it will change into some other kind of system. In this sense, then, institutions, cultural activities, and other cultural complexes are understood or explained not merely by specifying their relationships to some larger system in which they are implicated. They also are understood by demonstrating that these relationships contribute to the maintenance of the larger cultural system or some part of it. Kaplan and Manners stress that the functional theory of culture is hampered in its effectiveness because functionalists are forced to argue from some general systemic requirement or need for the presence of a specific institution which meets this requirement. Unless the functionalists can demonstrate that the institution in question is the only one capable of performing the function attributed to it, the theory is inconsistent. However, the same social function may be performed often by a variety of institutions, or the same institution may perform a variety of functions. Kaplan and Manners believe that the argument for culture and its institutions and customs from a functionalistic point of view provides a shaky theory on which to rest culture study and theory if used without other theoretical perspectives (1972:56-60).

In 1950, David F. Aberle and other social scientists developed a generalized model of human society which included a list of the "functional prerequisites" of *all* human societies, justifying the inclusion of each prerequisite by demonstrating that in its hypothetical absence the society could not survive. These prerequisites include provision for an adequate relationship to the environment and for sexual recruitment, role differentiation, role assignment, communication, shared cognitive orientations, shared and articulated set of goals, the normative regulation of means, the regulation of affective expression, socialization, and the effective control of disruptive forms of behavior (Aberle, 1950:100-111). Kaplan and Manners challenge generally the ability to gain precise empirical results from functional studies of culture. More precisely, they challenge the ability to determine whether a society or culture actually dies when one or more of Aberle's stated prerequisites for societal survival is missing. They question when one can determine precisely whether the society is dead, especially if many of its functions survive for the development of a new society (1972:63-67). If, as Harold Innis suggests in *The Bias of Communication* (1973), Roman society dissolved gradually after the fall of Rome into the forms and functions developed by the Roman Catholic Church as a major cultural institution, we might ask whether it is fair to assume that the earlier culture and its functions actually died and disappeared entirely.

Kaplan and Manners argue that statements which appeal to such universal functional requirements cannot be empirically tested, and in fact, are *definitions of society*. Thus, they believe that because cultural systems are subject to relatively rapid qualitative change, we have to be able to ask: At what point does a culture cease to be one kind of system and become transformed into some other kind? Based on this question, Kaplan and Manners draw up a basic set of requirements for an adequate functional analysis of culture: a conception of a system; a list of the functional requirements of that system; definitions of the various properties or states of the system being maintained; a statement of those external conditions of the system which can conceivably affect these properties and states, and which must therefore be controlled; and some knowledge of the internal mechanisms by which such system-properties are maintained or kept within specific limits. They contend that in dealing with cultural systems, these functional requirements simply cannot be met on a regular and consistent basis. Functional approaches to culture must be combined with other approaches which provide basic understandings of culture (Kaplan and Manners, 1972:63-67).

Cultural history and the contemporary history of a culture

In considering the usefulness of *historical* and *ethnographic* approaches to culture, Kaplan and Manners suggest that *functional, evolutionary,* and *historical* perspectives are most effectively wed. If we are interested in more than simple chronology or narrative, we must engage in the process of classifying, categorizing, and positing possible relationships among *types* of events. When the historical data are not placed in a functional-evolutionary framework, the history remains mere narrative or chronology. In short, *all study of culture is a study of history, and moreover, a study of contemporary history.* It is contemporary in the informants, documents, artifacts, and other historical evidence available from whatever period of history a culture is being studied. Kaplan and Manners claim that the most important point in the development of any theory about culture is *that no theory can possibly explain the operation of a concrete system unless the general nature of the theory is restricted and supplemented by a statement of the relevant initial boundary conditions of the system to which the theory is being applied* (Kaplan and Manners, 1972:63-75). Additionally, they argue, it is history which provides us with the appropriate data for formulating relevant restrictive and supplementary conditions in studying culture. In this way, we maintain that the fundamental issues we have developed earlier are the true subjects of historical study.

If all cultures were similar both in time and space dimensions, we would not need comparative studies. If cultural and individual conflict and control were not factors in cultural development, we would not need to chronicle such human events. If total cultural assimilation and stability were assured, historical study would have no value. History, if it is anything, is the study of cultural pluralism and change. Finally, a chief purpose of the study of history is to compare the interaction between traditional and technologically developing societies, cultural stability and change, and cultural imperialism and dependency.

Nevertheless, just as attention only to cultural evolution or cultural functionalism causes methodological problems for the student of culture, a purely historical approach has led such anthropologists as Frank Boas to dead ends in their research. However, Kaplan and Manners believe that the use of history (among other orientations) to study culture does provide an important methodological focus for investigators to see, review, and analyze the data with insights that would have been missing from a single approach. In general, they conclude that those who are involved in historical research or understanding are often concerned with the search for similarities and differences, generalizations, and general processes which may lead to the formulation of broader theoretical statements about culture (63-75).

Cultural ecology stresses our interaction with our cultural environment

The final theoretical orientation emphasized by Kaplan and Manners is *cultural ecology*, which also directly relates to theories about culture developed by cultural evolutionists. They define cultural ecology as a concern with *adaptation* on two levels: first, with regard to the way cultural systems adapt to their total environment, and second, as a consequence of this systemic adaptation, with regard to the way the institutions of a given culture adapt or adjust to one another. The cultural ecologist maintains that focusing on these adaptational processes allows us to see how different cultural configurations emerge, are maintained, and become transformed. Generally, cultural ecologists have tended to emphasize technology and economics in their analysis of cultural adaptation. Herein the differences among cultures geographically through space, as well as the difference over time within a culture, are most apparent. Our control over our environment has changed dramatically since the Ice Age. This increased control can be largely attributed to improvements in the technological means available to us, and to the growth of scientific knowledge. While modern societies can still adhere to moral philosophies 2,000 or more years old, as they do, for them to adhere to the technological and scientific knowledge of that time would strip away most of contemporary culture of the last quarter of the twentieth century (Kaplan and Manner, 1972:76-77). While morality may be a constant, technological and scientific development must always remain in a state of flux.

Kaplan and Manners generalize that cultural ecology takes its inspiration from a long-range view of humanity. It is a view that sees the human species as a product of biological evolution, but a wholly unique product. We are unique because we come to terms with our environment in ways that differ profoundly from those of all infrahuman species, especially because we progressively and cumulatively develop cultural characteristics not available to the infrahuman levels of life. We play an active role in our environment, while animals play an essentially passive role. We act upon our environment and shape it, while lower animals are acted upon by the environment. Kaplan and Manners argue that: The enabling device is what we call *culture*—the primary mechanism through which humans begin by adapting to and end by controlling their environment. This environment in which humans live has become a cultural environment, so that whatever biological change may occur in the species, the direction of causation seems to be much more from culture to biology, rather than the other way around. Thus, *cultural* ecology, unlike *general* ecology, is not concerned simply with the interaction of life forms in a particular ecosystem, but with the way in which humans through the instrumentality of culture manipulate and shape the ecosystem itself (Kaplan and Manner, 1972:76-77). A key term is *homo faber*, man the maker. We do not simply make tools. We make tool-making tools. This is the height of symbolic competence.

Two fundamental concepts in cultural ecology are perceived by Kaplan and Manners as *environment* and *adaptation*. The environment that figures in the cultural ecology perspective is always a culturally modified environment. Such a formulation, they suggest, implies an inescapable element of circularity: *environment > culture,* or *culture > environment.* Thus cultural ecology stresses the distinction between the habitat as given, and the habitat as we modify and utilize it. We convert more and more of the natural habitat into a cultural environment. According to Kaplan and Manners a *basic tenet of cultural ecology, then, is the distinction between the environment by itself, and the effective environment with the latter which is seen as the environment as conceptualized, utilized, and modified by humans* (Kaplan and Manners, 1972:76-66). Edward Leach offers a highly plausible hypothesis: "The environment is not a natural thing; it is a set of interrelated percepts, a product of culture. What this environment is is not discoverable objectively; it is a matter of perception. The relation between a society and its environment can be understood only when we see how the environment is organized in terms of the verbal categories of those who use it" (1965:25, 37-38). This is what we call *subjective culture.* Kaplan and Manners argue further, however, that the way in which a people are able to utilize their verbal categories is also affected by the objective properties of the environment, and also the knowledge and techniques a people use in coping with these objective properties. Thus Kaplan and Manners do not accept entirely such a *cognitive* argument as proposed by Leach (1972:76-77).

Major proponents of *cognitive anthropology,* which emphasizes subjective culture, argue that culture is located in human minds and hearts. Thus it consists of whatever one has to know or believe in order to operate in a manner acceptable to its members. Clifford Geertz objects that what follows is a view of describing what it is—the writing out of systematic rules, an ethnographic computation, which if followed, would make it possible to operate, to pass (physical appearance aside) for a native. Geertz contends that the cognitivist fallacy—that culture consists of mental phenomena which can be analyzed by formal methods similar to those of mathematics and logic—is as destructive of an effective use of the concept as are the behaviorist and idealist fallacies to which it is a misdrawn correction. He argues that knowing how a native thinks and acts in another culture does not make one a member of that culture, or able to act and think precisely like the native (1973:12).

To clarify his own position in *The Interpretation of Cultures,* Geertz stresses that we generally are not trying to become natives of a particular culture, but to widen the universe of social dialogue for and to members of the specific culture:

Culture is not a power, something to which social events, behaviors, institutions, or processes can be casually attributed; it is a context, something within which they can be intelligibly—that is, thickly—described. . . . Understanding a people's culture exposes their normalness without reducing their peculiarity. . . . The ethnographer "inscribes" social discourse; *he writes it down.* In doing so, he turns it from a passing event, which exists only in its own moment of occurrence, into an account, which exists in its inscriptions and can be reconsulted (14,19).

Geertz calls culture those webs of significance which humans have spun for themselves (5). He suggests that the symbol-making, tool-making, symbol-using, laughing, lying animals which we call humans are incomplete, or are self- completing animals. In effect we create ourselves through our culture. Geertz argues that the Ice Age appears to have been a time not merely of receding brow bridges and shrinking jaws, but a time in which were forged nearly all of those characteristics of our existence more graphically human. Our nervous system does not merely enable us to acquire culture, but it positively demands that we do so if we are to function (67-68, 218). Geertz labels culture an ordered system of meaning and of symbols, in terms of which social interaction takes place and develops social structure. It relates to culture, but is not synomomous to it. He contends that *culture is the accumulated totality of cultural patterns, organized systems of significant symbols, not just an ornament of human existence, but the principal basis of its specificity, and an essential condition for it.* To become human is to become an individual, and to become an individual is to do so through the guidance of cultural patterns in a social setting. Culture shapes us both as members of a single species and as individuals (144-145; 46; 52).

Finally, as it relates to cultural ecology, Kaplan and Manners acknowledge the difficulty in determining when a *system* ends and the *environment* begins, or even in determining the precise *boundaries* of any system which are natural rather than artificial, such as those created through technology. Therefore, when we consider culture from the cultural ecology perspective, we must be aware that such concepts as environment, system, and adaptation are of considerable importance. However, like many instruments in studying culture, they generally lack highly precise operational definitions and limits. Kaplan and Manners contend, nonetheless, that cultural ecology remains one of the most suggestive and fruitful orientations in the study of culture: "The anthropological ecologist must always be a *cultural* ecologist, for he should never lose sight of the fact that man adapts primarily through the mechanism of his culture, and that, as a consequence, his mode of adaptation is unique (79-87).

Theoretical orientations towards culture distinguish cultural units

Theoretical orientations toward culture, including those we have just discussed (cultural evolutionism, cultural functionalism, cultural history, and cultural ecology, as well as the concept of subjective culture) provide various useful approaches toward the study of culture. While each orientation may be insufficient in itself, together they offer complementary ways of studying culture. Since we are most interested in social discourse and cultural dialogue, an understanding of these orientations assists us in defining cultural parameters and components. Then, it becomes possible to combine the fundamental issues which we addressed initially with the emerging interrelationships between communication and culture. This combination should blend into the needs that we have as potentially frequent cultural communicators and as members of cultural groups, which are represented for us by cultural spokespersons. With this broader treatment of orientations toward an understanding of culture, it is possible to begin to distinguish cultural units.

Cultural maximizers assure the culture's survival

Jules Henry proposes that in all cultures people commit most of their resources to where the main components of culture meet. It is also the place where the greatest cultural conflict and control occurs. Cultural maximizers are persons able to assure cultural survival and the passing down of traditions and values. They are called into service when such conflict develops. Often cultural maximizers are the most powerful members of the culture in terms of assuring cultural survival and the passing down of cultural traditions, customs, norms, and values, especially since these two concepts are chief values of all cultures. They also exert major influence in cultural control.

Within different cultural systems and at different levels of culture, the cultural maximizers play different roles. Since the family typically serves as an important framework in the promotion of these values, its members play important roles within that structure for promotion of the larger cultural customs, norms, and values (Henry, 1963). As Margaret Mead has suggested, in the postfigurative culture the family's cultural maximizers would be the grandparents. In the cofigurative culture, the grandparents would essentially be absent or not creditable as cultural maximizers. Instead, the cultural maximizers might be the parents, just a generation removed from those to whom the values are being passed down, or they might even be precise peers, as in modern technological societies where peer pressure and influence are considerable (1970). In the unknown prefigurative culture, the cultural maximizers might themselves be unknown, either in the sense of an Orwellian 1984 "Big Brother" controlling the culture, or in the sense of countercultural groups seeking to build their own Utopias, or to use the analogy of the mythical phoenix bird, to build the new culture from the ashes of the old culture that they destroyed.

Cultural maximizers include educators, religious leaders, politicians, legislators, judges, media controllers, and in the very complex society, often scientists and engineers. Most such cultural maximizers have high status, especially in manipulating the collective aspects of communication and culture. When various high-status persons clash in their efforts to control the cultural customs, beliefs, and values for their followers, conflict emerges. In the technological society, when the scientist and engineer clash with the clergy or moral philosopher/teacher, the scientist and engineer are more likely to win than the latter: the scientist and engineer have greater controls over technology and technological channels and media than do moral guides and philosophers. Between cultures, the greater the technological power that a specific culture or society holds, the more likely its cultural spokespersons can control the members of the other culture imperialistically. While the ideal world community with effective global communication would be represented in the United Nations by the Secretary General, the justices of the International Court of Justice, and the representatives of individual member countries all working together to promote peaceful coexistence, equality, and human dignity, this would be a Utopian view of the world community. The more realistic view is that various cultural maximizers seek to control members of other cultures in such an organization both through their command over social discourse and cultural dialogue and by their technological power over the others.

The quantum of culture is the accumulation of the culture's customs, traditions, norms, and values

The concept of the *Quantum of Culture* represents the totality of customs, traditions, norms, and values at the broadest levels of human social development. It emphasizes *Humanity* and *Culture Writ Large* as seen both from the theoretical orientations stressing cultural evolutionism and cultural ecology. It includes all of the uniquely human characteristics which have been culturally influenced since the beginning of the human ability to shape and share culture. On the other hand, the *quantum of culture* suggests *culture writ small*, or individuals interacting within their own specific culture. The same kind of totality of experience is suggested in both concepts. Preservation of the strongest and best features in human society, and elimination of the weakest and worst features both play a role in these concepts. The differences between Culture and culture are not necessarily in kind, but in degree. The sum total of the experiences of *Culture Writ Large* are naturally comprehensive of human experience and encompass the experiences of *culture writ small* (Stewart, 1974a).

The central question of "Who am I in my cultural setting?" is relevant to both concepts. Members of a specific culture sometimes cannot define their roles in a specific culture, or may not realize that they function also as members of a larger Culture. Members of certain cultures literally do not know who they are as a people, or believe that no other culture exists besides theirs. Many North Americans are reluctant to identify with their collective culture or society. When asked the "Who am I?" question, articulate members of developing third world countries in contact with the technological societies may very readily identify themselves by nationality, and possibly by their moral, ethical, or religious traditions, such as "Palestinian and Moslem," or "Islamic Arab," or "Lebanese Christian." North Americans may call attention to the quantum of their specific culture only if prodded. Edward Stewart indicates that the uncertainty of North Americans with their own cultural identity supplies a basis for the inference that the *individual* and *individual consciousness* may be the *quantum* of North American culture in general. North American language patterns among those who speak English predominantly, their customs, beliefs, values, and their thought-patternings all point to the individual identity. In other cultures, the quantum may coincide with a *set of rules, a group* of some sort, *a family, clan, caste,* or some other collective unit. In short, English-speaking North Americans may perceive the totality of their culture as residing in themselves, while members of another culture may see the totality as residing in themselves only in the broader context of the whole culture (Stewart, 1974a).

As an aspect of *Culture Writ Large,* cultural universals play an important role

Arguments that a world culture is emerging with its global communication have already been cited. As an aspect of *Culture Writ Large,* the assumption can also be made that there are *cultural universals* which link humanity more by their similarities than their differences. Such assumptions require us to reexamine all cultural systems as actually or potentially open rather than closed systems, in which there is a constant interchange of customs and values. The diffusion of cultural characteristics is certainly found widely throughout the world. We have already considered the importance of language universals and generative grammar as leading theories among sociolinguists today. This diffusion implies contact rather than isolation. George Murdock and other anthropologists in the early post-World War II era began developing the concept of cultural universals, or cultural traits common to all cultures, past and present, whether or not contact with other cultures was involved. Such traits were seen as categories relating to doing and thinking that could be applied in all locations and time periods for all people. Among the several dozen cultural universals which Murdock identifies as being found in all cultures are customs relating to the cycles of life: birth, adolescence, courtship, marriage, maturation, and death; bodily care: such as bodily adornment, cleanliness, hygiene, modesty, and sexual customs and restrictions; relations with others: such as governance, kinship, cooperative labor, community organization, education, law, and status differentation; and customs relating to the supernatural: such as magic, ethics, religious ritual, and soul concepts (Murdock, 1945: 123-142). The theory of cultural universals is important and widely held. It is useful for us to understand how social discourse interculturally and crossculturally can be made more workable by understanding in the principle of similarities and differences those things that help to unite us and bring us together.

However, despite the value and importance of an understanding of cultural universals as an aspect of Culture society or culture at the broadest level, Clifford Geertz warns against an uncritical acceptance of such universals. He stresses that the concept, sometimes called the *consensus gentium*, is an effort to peel off the layers of the human individual, layer by layer, to find Man (or Woman) in Culture rather than specific persons in specific cultures whose differences may be more profound than their similarities. Geertz believes that humans stripped layer by layer of their culture until they can be seen as the basic early human may in fact be an unworkable cultural entity. Geertz challenges Clyde Kluckhohn's statement that "some aspects of culture take their specific forms solely as a result of historical accidents; others are tailored by forces which can properly be designated as universal" (Kluckhohn, 1962:280). The danger, Geertz argues, is that such an approach splits our cultural life in two. He claims that for the theory to be entirely valid, a dualism between empirically universal aspects of culture rooted in subcultural realities and empirical variables which are not so rooted must be established. To do so, the universals proposed must be substantial ones, and not empty categories. They must be specifically grounded in particular biological, psychological, or sociological processes, not just vaguely associated with "underlying realities" (Geertz, 1973:39-44).

Geertz insists that generally the cultural universals theory does not meet those minimum tests. To say that religion, marriage, or property are empirical universals is to say that they have the same content in every culture. The difficulty in the common definition that all people have religion, marriage customs, or property becomes meaningless beyond the simplest statement that all humans have some form of value orientation toward abstract notions of religion, marriage, and property. Geertz warns that at this level such universals may be fake or unimportant in trying to get the clearest picture of the human. Geertz asks us to consider what value there is in saying that morality is a universal, and so is enjoyment of beauty, and so is some standard of truth, if we are forced in the very next statement to say that the forms which these concepts take are but the products of the particular cultural historical experience of the societies and cultures which exhibit them. Further, Geertz argues that while it is possible to demonstrate universal biological, psychological, and sociological processes in general, it is much more difficult to state these relationships in an unequivocal form beyond the minimum statements. Geertz concludes:

Even if I am wrong (as, admittedly, many anthropologists would hold) in claiming that the *consensus gentium* approach can produce neither substantial universals nor specific connections between cultural and noncultural phenomena to explain them, the question still remains whether such universals should be taken as the central elements in the definition of man, whether a lowest-common-denominator view of humanity is what we want anyway. . . . In short, we need to look for systematic relationships among diverse phenomena, not for substantative identities among similar ones (1973:39-44).

As we can see, the issue of similarities and differences continues to face us at every point when we consider either communication or culture and its interrelationships. It is my feeling that the idea of cultural universals can best be supported as a theory when we are better able to collect a more complete data bank across cultures, as is being attempted presently in Osgood's efforts in twenty-five cultures which he and others describe in their *Cross-Cultural Universals of Affective Meaning* (1975).

The cultural placenta provides the interaction for social discourse

Stewart suggests that since culture refers to attributes of individuals as they are influenced by the relationships between them and their cultural setting, the interaction is the junction between individuals and their society. Men and women engage in that interaction through social discourse. This interaction may be described as the *cultural placenta* (Stewart, 1974a:29-30). It is essentially a cultural ecology position. Stewart notes that on one side of the placenta, American society places the full range of individual experience, and on the other side of the placenta, the total cultural system is seen as important. The cultural placenta does not establish structure but supplies the juncture and the limits of the interface. For Americans, Stewart believes that the scope of the interface between the culture and the individual ranges over the full gamut of experience. While the interface between the individual and the total cultural setting emphasizes the individual in American society, the cultural placenta differs for other societies. Stewart comments: "On one side of the cultural placenta only a brief range of the individual's experience may lead to the culture, but within that range, complete conformity may be required to the community or to the family or to some other aspect of cultural life which is defined to be critical. Once the responsibilities, duties and privileges have been exercised in these areas, the individual may experience a freedom of action which startles many Americans who have noticed the conformity in the critical areas" (1974a:29-30). Just as the cultural placenta refers to the interaction between individual and the totality of their culture, the *Cultural Placenta* can be used to describe the interface of all human individuals and the total accumulation of *Culture.*

The cultural quantum of communication is the direct interaction between communication and culture

We can identify a *cultural quantum of communication* as the direct interaction between communication and culture. Such a

concept emphasizes the totality of the interacting communication and cultural components within and between cultures. On
a comparative crosscultural basis, the concept identifies the
emphasis that the culture gives to various facets of communication. Since the term communication by itself has very different
meanings, and applications in different societies, assumptions
about it will also differ from culture to culture and society to
society. In North American society and culture, Stewart suggests that communication is often treated as a surface
phenomenon or an exchange of information. North Americans,
culturally, often tend to minimize symbolic and implicative
meanings of communication and rivet their attention primarily
on what was said and secondly on how it was said. Stewart
notes a set of conventional North American cultural beliefs
that communication encourages participation, reduces conflict, and enhances the resolution of interpersonal problems.
From the systems approach to conflict mentioned in our earlier
discussions, the notion that communication helps to resolve
conflicts which ought to be avoided in any case would be consistent with this potential North American version of conflict
and its resolution. However, the more acceptable version of
conflict resolution is that seen from the actor-orientation approach, where every conflict has a winner and a loser, depending upon how the resource pie is divided. Using this perspective, communication could just as well intensify the conflict as
resolve it (Stewart, 1974a).

The evident distrust—or at least implicit rather than explicit treatment—which communication receives in other
cultures offers a stark contrast for the cultural quantum of
communication for those societies as compared to North
American culture. Even when we consider this concept in relation to Western capitalistic and socialist Marxist-Leninist
societies, the cultural quantum of communication is considerably different. Again, where it must be seen with an emphasis on the individual in the United States, its stress in Soviet
society is on the communicative responsibility of the individual
within the guidelines of the society.

Thus, on a spectrum of controls on the freedom of
communication messages, communicators, codes, and channels, North American society tends to favor the individual,
while Societ society tends to favor the society. As we extend
such concepts as the quantum of communication from a
specific culture to *Culture Writ Large*, a *Cultural Quantum of*

Communication would be the totality of unconscious and conscious emphasis and utilization of communication accumulated in all cultures as aspects of *Culture.*

Each culture has its own bias toward communication

Related to the concept of a cultural quantum of communication is Harold Innis' assertion that each age, each civilization, and each culture has its own bias of communication. In *Empire and Communications,* Innis states: "Concentration on a medium of communication implies a bias in the cultural development of the civilization concerned either towards an emphasis on space and political organization or towards an emphasis on time and religious organization. Introduction of a second medium tends to check the bias of the first and to create conditions suited to the growth of empire" (Innis, 1972:170). Thus, he sees the historical dominance of parchment in Western culture giving a bias toward ecclesiastical institutional organization, which led to the introduction of paper with its bias toward political organization. As printing increased, the vernacular languages became strengthened over official literary, political, and ecclesiastical languages. This development in turn gave rise to nationalism. Eventually the dominance of the Roman Catholic Church in Western culture through parchment and the oral-aural traditions was superseded by printing, and Protestantism began to break the Catholic control over communication. As new religious thought started to prevail, the accompanying trend towards industrialism and nationalism started to take effect. In the United States, the initial dominance of the newspaper emphasized the large scale-development of communication monopolies in terms of space, neglecting emphasis on the problems of time. Radio, and later television and satellite communication, served as a check on the spatially dominated media of Western culture, and has reemphasized time as a dominant cultural construct (Innis, 1972:170). Space and time are again joined in such audio-video techniques as television, especially as it is transmitted by space satellites. The cultural quantum of communication, or the totality of its communicative potential and accumulation thereby becomes emphasized by the particular bias of communication which the specific culture develops.

Summary

Several definitions of culture are possible. A chief contribution of such definitions can lead us to Clifford Geertz's important statement that without humans, no culture, but more significantly, without culture, no humans. We have identified four theoretical orientations which provide current theories of culture: cultural evolutionism, cultural functionalism, cultural history, and cultural ecology. We have stressed that cultural evolutionism refers to the cumulative, collective experience of humanity, *Culture Writ Large*. Cultural functionalism emphasizes the society or culture as a working system, which indicates that if all aspects of the system are not at work, the system itself will disintegrate. Cultural history ethnographically studies the contemporary history of a culture as seen through time and space. That is, all cultural history is a study of contemporary history whenever it took place. Cultural ecology stresses our interaction with our cultural environment. As an aspect of cultural ecology, we have briefly explored the role of cognitive or subjective culture which is defended by cognitive anthropologists as getting into the minds and hearts of members of the culture to know it more fully. Two fundamental aspects in cultural ecology have been seen to be environment and adaptation.

These theoretical orientations towards culture have allowed us to begin to distinguish cultural units. Among the cultural units which we have explored are cultural maximizers, the quantum of culture, cultural univerals, the cultural placenta, the cultural quantum of communication, and the cultural bias toward communication. We have noted that in any culture, cultural maximizers assure the culture's survival and the passing down of traditions and values, two key values for every culture. We have seen the quantum of culture as the accumulation of the culture's customs, traditions, norms, and values. As an aspect of *Culture Writ Large*, we have isolated the important role which cultural universals play and have noted criticism of the concept. Since we are chiefly interested in social discourse, we have suggested that the cultural placenta provides the interaction for such discourse. Finally, we have identified the cultural quantum of communication as the direct interaction between communication and culture. This concept, linked with the notion of a cultural bias of communication as seen by different cultures, ties directly into the early issues which we raised, and emphasizes the importance of these linkages between communcation and culture which we have sought to make.

References

Aberle, David F., et al., 1950. "The Functional Prerequisites of a Society." *Ethics*, 60, 100-111.

Davis, Kingsley, 1959. "The Myth of Functional Analysis as a Special Method in Sociology and Anthropology." In *American Sociological Review*, 24, 752-772.

Geertz, Clifford, 1973. *The Interpretation of Cultures*. New York: Basic Books.

Henry, Jules, 1963. *Culture against Man*. Middlesex, England: Penguin.

Innis, Harold A., 1972. *Empire and Communications*. Revised by Mary Q. Innis. Foreword by Marshall McLuhan. Toronto: University of Toronto.

Innis, Harold, 1973. *The Bias of Communication*. Toronto: University of Toronto.

James, William, 1950. *The Principles of Psychology*. New York: Peter Smith.

Kaplan, David, and Robert A. Manners, 1972. *Culture Theory*. Englewood Cliffs, New Jersey: Prentice-Hall.

Kluckhohn, Clyde, 1962. *Culture and Behavior: Collected Essays of Clyde Kluckhohn*. Edited by Richard Kluckhohn. New York: Free Press.

Mead, Margaret, 1970. *Culture and Commitment; A Study of the Generations Gap*. Garden City, New York: Doubleday.

Murdock, George, 1945. "Common Denominator of Cultures." In *Science of Man in the World Crises*. Edited by R. Linton. New York: Columbia University.

Nieburg, Harold L., 1973. *Culture Storm: Politics and the Ritual Order*. New York: St. Martin.

Osgood, Charles E., William H. May, and Murray S. Miron,

1975. *Cross-Cultural Universals of Affective Meaning.* Urbana, Illinois: University of Illinois.

Russel, Bertrand, 1959. *My Philosophical Development.* New York: Simon and Schuster.

Stewart, Edward C., 1974a, "An Overview of the Field of Intercultural Communication." Mimeograph released by Intercultural Communications Network. Pittsburgh: University of Pittsburgh.

White, Leslie, 1959. *The Evolution of Culture.* New York: McGraw-Hill.

CHAPTER 9

Cultural Values and Value Orientations

Values are the patterns in individuals and groups which are structured primarily through cultural communication. They are the most deep-seated aspects of culture, and we assume that all humans have values.

Munro S. Edmonson accepts the structuralist application of culture: that is, the theoretical orientation toward culture described as cultural functionalism. It suggests that the most important result of culture is the creation of structure. This structure provides for an increased intensity in cultural communication. Edmonson stresses that among the many kinds of cultural structures, the most difficult to identify precisely are those which have led us to the study of values. He calls values the most cultural of cultural structures. Communication acts to spread the simplest and most diffusable ideas to all cultures, which builds up a generalized structure-creating similarity from culture to culture. Objective ideas spread rapidly throughout a culture and between cultures on an explicit and outward basis, especially with the advances in technology. For example, skills and precise artificial coding systems, such as musical symbols or mathematics, transfer very easily from culture to culture. Subjective ideas spread more slowly on an implicit and intrinsic basis. Religious or political philosphies and ideologies are examples (1973:192-196). Edmonson notes that this intrinsic dimension of culture has been called "values." Edmonson suggests that the common denominator of all culture is its communicative process, because it is through cultural communication that values are passed on within the culture and are shared with others in other cultural settings. In this sense, both cultural ethnocentrism, where individuals in the culture seek to hold on to their most deep-seated cultural patterns, and cultural ecology, where individuals in and between cultures seek to maintain a balance between their main structures of culture, play an important role in cultural communication (1973:192-196).

Some values and normative systems are shared broadly throughout the world, as suggested by the Universal Declaration of Human Rights. Others are culturally specific and provide an opportunity to apply the standard of differences in the principle of similarities and differences. Still others are peculiar expressions or deviations of individuals within cultures. These are also called aspects of subjective culture. We have suggested that the multicultural man or woman is on the boundary of his or her culture and other cultures as well. This means that he or she is also on the boundary of specific cultures' value systems and patternings.

On a relative range of easier to more difficult problems which might be faced in the intercultural context, we might assume that greater differences would increase potential breakdowns. From the least to most difficult, we might place various cultural and communicative components, for example structural or grammatical linguistic codes, semantic and symbolic language problems, and nonverbal patterns at the less difficult end; in the middle, stereotypical and prejudicial concerns; and at the most difficult end, values and thought-patterning. While problems may develop at each stage and none of them make intercultural communication a particularly easy task, values and thought-patterning are most difficult because here the most intense aspects of cultures clash sharply.

Various examples, including our early illustration of the value conflicts faced by the first American Peace Corps volunteers in the Philippines, have been cited. We have earlier suggested that the quantum of culture in the North American context focuses almost entirely on the individual, while in other societies and cultures, it revolves around group interdependence. In many postfigurative cultures and the great Asian cultures, people are born into a personal community—a group of intimates to whom they are attached in a symbiotic relationship for life. In the United States, people must create their own personal communities. Mobility here is so great that it is nearly impossible to develop a long-lasting personal community, even with members of one's own family (Henry, 1963:129). The mobility of Americans allows them to lose or thrust off unwanted values and normative standards (with which they have been acculturated at a younger age or in a different setting) much more easily than in a static cultural environment. Technology weakens old value structures and builds new ones.

Values and value orientations can be applied in a practical way

Clyde Kluckhohn, an important American thinker about values and value orientations, argues that values and value orientations can be applied in an entirely practical way. His definition of a value "is a conception, explicit or implicit, distinctive of an individual or characteristic of a group, of the desirable which influences the selection from available modes, means, and ends of action." He suggests that key words of the definition are *desirable, conception,* and *selection.* A conception identifies values as a logical construct comparable to culture or social structure. Just as one cannot directly observe culture, neither can one precisely observe a value in operation. However, one can observe the behaviors which result from accepting the value. Values are preferences which are justified "morally," or by reasoning or by aesthetic judgments, and often by two or all three of these. Whether values are explicit or implicit, they can always be rationalized by verbal behavior (1962:394-403).

The term *desirable* in this case means that values are normative terms implying the opposites of right and wrong, better or worse, and should or should not. Values define the limits of permissible cost of impulse satisfaction, and serve as codes of correct, moral, or appropriate long-term goals. The term *selection* implies the ability to choose between alternatives, though this is the very point in Kluckhohn's work which Munro Edmonson challenges: he argues that if values are only culturally motivated, the individual has little or no freedom of choice in the process of selection (Edmonson, 1973). Kluckhohn summarizes his position at this stage in his thinking by identifying any given act or behavior as a compromise between motivations, situational conditions, available means for action, and the means and goals of action interpreted in value terms. Since all values are arrived at on an evaluative basis, often culturally fixed, the realm of value is conduct which is culturally approved or disapproved, reinforced, supported, or challenged through both linguistic and nonverbal codes (1962:394-403).

Stated in the most practical terms, Kluckhohn emphasizes that the observer who is striving to determine cultural values on the basis of behavior needs to observe patterned recurrence in various members of the culture. This is the structural approach to values mentioned by Edmonson. The observer also needs to ask not only for the behaviors which receive approval and disapproval, but also for those behaviors which elicit a strong emotional response. For example: What, in a given society, is considered worthwhile to die for? What is worth great trouble to protect? What frightens people—particularly when the act is interpreted as a threat to the security or stability of the system? What are considered proper subjects for bitter ridicule? What types of events seem to weld a plurality of individuals suddenly into a solitary group? How is tacit approval-disapproval of particular values molded in the framework of gossip? After addressing these important questions, the observer needs to determine what motivations and values people work hardest to achieve. Kluckhohn suggests that in the North American society most North Americans tend to strive hardest and suffer the most hardships for success in the occupational system. Members of other cultures give their fullest energies only to preserve a received tradition or to types of self-fulfillment that do not expose them to public notice. There are, of course, significant examples of the latter types of persons also in the North American setting. Finally, Kluckhohn states that the observer ought to note when more than one alternative is open for selection. When individuals or groups show a consistent directionality in selections, the generally consistent alternative chosen gives a vivid description of an explicit or implicit value system. Dominant and variant value systems may exist side by side within the same culture, as long as the variant systems do not seriously threaten the dominant system (1962:405-409).

Value orientations are generalized, organized, and existentially judgmental

Gregory Bateson defines human individuals as endlessly simplifying, organizing, and generalizing their own views of their own environment; they constantly impose on this environment their own constructions and meanings; and these constructions and meanings are characteristic of one culture, as over against another (Bateson, 1944:723). The term "philosophy of life" applies to every individual, except those who are affected by total valuelessness, a relatively rare phenomonen. B. F. Skinner argues that when value controls in a culture are evaded or destroyed by the cultural maximizers, then only the most personal reinforcers are left. When this happens, if the individual's moral and normative ties are weak, he or she might turn to immediate gratification, possibly through sex, drugs, violence, apathy, or suicide. When he or she suffers from a very serious lack of values, or valuelessness, the condition may be described as amorality, rootlessness, emptiness, hopelessness, or the lack of something to believe in and be devoted to (1971:118). If we accept the potential negative aspects of value loss as Skinner describes it, then we might say that values consist of something to believe in, to be devoted to, to hope in, by which to structure our morality, and something to give us roots. Even though we have described the multicultural person as the one on the boundary, presumably including the boundary of value systems as well, we would assume that even this person would be searching for sets of values to believe in. The term "philosophy of life," which implies a positive set of values, also applies to every relatively homogeneous group, such as a culture at any given point in the spatial or temporal aspects of its history. This philosophy of life provides the culture members a sense of unity and completeness, either explicitly or implicitly, both in their cognitive and emotional acceptance of the philosophy's main tenets.

While individual, particular, and creative tendencies may challenge or change this philosophy, Skinner argues that even the cultural change agent is bound by the traditional values and norms of the culture which he or she wishes to replace (1971:164). Jules Henry emphasizes that the creative tendency to alter radically cultural forms marks the unusual rather than the ordinary members of a culture, especially since the greater the creativity, the more cultural stability is threatened. In fact, Henry concludes pessimistically that: "Creativity is the last thing wanted in any culture because of its potentialities for disruptive thinking; . . . creativity, when it is encouraged (as in science in our culture), occurs only after the creative thrust of an idea has been tamed and directed towards socially approved ends. In this sense, then, creativity can become the most obvious conformity" (1963:237). Even the certain culturally approved forms of creativity, the underlying principles of a "philosophy of life" are ordinarily culturally shaped (Kluckhohn, 1962:409).

Generally, Clyde Kluckhohn formulates and Florence Kluckhohn expands and tests the concept of value orientations for specific cultures growing out of their philosophy of life. Clyde Kluckhohn postulates that it should be possible to construct the views of a given group regarding the structure of the universe, the relation of humans to the universe, both natural and supernatural, and the relations of one human to another. These views will represent the group's own definition of the ultimate meaning of human life, including its rationalization of frustration, disappointment, and calamity.

As early as the time of Plato and Aristotle, notions were being formed about the ultimate value. Plato's concept of idealism provided such descriptions of values as "idea," "idea culture," and "ideology." Plato called the ultimate value in human terms *happiness*; later Thomas Aquinas defined it in divine terms. Such a "definition of the life situation" for the group contains more normative "should" or "ought" statements; it contains also existential propositions about the nature of "what is." The relationships between normative and existential propositions are two-way. On the one hand, the normative judgments must be based on what in fact exists, and on the other hand, the group's conception of what exists or what seems natural or obvious also depends upon prior normative statements about what ought to be. The process is thus circular. The values of the group, when institutionalized and internalized, have for its members a practical kind of existential reality. Value becomes a part of the situation of what ought to be and what is. The statement of a given group's definition of the meaning of life, a statement comprising both existential and normative postulates, will provide an understanding of the general value-orientation of the group (Kluckhohn, 1962: 409-411).

Formally, Kluckhohn defines a value-orientation as a generalized and organized conception of nature, of the human's place in it, of his or her relation to other humans, and of what is desirable and nondesirable in relating as individuals to humans, their environment, and to their interhuman relations (1962:409-411). Essentially, this means that as humans we may have generalized preferences toward certain values potentially derived on a universalistic basis because we are humans. If, for example all humans believed in the sanctity of human life, this value orientation would be reinforced positively in every culture and society. Other value preferences may be similar in certain types of cultures, such as traditional or heavily technological societies. If, for example members of traditional oral-aural societies typically believe that they are an integral part of nature, and if members of advanced technological societies believe that nature is meant to serve humans, then these value orientations would be culturally specific to the cultures fitting each description. When we suggest that most North American cultures place a heavy value on individualism, it is of course possible that specific cultures within this setting or individual members might have specific value orientations which place a greater emphasis on community interdependence than upon individualism. The principle of similarities and differences is applied in determining the range between cultures in their approach to value-orientations.

Florence Kluckhohn and Fred Strodtbeck define value orientations as complex but definitely patterned or rank-ordered principles which result from the interplay of three distinguishable elements of the evaluative process—the cognitive, the affective or emotional, and the directional elements—which give direction to the constant stream of human acts and thoughts as they relate to the solution of "common human" problems (1961:4-8). They suggest that these principles are variable from culture to culture in degrees of conscious awareness that individuals have of the value orientations. These orientations influence their behavior and beliefs on a continuum from the completely implicit or hidden, to the completely explicit or clearly expressed notions. More importantly, they argue, the main variables occur only in the ranking patterns of component parts which are themselves cultural universals. The most important aspects which they claim for their definition are the variable of rank-patternings from culture to culture, and the primary importance of the directive aspect of the total process. It is not enough to assume that one cognitively knows and affectively acts upon cultural values and value-orientations (Kluckhohn and Strodtbeck, 1961:4-8).

The concept of directiveness in value-orientations relates to the influence of communicative and cultural control. Since both communication and culture are processes, the concept of directiveness can be seen as the "moment of time" interacting on individual members of a culture within the broader context of the cultural process. That is, when value orientations clash, how is control exercised either communicatively or through the culture itself to force cultural members to accept one value orientation over the other? In a culture where group interdependence is the norm, how does the culture direct or control the members who seek to demonstrate their individualism? Florence Kluckhohn and Strodtbeck stress that there would be no value system which distinguishes human behavior from that of pure animal instinct without the human ability to build and use symbols, and practical affective attempts to use the value system through behavior. It also seems apparent that there would be no ordered, systematic value system without a directive tendency based both in biological human needs and in culturally controlled and directive tendencies. These tendencies aid in the selection among possible value systems and give continuity to the total system (1961:4-8).

Value orientations can be classified as crucial

At the level of cultural universals, Florence Kluckhohn and Strodtbeck formulate a set of basic assumptions in considering value-orientations based on the culturally specific premise that ordered variations exist among cultures. They assume initially that there is a limited number of common human problems for which all peoples at all times and in all locations must find solutions. While there is variability in solutions, the alternatives of all solutions are present in all societies at all times but are differentially preferred from culture to culture. Every culture has a dominant value-oriented profile, and also numerous variant or substitute profiles. There is almost always a rank-ordering of the preferences of the value-orientation alternatives. It is in intercultural and crosscultural communication where such value orientations usually clash. A complementary overlapping also exists (1961:10).

Kluckhohn and Strodtbeck have isolated five basic problems common to all human groups and cultures. By posing five questions and offering a specific value-orientation to refer to each question, they sum up their approach to a major research problem: 1.) What is the character of innate human nature (human nature orientation)? 2.) What is the relation of humans to nature and supernature (human-nature orientation)? 3.) What is the temporal focus of human life (time-orientation)? 4.) What is the modality of human activity (activity orientation)? 5.) What is the modality of humans' relationship to others (relational orientation)? In their study, a sixth problem is posed but was not tested. This is the human conception of space and his or her place in it (1961:10-11). In Edward Hall's *The Hidden Dimension*, he attempts a nonempirical description of such spatial relationships (1966).

In approaching the human nature orientation, Kluckhohn and Strodtbeck ask whether human nature is inherently evil, or good and evil, or good. These distinctions allow several possibilities in various cultures: human nature can be conceived as evil and unalterable; or evil and perfectible; or it can be seen as good and unalterable, or good and corruptible; or a mixture, subject both to positive and negative influences. The authors illustrate these possible orientations in American life by suggesting that the orientation inherited from the Puritans emphasized an evil but perfectible human nature for which constant control and discipline were necessary. However, in the United States presently, they suggest that a growing number of persons lean toward the view that human nature is a mixture of good and evil, which is an orientation shared generally by other cultures in the world. The totally good human nature is seen as a variant in various cultures and societies but does not appear to dominate their orientations (1961:13).

The human-nature (supernature) orientation varies from subjugation-to-nature, harmony-with-nature, and mastery-over-nature orientations. Kluckhohn and Strodtbeck note that the Spanish-American culture in the American Southwest provides an example of a very definite subjugation-to-nature orientation, as do many traditional peoples in Latin America, Africa, and Asia. In societies which believe that humans are subjugated to nature, such as in the Spanish-American culture tested by Kluckhohn and Strodtbeck, they found that a pervasive sense of fatalism prevailed, and it was assumed that droughts, floods, storms, and other "acts of God" could not be controlled and that there was little sense in trying to overcome nature (1961). The earlier example of the Philippines stresses the impact that their fatalism had upon the social and cultural changes which the Peace Corps volunteers first tried to initiate there. Most studies of social change in the more traditional society indicate the same influence.

If the conceptualization of the human-nature relationship is that of harmony, there can be no real separation of the individual, nature, and supernature. One is an extension of the other, and a conception of their wholeness derives from their unity. Florence Kluckhohn and Strodtbeck suggest that this is the dominant orientation for much of Chinese and Japanese history, as well as the Navajo Indians, and until recently, the Mormons (1961).

The mastery-over-nature is the priority of most North Americans, and increasingly so of most highly industrially advanced peoples. The pre-Christian notion of Protagoras, "Man is the measure of all things," was reemphasized during the eighteenth-century Enlightenment, and again earlier in this century. However, as the twentieth century draws to a close, our attempts to overcome all obstacles has led to a great emphasis on technology. We have suggested earlier that technology is the metaphysics of the twentieth century. While many industrially advanced peoples continue to have strong value preference towards the supernatural, there is often serious conflict between the technological ability to overcome natural and apparently supernatural forces, and a conviction that God is the ruling force of the universe and of individual lives. Although the Soviet system officially promotes atheism instead of theism as a dominant value orientation, there are still many Soviet citizens for whom the theistic value orientation is dominant. This demonstrates how difficult it is for those who control communication and culture effectively to change deep-seated cultural values and beliefs even over an extended period of time.

The time orientation breaks easily into the range of past, present, and future. Kluckhohn and Strodtbeck suggest that not many meaningful cultural differences have been demonstrated to prove that folk peoples have no time sense and no need of one, while urbanized and highly technological peoples must have one. All cultures and societies must deal with all time problems, and therefore have conceptions of past, present, and future. They differ, however, in their preferential treatment to the alternatives, and much can be learned about the culture or society by knowing what their rank-order preference is. The authors suggest that the Spanish-Americans in their study placed the present in first rank, as do the Filipinos and many Latin Americans. The slogan "Live for today; eat, drink, and be merry, for tomorrow you may die" expresses this concept very well. Ancient China gave first-order value preference to the past time orientation especially in the form of ancestor worship and strong family tradition in which the grandparents played very important parts (the postfigurative type of culture would be an example). Even an industrially advanced society such as the British, as well as many other Europeans, have strong past time orientations, and differ in one significant way from the North Americans who tend to have much less sense of tradition. However, the American celebration of their Bicentennial suggested considerable emphasis on their past traditions. North Americans, more strongly than others, place an emphasis on the future—a future which is expected to be bigger and better. Buying life insurance is an expression of this view. This view encourages a high regard for change rather than stability, provided that the change does not destroy the North American way of life (1961:13-14).

The modality of human activity can also be seen with a three-fold range, according to Kluckhohn and Strodtbeck: being, being-in-becoming, and doing. The range of alternatives of the activity orientation varies independently from those of the human-nature, time, and human activity orientations. The activity or doing orientation centers solely on the problem of the nature of human means of self-expression in activity. North Americans are essentially a "doing" society. Compared with the being-in-becoming orientation and the doing orientation, the being orientation is a nondevelopmental model of activity. The human being is valued for what he or she is rather than for what he or she can accomplish. Intergroup harmony is a key feature of such an orientation. It is more important not to offend than to be proven right or wrong. This suggests the spontaneous nature of expression in activity of impulses and desires. Kluckhohn and Strodtbeck note that while the Mexican fiesta exemplifies the concept through its spontaneity, there is never pure impulse gratification as other value demands from overlapping orientations provide very definite controls on actions. Where such controls are not in effect, we have suggested the problem of rootlessness. The being-in-becoming orientation is similar to the being orientation in that emphasis is placed on what the human being is rather than what he or she accomplishes. However, the being-in-becoming orientation further stresses that kind of activity which has as its goal the development of all aspects of the self as an integrated whole. Western monastic life suggests this type of prevalent view. There is a spiritual goal of inner harmony and peace, with a very low emphasis on material accomplishments. Activity is undertaken to achieve these goals, but a large portion of the time is spent in simple communication with God. The doing orientation is characteristically the dominant one in North American and much of European society. Its most distinctive feature is the demand for the kind of activity which results in explicit accomplishments that are measurable by standards conceived to be external to the acting individual (1961). It leads to the drives suggested by Jules Henry such as competitiveness, expansiveness, and achievement, which are seen as values by many but are in constant conflict with more positive values such as cooperation, gentleness, and kindliness (Henry, 1963).

The final orientation developed and tested by Kluckhohn and Strodtbeck is the relational one. This orientation describes the human's relation to other persons. It has three subdivisions: the lineal, the collateral, and the individualistic orientations. Kluckhohn and Strodtbeck suggest that all societies and cultures must give heed to all three relational principles. Individual autonomy is always found, even in the most extreme homogeneous societies and cultures. Collateral relations or group interdependence are also found in all societies. The human being must be a part of a social order, and one type of social grouping is that which results from laterally extended relationships. Finally, since all societies and cultures are related culturally and biologically through time, there is always a lineal relation according to Kluckhohn and Strodtbeck, though the linear notion itself is a very Western perspective. There are cultures which have no such relationships, as they think they are the only people in the world: until the intrusion of white Europeans, Eskimos always called themselves "The People," with the assumption that there were no others.

When individualistic principles are dominant, individual

goals have primacy over the goals of specific collateral or lineal groups. In this setting, each individual's responsibility and place in the total society are defined in terms of goals and roles which are structured as autonomous, in the sense of being independent of either specific lineal or collateral groupings. A dominant collateral orientation calls for a primacy of the goals and welfare of the laterally extended group. The extended families of the Navajo or even of the Irish families of Newfoundland are examples of this principle. If the lineal principle is dominant, group goals have primacy, as in the collateral orientation. There is the additional factor that one of the most important group goals is continuity through time. Continuity of the group through time and an ordered positional succession are crucial issues in the lineal relationship (1961).

Empirical testing for dominant and variant value orientations is possible

Kluckhohn and Strodtbeck and other researchers extensively tested the five sets of value orientations in what was called the Comparative Study of Values in Five Cultures. Five communities within fifty miles of each other living on subsistence agriculture in the American Southwest were chosen: a Navajo Indian community living off the reservation, the Pueblo Indian community of Zuni, a Spanish-American village, a Mormon village, and a recently established farming village of Texan and Oklahoman homesteaders. The five communities were substantially different culturally, and at the time of the study, the Zuni were the most self-contained. The least self-contained were the Navajo, who had the most contact with the other communities and with other outsiders.

Florence Kluckhohn had been studying these communities for fifteen years before 1951. When the major aspects of the study were undertaken, she made value orientation predictions for each community based on the five sets of value orientations. At the most general level, the predictions were verified, especially at the first-ranking priorities of orientations. Complementary overlapping was also generally predicted with considerable accuracy. In only a few instances was there a marked discrepancy between the prediction ventured and the result observed. A great majority of both the consistencies and inconsistencies of patterning in ranking patterns emerged with predictable accuracy. Since the study has been completed, each of these cultures has changed considerably. In one case the cultural group has virtually disappeared, but it was already very small at the time of the study. In completing their study, Kluckhohn and Strodtbeck warned against assuming that accuracy of predicted results necessarily assured that these value orientations would remain constant in these cultural groups over time and space. Nevertheless, reliable trends of dominant, variable, and complementary value orientations are possible to predict and test on the basis of the Comparative Study of Values in Five Cultures project (1961).

Value orientations may be considerably expanded and applied to contrast cultures

The influence of Clyde and Florence Kluckhohn on value and value-orientation studies has been considerable. For the student in intercultural communication, Condon and Yousef have clarified the notion of value orientations further by expanding the list from the original five to twenty-five. These include the *self*, with added orientations relating to individualism-interdependence, age, sex, and activity; the *family*, with added orientations toward relational interaction, authority, positional role behavior, and mobility; *society*, with orientations toward social reciprocity, group membership, intermediaries, formality, and property; *human nature*, with orientations toward rationality, good and evil, happiness and pleasure, and mutability; *nature*, with orientations towards the relationship of humans and nature, ways of knowing nature, structure of nature, and the concept of time; and the *supernatural*, with orientations toward the relationship of humans and the supernatural, the meaning of life, providence, and knowledge of the cosmic order (1975:60-62).

To demonstrate how value orientations work, Edward Stewart's *American Cultural Patterns: A Cross-Cultural Perspective* (1971) utilizes two cultures, the Filipino and the North American cultures, to demonstrate contrasting assumptions and values for nearly opposite cultural groups. As do other writers, Stewart acknowledges his indebtedness to the pioneering work of Florence Kluckhohn and her colleagues. Like others, he also seeks to expand the concept. The following chart summarizes the key assumptions, values, and value orientations isolated by Stewart for the two cultures.

Assumptions and Values in North American and Filipino Cultures Offer Striking Contrasts

	North American	Filipino
I. *Perception of the Self and the Individual*		
A. General perception of self	Human being of a particular self	Self perceived in context of family
B. Self as point of reference	Autonomy encouraged; solve own problems, develop own opinions	Dependence encouraged; point of reference is authority, older members of family
C. Nature of humans	Evil but perfectible; notion of progress: humans can change and improve and it is their responsibility to do so	Evil, but there is not too much that can be done: "ganyan talaga ang buhay" (such is life)
D. Cultural variation of self-concept	Self is identified with individual; behavior aimed at individual goals	Point of reference is network of obligations among members of a group summarized in concept of "face"; behavior aimed at preserving group affiliations and maintaining smooth interpersonal relationships
E. Self-reliance	Old self-reliance value still believed upheld (although American often now functions best as member of organization)	Dependence not deplored because it strengthens relationships among people

II. Perception of the World

	North American	Filipino
A. Individual's relation to nature	Separate from nature	Separate from nature
B. Materialism and Property	Clear distinction between public and private property; materialism is big value	Public property divertible to private hands with little guilt; spiritual, religious things are more important than material things
C. Progress related to concept of time	Time moves fast, from past, to present, to future; one must keep up with it, use it to change and master environment	Time moves slowly; one must integrate oneself with the environment, and adapt to it rather than change it
D. Progress and optimism in contrast to limited good	Optimism exists that there is enough for everybody; economics is final arbiter	[Peasants only]: there exists a finite amount of good that can be divided and redivided but not augmented; therefore phenomenon of sociostat: if one member of a community increases wealth, it is seen as a threat because of the concomitant loss to other members; tendency for community to pull person down to old level by temporary ostracism
E. Quantification	Stress on measurement and concreteness	Stress on qualitative feeling
F. Comparative judgments	What is not American is bad	What is not Filipino is different or American; moral judgments not as easily made

	North American	*Filipino*
III. Motivation		
A. Achievement as self-motivation	Fulfillment in personal achievement; status is achieved	Fulfillment in smooth interpersonal relationships; status is ascribed
B. Fragmentation and totality of personality	Personalities can be fragmented; totality of other person does not need to be accepted in order to be able to work together	Personalities reacted to in their entirety; tendency to accept or reject person completely
C. Competition and affiliation	Competition is primary method of motivation	Communal feeling towards one another excludes the incentive to excel over others
D. The limits of achievement:	Expansive view of achievement: "Where there's a will, there's a way"	Achievement is a matter of fate
IV. Form of Relations to Others		
A. Characteristics of personal relations	Friendships are numerous but not deep or permanent; social obligations avoided	Social obligation network: "utang na loob"
B. Equality	Equality is mode of interaction	Continual shift from high to low status, depending on other person

	North American	Filipino
C. Confrontation	Face-to-face confrontation	Confrontation through an intermediary to avoid "losing face"
D. Informality and formality	Informal and direct	More formal; social interactions more structured
E. Specialization of Roles	Specialized roles distributed among members of group	All functions vested in leader
V. Form of Activity		
A. Doing	"Doing" and being active are highly valued	"Doing" not emphasized as much, especially in rural areas; it is just as important to "take it easy"
B. Decision-making	Decisions made by individual; every member feels responsible for group decisions	Decisions made by authority or group; group decisions are usually product of key group members even if they are apparently made by all
C. Work and play	Dichotomy of work and play	Work and social life are not separated
D. Temporal orientation	Stress on future	Stress on present and past; life is lived from day to day

Edward C. Stewart, *American Cultural Patterns: A Cross-Cultural Perspective.* "Dimensions of International Education," No. 3. The Regional Council for International Education, April 1971. Reprinted with kind permission.

A culture's values of truth and reality are symbolized by ritual

H. L. Nieburg suggests that culture is the precursor of political and institutional change. Values change first, then everything else becomes possible. However, it is sometimes hardest to get values to change since they are deep-seated and not easily subject to quick change. In a cause-effect relationship, he argues that culture comes from the reciprocal exchange of values that goes on simultaneously at all levels of social organization. Today, with the increased contact between cultures, this reciprocal change goes on at an accelerated intercultural rate. It involves all values and resources in a web of interpersonal and intergroup interaction. The sum of these interactions at any moment in time or across spatial boundaries is embodied in values that continue to be subject to challenge and further change. Each culture's method of defining its truth and reality depends upon its values and their relative preservation or change through an acceptable framework. All of the components of communication and culture interact to define the values of truth and reality through the social structure of ritual. Though modern people scoff at the ritual of ancient and preliterate peoples as magic and superstition, our own technological advances have provided us endless new rituals to symbolize our own assumed rational behaviors, which become our values of truth and reality (Nieburg, 1973:3-30).

One way to discover a culture's or subculture's values is to strip away its ritual. Just as values may be both explicit and implicit, so too is the pervasive influence of ritual in our own lives. Many of the linkages between communication and culture are inherently ritual. Ritual almost cannot be separated from nonritual and cannot be separated from culture. Nieburg notes: "All of the forms of ritual behavior are parts or dimensions of culture; they are expressions, often nonverbal, of the values, attitudes, theories, interpretations, potential actions, and expectations of individuals in a community . . . (Nieburg, 1973:3-30).

Ritual is the acting out of the "subjective content of culture"

Virtually every ritual designed to accentuate or isolate positive values, such as a group's hold on the truth or reality, is contrasted by opposing ritual designed to weaken the values or to change them dramatically into another form.

The ritual of patriotism is opposed by the ritual of destroying draft cards or profaning the flag. The ritual of ending a widely unpopular war is countered by massive acts of ritualistic protest. The modern industrial society has denied the old rituals which expressed the truth and reality values of an earlier age. As we have suggested before, the metaphysics of one period was God; of another, the human being; and of the twentieth century, it is technology. Recently members of countercultures have attempted to provide new ritual to replace that of today's dominant technologically oriented cultures. Attempting to overcome the technological culture's concepts of truth and reality as rational and scientific precision, the members of the counterculture express their new ritual through their intensely different music, dress, dance, and life styles. Some aspects of their countercultural values have been adopted into the mainstream of the dominant culture, especially for the younger members of it. However, as Eugene Goodhart stresses, in trying to establish a new ritual as a symbol of a new value system, the prophetic tendencies of their music, dress, dance, and life styles have been seduced by technology itself. This seduction is exemplified by the technocracy required to produce their ritual, and by the wholesale taking over through technical imitation of chief aspects of their own new ritual into the mainstream dominant culture (1973:37).

Summary

In this chapter, we have seen that values are the patterns in individuals and groups which are structured primarily by cultural communication. Values can be delineated at the level of cultural universals, cultural specifics, or of individual deep-seated conscious and unconscious expressions of the whole notion of culture itself. They are the most cultural of cultural structures, and underlie the emphasis on the principles of similarities and differences as the starting point for studying intercultural communication. Values can be defined from philosophical, psychological, culturological perspectives as well as a number of other ways.

Kluckhohn defines values as conceptions of the desirable for a group in its selection of modes and means of conduct, and stresses that while it is difficult to observe the values themselves. it is less difficult to see the actual behaviors which come out of such values.

Value orientations have been described as making it possible to construct the views of a given group regarding the structure of the universe, their relations to the universe, both natural and supernatural, and their relations to others. Such views represent their definition of the ultimate meaning of life, including their rationalization of its frustrations, disappointments, and crises. Such orientations provide the normative "should" or "ought" to statements, as well as their view of what life really is, and what truth and reality actually means for them. Florence Kluckhohn and Fred Strodtbeck place the importance of value orientations for intercultural communication as the variables of rank-patternings toward specific orientations from culture to culture, and the primary importance of the directive aspect of the total process for one culture against another culture. Thus, value orientations can be classified as the primary and crucial values which are common to all human groups, but differentiated culture by culture through the specific emphasis placed on different orientations. The clash occurs between cultures over their deep-seated values and value orientations in such a way that intercultural and crosscultural conflict and breakdowns occur. They isolate five such orientations: human nature, human-nature, time, activity, and relational. They suggest a sixth—space—but do not test it.

Kluckhohn and Strodtbeck's primary testing of these hypotheses occurred in the American Southwest among five distinctly different cultures living within close proximity of each other. They proved the validity for most of their predictions and hypotheses for those cultures in the specific spatial and temporary setting in which they worked. Others have expanded the value orientations to include many more orientations which might be tested. As an extended example of applying the value orientation concept to contrast cultures, we have utilized Edward Stewart's contrasting chart of basic assumptions and values as seen in North American and Filipino cultures. The last point in this chapter has been that a culture's values of truth and reality are symbolized by ritual which can be described as the expressions of the collective representation of the group with its sacred and profane aspects.

References

Bateson, Gregory, 1944. "Human Dignity and the Varieties of Civilization." In *Conference of Science, Philosophy, and Religion.* 3rd Symposium.

Condon, John C., and Fathi Yousef, 1975. *An Introduction to Intercultural Communication.* Indianapolis: Bobbs-Merrill.

Edmunson, Munro S., 1973. "The Anthropology of Values." In *Culture and Life: Essays in Memory of Clyde Kluckhohn.* Edited by Walter W. Taylor, John L. Fischer, and Evon Z. Vogt. Carbondale, Illinois: Southern Illinois University.

Goodheart, Eugene, 1973. *Culture and the Radical Conscience.* Cambridge, Massachusetts: Harvard University.

Hall, Edward, 1966. *The Hidden Dimension.* Garden City, New York: Doubleday.

Henry, Jules, 1963. *Culture against Man.* Middlesex, England: Penguin.

Kluckhohn, C., 1962. *Culture and Behavior: Collected Essays of Clyde Kluckhohn.* Edited by Richard Kluckhohn. New York: Free Press.

Kluckhohn, Florence Rockwood, and Fred L. Strodtbeck, 1961. *Variations in Value Orientations.* Evanston, Illinois: Row, Peterson.

Nieburg, Harold L., 1973. *Culture Storm: Politics and the Ritual Order.* New York: St. Martin.

Skinner, B.F., 1971. *Beyond Freedom and Dignity.* New York: Knopf.

Stewart, Edward C., 1971. *American Cultural Patterns: A Cross-Cultural Perspective.* Pittsburgh: University of Pittsburgh.

CHAPTER 10

The Individual Processes of Culture:
Subjective Culture

We have stressed that separate from the social group, in which social discourse may occur, we have no culture. We have suggested that our innate capacity to become builders and users of symbols and tools has given us the potential of becoming 10,000 different cultural beings. Each of us as an individual has in fact only become one such being. Clifford Geertz comments: "Becoming human is becoming individual, and we become individual under the guidance of cultural patterns, historically created systems of meaning in terms of which we give form, order, point, and direction to our lives. As culture shaped us as a single species—and is no doubt still shaping us—so too it shapes us as separate individuals. This, neither an unchanging subcultural self nor an established cross-cultural consensus, is what we really have in common." (1973:52).

All individuals are influenced by *Culture Writ Large*, by our cultural civilization, by our cultural institutions, by the technological impacts upon our culture, by the political culture which surrounds us, by the cultural maximizers in our own culture, by the ethnocentric influences upon us as cultural beings, and by our own unique development. As Charles Osgood and his colleagues argue, it is possible to study both *objective* and *subjective* culture. Both have their impact for the student of intercultural communication, but the latter is even more compelling than the former. They define the comparative study of objective culture as comparing either artifacts and the technologies that produced them (such as tools, habitations, transports, paintings, and the availability of media) or observable human activities (such as general norms of behavior, interpersonal roles in a culture, child-rearing practices, and institutional structures). They define subjective culture, on the other hand, comparatively as the study of human cognitive processes, which may be nonlinguistic (such as perceptual styles, motivational patterns, and skills) or linguistic (such as meanings, beliefs, and the linguistic structures which express them) (1975:335). Their distinctions are closely paralleled by Ward Goodenough's description of culture: ". . . culture 1, the recurring patterns which characterize a community as a homeostatic system, and culture 2, people's standards for perceiving, judging, and acting. Culture 1, moreover, is an artifact or product of the human use of culture 2 . . . individuals can be said to possess culture 2 but not culture 1, which is the property of a community as a social-ecological system" (1961:522).

Taken alone, we have already noted the criticism of Clifford Geertz toward the tenets of cognitive anthropology as a destructive fallacy. We could also note Jerry Burk's criticism: "Cognitive anthropologists seem to deny the strengths of other human scientists while endorsing their weaknesses. The case of cognitive anthropologists seems to be one of idealism gone to seed" (1974:34). Nevertheless, just as the study of language and values play an important role in linking communication and culture, so too does the study of the cognitive aspects of culture, or subjective culture.

The memory of past structured, stable, and meaningful experiences forms our present perceptions

In this chapter, we shall stress the role of perception and its linkages culturally and personally with other cognitive aspects of subjective culture. We have earlier suggested that Bertrand Russell's definition of culture is a collection of events connected by a memory chain, backwards and forwards. It emphasizes the collection of events involving the individual which he or she remembers better than any other events. As a value orientation, we have pointed out that some cultures tend toward the past, others toward the present, and still others, such as North Americans, toward the future. Another value orientation stresses the individual in contrast to the collective social group. The overlapping in such value orientations is considerable. The events of the past are discontinuous, but as Nieburg argues, it is in the very nature of culture to maintain an arbitrary and abstract stability in the face of the flux and perversity of nature. Within the individual, Nieburg suggests, the period of tranquility between events allows him or her to make past experiences seem structured, stable, and meaningful rituals which both cultures and individuals develop to make sense out of life. Reality for the individual lies in the legitimacy of a specific culture form or process in a given population over a period of time (1973:52-58).

Perceptually significant experiences are always culturally derived

As a cultural universal, perception can be seen as an inherent capability of all human beings whose cognitive abilities are functioning in a normal fashion. Each culture also helps to shape this capability according to the experiences which are common in that particular culture. As individuals both are acted upon by our culture and act upon it, so too do we perceive through our cultural experiences. A. I. Hallowell contends that what becomes perceptually significant to the human

cannot be considered apart from a continuum that views the human individual as an adjusting organism, motivated, goal-directed, and psychologically structured as a functioning unit in a socio-cultural system. . . . The psychological field in which human behavior takes place is always culturally constituted, in part, and man's responses are never reducible in their entirety to stimuli derived from an "objective" or surrounding world, in the physical or geographic sense. . . . The fact that the human organism becomes selectively sensitized to certain arrays of stimuli rather than others is most certainly a function of the individual's membership in one cultural group, rather than another, whatever other factors may be involved (1972:51).

Hallowell argues that since perception, based on group or individual experiences, is mediated symbolically within and between members of cultures, several key cultural aspects come to bear upon its development in the individual. Among these aspects are the cultural relationships of perception to language, art forms, belief, and personality factors

(1972:51-67). We could add thought-patterning and intelligence in general.

Language is an integrative factor in the functioning of perceptual discrimination

If we were to accept the Sapir-Whorf hypothesis of language, as Hallowell does, language becomes an integrative factor with respect to the functioning of perceptual discrimination, conceptualization, evaluation, and motivation in the context of each individual culture, and in a different way from culture to culture. Sapir argues: "The 'real world' is to a large extent unconciously built up on the language habits of the group. No two languages are ever sufficiently similar to be considered as representing the same social reality. The worlds in which different societies live are distinct worlds, not merely the same world with different labels attached. Even comparatively simple acts of perception are very much more at the mercy of the social patterns called words than we might suppose. . . . We see and hear and otherwise experience very largely as we do because the language habits of our community predispose certain choices of interpretation" (1929:209-210). Examples of the cultural influence of language on perception can be demonstrated by the fact that North Americans perceive the stellar constellation "the Big Dipper" while other cultures perceive it as a "plow" or "the bear" because this is the way that it is described by their languages. Members of the other cultures do not see a big dipper at all, nor do North Americans see a plow or bear. Such examples are primarily inferential rather than empirical, but it does seem clear that the cultural dimensions of language on perception do play an important role.

Art smashes open the doors of perception

T. S. Eliot has remarked: "The poet dislocates language into meaning. The artist smashes open the doors of perception" (1970:44). Nieburg comments "that the frontier of art is a self-contained ritual of rebellion, a crowd of infinite possibility that erupts as a random mob, looting the psychic storehouse of images, toppling identities and monuments along the mental streets and squares of sensibility." Culture itself, Nieburg asserts, is stylized and learned as the trail left by art: "Art is an anti- or counter-environment through which man can perceive the environment itself. As antienvironment, it is a means of developing perception and judgment. McLuhan goes a step further and holds that art is at once a step behind the present and a probe of the future. Existing environments are always taken for granted and embodied in un-self-conscious behavior. Only as the environment changes does it provide materials for art" (Nieburg, 1973:177). Thus, the perception of experience within a cultural context is affected by the artistic efforts permitted, and encouraged in that culture, and it shapes the notion of truth and beauty which the culture gives its members. At the same time, this perception of truth and beauty encourages artists to probe into the future and consequently to assist in developing an environment which will be artistically changed by new perceptions. Nieburg argues that bringing experience into the realm of perceptual consciousness through art's variety of symbolic processes makes art not only useful but absolutely necessary to social life, as it is at the heart of the cognitive aspects of culture (1973:179-180). Kenneth Burke sees all art as spokes on the hub of ritual drama. All art, whatever its subject matter, receives its significance as part of a complete ritual drama. The underlying ritual drama celebrates the forces of good and evil, which are at the center of a culture's cognitive expression (1964:20-21). Every age and every culture gains and invents perceptions through its ritual drama, and thus, ritual drama can be seen as a major symbolic identification of subjective culture.

Belief and perception link tangible and intangible experiences

Beliefs become an important expression of values and value orientations, and are structured out of experiential perceptions. Many of our values about natural and supernatural forces are identified in sets of beliefs which must be taken on faith rather than on an empirically provable basis. Entities which "have no tangible or material existence may become perceptual objects in the actual experience of individuals. The reality of what to outsiders are only symbolically mediated and concretely elaborated images may receive perceptual support through the experiences of individuals for whom such entities exist in an established system of traditional beliefs. Under these conditions," Hallowell notes that it is "predictible that some persons will not only report perceptual experiences involving such entities, but will *act* as if they belonged in the category of tangible or material objects" (1972-58). We tend to identify religious beliefs of ancient people as superstitions and assume that their perceptions have no factual reality, while our religious beliefs have a firm experiential and perceptual basis in reality. In fact, religion, race, and nationalism perhaps have more direct cognitive and objective impact upon culture than any other factors. More dissension between cultures exists at the level of values, beliefs, perceptions, and experiences because of religion, race, and nationalism as cognitive contructs than for any other such ideas. This dissension is often demonstrated behaviorally by prejudices and biases about persons of other religions, races, and nationalities. At the same time, these constructs also make cultural diversity far richer, and provide greater opportunities for genuinely effective intercultural communication than do many other cognitive cultural theories and ideas.

If all aspects of cultural life are intimately and constantly tied up with experiential perceptions dealing with either religion, race, or nationalism, the relation between belief or faith and perception becomes very closely linked for both tangible and intangible events. Without offering the many examples where belief and perception are linked culturally on the basis of intangible religious factors in ancient culture, we can note that often devoted American Roman Catholics perceive nonreligious experiences on a rational and empirical basis. However, when the priest states at the center of the Mass, while elevating the small round bread host, "This is the Body of Christ," and when he lifts the chalice filled with wine, saying, "This is the Blood of Christ," the truly faithful believer perceives the experience of a real conversion from bread and wine to the body and blood of Christ. The reality of this perception for the faithful Catholic provides a major stumbling block in Christian dialogue, since many other Christian churches perceive the same statement and experience as the symbol of Christ, but not the reality of Christ.

If this combination of religious belief and perception seems strange, we need only consider the perceived reality of the American flag, the national anthem, and the draft card for many otherwise nonsentimental Americans. Many Americans continue to believe that the defilement of one of these symbols of American society is a defilement of the society itself. Reality thus becomes a perceived reality, which is culturally oriented and generally meaningless in other cultural settings. Hallowell's emphasis in linking belief and perception is that the latter serves as "one of the chief psychological means whereby belief in reified images and concepts as integral parts of a cultural order of reality are *substantiated* in the experiences of individuals. It is through the activity of the same sensory modalities that always have been considered sufficiently reliable in bringing us into contact with the 'reality' of the outer world that the 'reality' of objects that have their roots in the individuals inner world are reinforced" (Hallowell, 1973:63).

We perceive every situation in a manner determined by our past cultural and personal experiences

Victor Barnouw defines personality as a more or less enduring organization of forces within the individual associated with a complex of fairly consistent attitudes, values, and modes of perception. They account, in part, for the individual's consistency of behavior. Despite the cultural impact and the fact that cultures themselves have a personality or an ethos, it is the personality of individuals which Barnouw considers the most real, as cultures can only be mediated through individual personalities. Just as there is consistency and change in culture, there is also consistency and change in individual personalities. As adult individuals we have carried over certain characteristics from our childhood, but we are still different persons than we were as children. Thus, our methods of perception as children and as adults have gone through consistent development and have changed.

While one set of religious believers interprets perceived reality in one way, another set of religious believers who share the same faith with the first set interprets its perceived reality in an entirely different way. As an example, the Roman Catholic experience is shared throughout the world in various communities and cultures, but members of each culture may interpret fundamental dogma on the basis of a different set of perceptual experiences. Even within the same culture, such differences may exist between various members (Barnouw, 1963:26-27). As Barnouw suggests, personality is affected by many determining factors. Its linkage culturally with perception has many other influences, but essentially, human beings are always in a particular situation, which we perceive in a manner determined by our past cultural and personal experiences. Our cultural baggage, which we carry along as we cross new cultural boundaries, is largely subjectively based on our past experiences. Personality and culture work in tandem to help shape the perception of experiences which each individual develops (1963:26-27).

Thought-patterning determines the way that perception operates individually

In *Conflicting Patterns of Thought*, Karl Pribram isolates four distinctive patterns of thought, or cognitive ways of arranging arguments for persuasive and influential effects, which are common to much of the Western world. The first is universalistic reasoning, in which "reason is credited with the power to know the truth with the aid of given general concepts," which can be attributed to French, Mediterranean, and largely romance language societies, including most of Latin America. The second is nominalistic reasoning, which is also called hypothetical reasoning and is characteristic of Anglo-American thought. This type of reasoning is distrustful of "pure reason" and broad categories. The emphasis is placed on inductive and empirical reasoning, and owes much of its continuing force to the impact of technology on such societies. The third is intuitional or organismic reasoning. It stresses the organic harmony between the whole and its parts, and utilizes many arguments from analogy and ancient authority. The intuitional aspects of thought are much more important than either inductive or deductive reasoning. Pribram asserts that this type of reasoning is important in the extremely nationalistic state, and is prevalent in Germanic and Slavic Central Europe. Based on our earlier emphasis on the cultural quantum of communication among the Eastern traditions, we could argue that this type of reasoning is also prevalent in such Eastern cultures as the Chinese and Japanese. Finally, dialectical reasoning resembles universalistic reasoning, in that it is systemic and deductive, but its system is located in assumed naturally antagonistic forces found in the work rather than "in the mind" of the one who reasons. This type of reasoning can be associated most closely with Marxism through Hegel, and also in the reasoning of the mind identified in Aristotle's *The*

Rhetoric, centuries before the birth of Christ (Pribram, 1949; cited and expanded by Condon and Yousef, 1975:227-228).

If members of one culture think in an entirely different fashion than members of another culture, certainly the influence of these contrasting thought patterns has a significant effect on the perceptual experiences of the members of each culture. At the crosscultural level, Edmund Glenn demonstrates by the use of English, French, and Russian translations of the same documents in the United Nations Security Council that these various thought-patternings do lead to a proper transmittal of immediate meanings which deal with diplomacy. However, latent meanings which may deal with broad patterns of national behavior, including collective processes of decision-making, simply do not transmit accurately. Glenn comments that because of the nominalistic or case-particular logic of the Americans, the universalistic logic of the French, and the dialectical or relational logic of the Russians, the Americans are likely to perceive experiences and thus formulate meaning by looking inwards to the observable particularity of the situation at hand; the French look outwards through the reference of particular situations to general standards; and the Russians direct their attention towards the relations joining the universals and the particulars. Glenn concludes his crosscultural analysis by suggesting: "It thus appears that the very gist of the underlying causes of conflict correlate with the communication that doesn't take place. As for the communication that does take place, it apparently correlates only with the immediate and the superficial. The latter may at times be enormously important, but the failure to communicate the former may have much to do with the impression of futility one often obtains when observing the debates of the world's highest council" (1972:123-140). Though Glenn's major emphasis is on semantic meaning, the assumption can also be made that if the specific thought patterns of these cultures differ so greatly as to make a major impact on meanings, it would seem clear that these differing patterns would also greatly influence the ways in which their cultures alllow them to perceive the latent aspects of the same experiences.

While perception is specific, intelligence is more universal

Jean Piaget distinguishes between perception and another cognitive structure—intelligence—in two fundamental ways:

those areas originating in the relations between subject and object, and those relating to structures and forms. Perception is subordinated to an object of which it supplies direct knowledge as determined by presented data. It is dependent upon experiences. By contrast, intelligence can evoke the absent object by means of a symbolic process, such as imagery or verbal connotations. Even in the object's presence, intelligence helps to interpret it by means of conceptual frameworks of the objects in general. Perceptual efforts are not only subordinated to the presence of the object, but also to limiting conditions of spatial and temporal proximity. Piaget notes that on looking at the full moon, he is not also able to see the missing half, but his memory or intelligence does allow an image to form of the missing half. He argues that perception is essentially egocentric from every point of view, and it is tied to the perceiver's position in relation to the object. It is strictly personal and incommunicable, except through the mediation of language or other nonverbal cues. This egocentricism is not only limiting, but is also the source of systematic errors. Intelligence, however, has a broader and more universal goal, and is independent of the ego, or of a particular individual's point of view. Primary perception is phenomenal, in the sense that it is concerned with the appearance of objects. Perception alone used to understand a closed box leads to the notion that it is three-dimensional and has an interior, but to decide on its content, other mechanisms other than those of perception must be used. Intelligence, though, even in the presence of the given object, constantly exceeds the data with interpretive reconstructions which go far beyond the actual perception. Finally, Piaget notes that abstraction plays no part in primary perception. Perception cannot retain certain elements or characteristics of the object while setting others aside. The essence of intelligence, on the contrary, is to select what is necessary for the solution of the intellectual problem. In a perceptual investigation, the subject is not asked to solve a problem deductively and therefore abstraction is not called for (1969:284-287).

Although both perception and intelligence are properly seen as individual processes of culture, both are linked and influenced by specific cultural experiences. When we note the impact culturally upon all of the cognitive aspects of subjective culture, they lead to an understanding of how they combine to develop intelligence both individually and culturally. Utilizing the definition offered earlier of culture as control, we can see that the individual culture shapes and regulates to a large degree the development and expression of intelligence from one culture to the next. Some cultural groups have been generally regarded as intellectually inferior in the past. Often because of their culturally dependent role in a culturally imperialistic society, the evidence seems to suggest that they have accepted this intellectually inferior role and have not permitted their members to achieve genuine intellectual achievements and superiority. In the American setting, the intellectual inferiority of blacks was for much of our history a given fact, both to some white and black Americans, as seen, for example, in the ABC television version of Alex Haley's *Roots*. Though this mistaken belief still persists today, equally for French Canadians as well as for American blacks, it is less prevalent than it has been in the past. The intellectual inferiority which they experience, which was shared by many other dependent cultural groups, was less a matter of innate inferiority than culturally dictated inferiority. When a culture does not allow or is not allowed to develop high-level abstractions, neither is it able to develop its systematic organization of perceived experiences properly. In this way, even though they function differently in other ways, perception and intelligence are linked both culturally and individually. The culture, on the other hand, which encourages high-level abstractions, also tends to allow its members to develop their systematic organization of perceived experiences in an enriching kind of way (Piaget, 1969:284-287).

Uniqueness attributes relate perceptually to the principle of similarities and differences

Much of the basis of perception is rooted in the structured, stable and meaningful experiences which we have in relations to things and objects. Hastorf, Schneider, and Polefka argue, however, that the same bases are rooted in the perception of persons. They contend that *person perception* is even more important than *object perception*, as it is this perception which provides a foundation for social discourse. By extension, we can argue as well that person perception takes on ever greater consequence for those interested in intercultural and crosscultural communication. Even though we regularly engage in behavior unconsciously, which becomes communicative in the perceived presence of others, a major factor in person perception is that we tend to perceive others in their role as causal, instrumental, and influential agents. We assume that they intentionally affect their own behavior. They may intend to do certain things, such as attempting to cause certain effects, either through their verbal or nonverbal codes. Because we see them as one source of their own actions, we consider them capable of varying their actions to achieve their intended effects. Our perception of their intentionality leads us to organize their behavior into perceptual units. We infer their intentions, and if we perceive a particular intent on several occasions, we tend to perceive another person as having an enduring personality trait. As we begin to categorize a person or a group of persons in terms of consistent or apparently consistent behavior, we begin to establish stereotypes which later form prejudices and biases (Hastorf and others 1970:10-12).

As we identify the consistent or apparently consistent behavior of others as structured, stable, and meaningful experiences, we also begin to stereotype them and their correspondent actions as favorable or unfavorable to us. Typically, if they are perceived favorably, we will tend to see them as similar to us, and if they are perceived unfavorably, we will tend to see them as dissimilar to us. As we have indicated earlier, many studies tend to show that the more similar we are with others, the more we perceive that we can communicate effectively, and the more different we are from others, the more we perceive that we will have difficulty in communicating effectively. As we have indicated, this principle is the heart of the study of intercultural and crosscultural communication. Meaning itself derives from familiarity. When we have coded a person's behavior similarly a number of times and have derived the same inferences about his or her behavior and its cause, and if we have seen other persons who are like the first person, especially on a cultural basis, we begin to extend our personal stereotype to group stereotypes. Thereby, we organize people into distinctive groups and then we impute certain characteristics to the groups. This process develops meaning in our experience of another's behavior. Group and individual stereotypes promote stability and meaning, but often the sample is too small to promote an accurate picture of members of the other group. When the linguistic and nonverbal patterns, the values, the norms, the traditions, the dress, and the behavior of members of the other group seem strange enough, the cultural dimensions increase and make it more difficult for effective communication to take place (Hastorf and others, 1970:1-18).

In contrast to the normal impression that similarity makes effective communication more likely, Howard L. Fromkin hypothesizes that all other things equal, perceptions of low degrees of interpersonal similarity between an individual and others may arouse positive affects, while perceptions of high degrees of interpersonal similarity may arouse negative affects. As a member of a group drawn together because of specific similarities in perception, attitudes, and beliefs, it may be considered important to be different from the others outside the group. The self-attribute of uniqueness is favorably reinforced because members of the group are different from others. The whole notion of status is involved in the perception of uniqueness as we have indicated earlier.

By definition, membership attributes serve to distinguish the goals of the reference group as distinct from other groups. By being similar to other members of the reference group, one is also distinctly different from members of other groups. At the cultural and individual level, this pattern leads to a conformity which makes communication with others who are different more difficult. At the same time, by being different from other members in the group itself in socially accepted ways, one may also gain special approval, status, prestige, and support from other members of the group. Additionally, persons are often members of different reference groups, and self-perceptions of uniqueness may be increased by the varying memberships when they do not represent precisely the same set of perceptual views of oneself and others (Fromkin, 1973:55-76).

Eric Fromm describes the societal forces which oppose each human's search for individuality. We gain our freedom through "awareness of self as distinct from nature and other people" (1941:21). In contrast, Riesman argues that we lose our freedom when we conform to avoid feelings of aloneness and powerlessness (1954). If dominant forces in society or culture focus on inhibiting the expression of individuality or uniqueness, then public expression of perceived unacceptable behavior of an individual nature typically invites mistreatment or rejection from members of the dominant group. The individual who is perceived as violating values, norms, traditions, or beliefs is often labeled a deviant, which leads to a self-image of deviancy. Nevertheless, Fromkin argues that there are a number of physical, material, informational, experiential, and perceptual attributes which are valued because they do define a person as different from members of his or her reference group and which at the same time are not so unacceptably deviant as to cause rejection and isolation from members of the reference group. Fromkin describes such attributes as *uniqueness attributes*. Among those which are important in linking perception to other cognitive aspects of subjective culture, he lists naming, scarcity, beliefs, and behavioral performance (1973:76-78).

Naming is the most important anchorage of self-identity

The perceived importance of names for self-identity is well known. Allport calls one's own name the "most important anchorage of our self-identity" (1961:117). It is not the material possession of the name itself, but the person who is being personalized by his or her initials and his or her name. Fromkin argues that names do more than simply identify a person. High-status communicators are more likely to give their children distinctive types of names; are more likely to call low-status communicators by first names; and are more likely to be called by their last names than are lower-class communicators. Members of dominant cultural groups also often distort or rename persons from dependent cultural groups. The difficult foreign name is often shortened by members of the dominant group, and often the foreigner feels compelled to change his or her own name to be more similar to the most common names of the dominant culture. The higher the status that communicators enjoy, the more likely their names will receive special recognition through awards and through mass media channels. Names acquire value in and of themselves. Fromkin points out how difficult it has been in the past in American society for a woman to retain her maiden name after marriage and how often she has been subjected to harassment by her husband, her family, her friends, and other women. Interculturally, women from societies which traditionally retain the maiden name find considerable problems when they enter a male-oriented name-culture such as American society. In American society, where there are many pressures for cultural assimilation, names still retain a measure of uniqueness for their bearers.

Scarcity of information, experiences, and material add to the symbolic perception of uniqueness

The whole notion of commodity theory, as distinct from economic theory, is cognitive and suggests that individuals perceive that unavailable commodities because of scarcity, whether they are informational, experiential, or material, add symbolically to their own uniqueness. Fromkin comments: "One possible explanation for the valuation of scarce commodities is that the possession of scarce commodities are in some way related to the self perception of uniqueness. In the early 1890s, William James remarked that 'the line between what is me and mine is very hard to draw.' . . .The self is established, maintained and altered in and through communication during social transactions. . . . [The] valuation of commodities increases when people perceive that they are a potential possessor of material objects, experiences, or information which is unavailable to other persons" (1973:84-88). The principle of similarity and differences is seen when members of one cultural group attempt to maintain a similarity of appearance, dress, linguistic, and nonverbal codes precisely so that they will appear different from other cultural groups.

American college students tend to believe that certain of their beliefs are uniquely theirs

We have already discussed beliefs as they relate to perception, but Fromkin and Demming have identified American college students as perceiving that their attitudes, beliefs, and values are "most unique about themselves" (1967). Fromkin reasons that we can assume that individuals covet a small compendium of beliefs which they think are highly idiosyncratic to themselves. In studies on this subject at Purdue University, Brandt and Fromkin found that for a 200-item questionnaire which included beliefs in categories such as religious, political, sexual, academic, economic, social, and moral values, the female subjects reasoned that their sexual beliefs were the most unique for them, and male subjects rated their religious beliefs as most unique. The researchers learned that there was little variation among all of the female subjects on their sexual beliefs, or among all of the male subjects on their religious beliefs. That is, while the subjects considered their beliefs in these areas to be unique to themselves, in fact, their beliefs closely paralleled those of other subjects of the same sex. The subjects were not really aware of the perceptions and attitudes of their own peer-group members. Probably these were areas which were not often discussed publicly by the subjects, and this avoidance led to their self-perception of uniqueness in terms of certain beliefs (1974).

Performance is perceptually motivated positively or negatively by the concept of uniqueness

As a final uniqueness attribute explored by Fromkin, he cites performance on the basis of perception of motivation. He speculates that the power of the desire to see oneself as unique might be demonstrated in the motivation to perform some tasks more or less efficiently in the effort to avoid absolute similarity with others (1973). Members of certain cultural groups may feel it necessary to humble themselves in the presence of elders or persons in authority to demonstrate the uniqueness which the higher-status persons have, or even to identify themselves as uniquely lower-status persons. Even in American husband-wife settings, it is often important that one member, typically the wife in the past, demonstrate that he or she is less capable of performing the same task as the partner so that this principle of uniqueness will not be lost. When the pattern is reversed, for example a successful married woman in political or business life, it becomes more difficult for the husband to accept the same negative perception of himself.

Gross and Osterman note, not only in relation to the uniqueness attributes suggested by Fromkin, but for other perceptual linkages with cognitive and subjective culture, that ". . . much of contemporary American social and political thought can be seen as a continuing debate over the problems and prospects of individualism in our national life . . . so basic is the concept of individualism to American society that every major issue which faces us as a nation invariably poses itself in these terms" (1971:xi). Technology itself appears to threaten the concept of uniqueness, and thus of the individual subjective and cognitive aspects of culture. The assembly-line process which is imposed on individuals by their cultural maximizers in many different phases of life leads to greater short-term efficiency, but affects adversely the feeling of uniqueness. Recognizing that every culture imposes its own norms and guidelines for membership in the group, and noting also that the value orientations of some cultures lean away from an expression of individuality, still it seems important to understand that in every society and culture it is the individual, through his or her subjective and cognitive culture, who interprets these norms and guidelines for himself or herself. In this sense, the characteristic of uniqueness plays an important part in the understanding of the cultural and communicative linkages which produce intercultural and crosscultural communication.

Summary

In this chapter, we have emphasized a chief aspect of individual subjective culture, perception and its relationships to other cognitive aspects of culture at the level of the individual. More important than genetic factors, an individual's perceptions of the external world are the experiential elements which help him or her to see the world as stable, structured, and meaningful. Both because of genetic and cultural environmental reasons, no two persons can completely share perceptions of themselves, the objects and things of their world, or other persons in their world. At the same time, everyone shares some such perceptions. When we apply the concept of individual perceptions to culture, there are reasons both to seek similar and dissimilar perceptions among individuals or collective groups who are communicating together.

Many perceptions are consciously coded and decoded, while many others are not. Marshall Singer (1971) suggests that it is precisely such shared, often unarticulated, and sometimes unarticulable patterns of perceptions, communication, and behavior which can be referred to as a culture. Group perceptions, however, do not necessarily recognize national or cultural boundaries. Groups which share the same perceptions to one degree or another develop and are intercultural or crosscultural in nature. Singer notes that the fewer group identities that a person shares, and the less intensely held the identities which exist with individuals with whom he or she must communicate, the more crossculturally he or she is operating on the basis of a perceptual continuum.

While greater dissimilarities of perceptions may exist between members of different classes within the same society than between members of the same class across societal or cultural boundaries, communication which occurs across both international and cultural boundaries often makes it even more difficult to adjust levels of expectation for effective communication in totally unfamiliar environments. Within an individual society, many familiar subtle cues inform the communicator of how to respond at different levels of sophistication. When the national and cultural boundaries are more sharply crossed, the cues and codes may be so different that the communicator has no idea of how to respond in the setting at all. While persons sharing identity groups appear to share the same perceptions, problems, and values, the deep-seated cultural impact may hinder the ability to communicate effectively. Even as they have certain things in common, they also have many more things which distinguish them culturally from each other. At home, the strain of uncertainty is not so great as in a foreign country or culture, until the concept of similarity becomes familiar enough to overtake the differences, particularly at the cognitive level which hinders effective intercultural communication.

References:

Allport, G.W., 1961. *Pattern and Growth in Personality*. New York: Macmillan.

Barnouw, Victor, 1973. *Culture and Personality*. Homewood, Illinois: Dorsey.

Brandt, J.M., and H.L. Fromkin, 1974. "Number of Similar Strangers and Feelings of Undistinctiveness as Limits for the Similarity Attraction Relationship." Unpublished paper presented at the Midwestern Psychological Association Convention (May). Chicago.

Burk, Jerry L., 1974. "An Explication and Evaluation of Cognitive Anthropology." In *International and Intercultural Communication Annual* I, 24-38.

Burke, Kenneth, 1964. *Terms for Order.* Edited by Stanley Edgar Hyman. Bloomington, Indiana: Indiana University.

Fromkin, H.L., 1973. *The Psychology of Uniqueness: Avoidance of Similarity and Seeking of Differences.* Paper No. 438. West Lafayette, Indiana: Institute for Research in the Behavioral, Economic, and Management Sciences, Krannert School of Industrial Administration, Purdue University.

Fromkin, H.L. and B. Demming, 1967. "A Survey of Retrospective Reports of Feelings of Uniqueness." Unpublished manuscript. Ohio State University.

Fromm, Eric, 1941. *Escape from Freedom.* New York:

Geertz, Clifford, 1973. *The Interpretation of Cultures.* New York: Basic Books.

Glenn, Edmund S., 1972. "Meaning and Behavior: Communication and Culture." In *Intercultural Communication: A Reader.* Edited by Larry Samovar and Richard Porter. Belmont, California: Wadsworth.

Goodenough, Ward, 1961. "Comments on Cultural Evolution." *Daedalus* 90, 521-528.

Gross, R., and P. Osterman, 1971. *Individualism: Man in Modern Society.* New York: Dell.

Hallowell, A.I., 1972. "Cultural Factors in the Structuralization of Perception." In *Intercultural Communication: A Reader.* Edited by Larry Samovar and Richard Porter. Belmont, California: Wadsworth.

Nieburg, Harold L., 1973. *Culture Storm: Politics and the Ritual Order.* New York: St. Martin.

Osgood, Charles E., William H. May, and Murray S. Miron, 1975. *Cross-Cultural Universals of Affective Meaning.* Urbana, Illinois: University of Illinois.

Piaget, Jean, 1969. *The Mechanism of Perception.* Translated by G.N. Seagrim. New York: Basic Books.

Pribram, Karl, 1949. *Conflicting Patterns of Thought.* Washington, D.C.: Public Affairs.

Riesman, D., 1954. *Individualisms Reconsidered.* Glencoe, Illinois: Scott, Foresman.

Sapir, Edward, 1949. *Selected Writings of Edward Sapir in Language, Culture, and Personality.* Edited by David G. Mandelbaum. Berkeley: University of California.

Singer, Marshall, 1971. "Culture: A Perceptual Approach." In *Readings in Intercultural Communication.* I. Pittsburgh: University of Pittsburgh.

Part Four
The Cultural Communicator in Dialogue: Observations on Japanese and American Cultures

I recently visited Japan to attend a joint Japanese-American intercultural communication workshop at a small Japanese resort spa north of Toyko. Sixty-seven Japanese and American professionals, teachers, students, and various agency representatives came together to explore and experience theoretical and practical aspects of cultural dialogue. The head of the Japanese delegation opened the workshop by recalling the constant warning that his impoverished parents had given him as a child: "Don't waste a single grain of rice!" Encouraging us to understand that just as every grain of rice was precious in his childhood, he stressed that so was every single moment during our nine-day workshop, even those moments which would seem frustrating and nonproductive.

In this part, we will move away from the heavily theoretical synthesis which has been provided in the earlier units. Instead, I wish to provide you with an interactional basis which will draw you into an actual cultural dialogue which involved Japanese and American participants in an intercultural workshop. The use of the extended illustration will demonstrate explicitly or implicitly many of the principles and concepts which we have offered or synthesized throughout *Cultural Dialogue*. Despite many superficial similarities in the Japanese-American workshop, we noted many differences between our linguistic and nonverbal codes, values, and perceptions. We were involved in intercultural communication at the most serious level. All of the cultural contrasts of time and space were present. Eating, sleeping, and behaving as much as possible as traditional Japanese, we were also strongly affected by the powerful impact of technology since our sessions were videotaped, monitored, played back, and preserved to some extent.

In Chapter 11, we set the stage by providing a view of the similarities and differences which affect a Japanese living in the United States in tangible cultural characteristics as life styles, social and human relationships, family and male-female relations, values and ethnical orientations, and what it feels like to be a marginal man. It is the perspective of Muneo Yosikawa, an expert in East Asian languages, a member of the workshop, and a person who finds himself moving between the traditional and modern cultures. If he is not the multicultural man, he is at least a symbol of the bicultural man.

Chapters 12 through 16 provide a subjective daily commentary which I wrote during my participation in the intercultural communication workshop. I had known that we would be asked to write a journal on our experience during the workshop so that these journals would collectively provide useful personal stimuli for our small discussion groups there. It would also individually allow us to record our own perceptions to check against our experiences with those of others. While many of my comments in *Cultural Dialogue* are interpretative of the writing of various other persons, this section is intended to offer practical first-hand applications of the positive opportunities offered by intercultural communication with a realistic description also of the problems which might hinder the achievement of such goals in an actual intercultural or bicultural setting. The following pages represent an illustrative, condensed, and autobiographical set of observations, perceptions, and evaluations about my involvement for two weeks of my life in such communication. You may have similar experiences to draw upon.

It is difficult to analyze a personal intercultural communication event fairly and objectively. I filter my perceptions through my own cultural biases. My observations may not be precisely what another person, even another American professional, involved in the same event might perceive, based on his or her cultural biases. The journal which follows lacks the character of data collected under carefully controlled circumstances. The base is too small in many cases for generalization on either of the two dominant cultural groupings included, or indeed, to other cultures, or to your own life specifically as an individual cultural communicator. We must take care not to assume that statements made collectively or individually by a small number of Japanese and Americans offer us greater cultural insight than intended. Still, the autobiographical and available potential data from such a brief dialogue may demonstrate how genuinely complex and frequently unpredictable communication often can be.

A two-week visit anywhere scarcely qualifies anyone as an expert on a culture or its peoples. The brevity of the experience was both useful and disadvantageous. At best the visit served to stimulate me to ask more questions about the similarities and differences between Japanese and American cultures. The perceptions which I gained are hampered by being first impressions, and the shortness of the visit prevented me from having the widest possible experiences in Japan. Later I checked these first impressions through interpersonal contacts and by reading the work of scholars on Japan. Helpful comments have also been made by several of the participants involved in the dialogue.

You may wish to write a journal for a brief period, especially if you have the opportunity for some unusual intercultural experience. It will provide you with a rich set of data for consideration and an interesting opportunity to look back at the development of your own thought-patterns at this stage of your life. You will also learn more about who you are, in terms of your cultural situation, as I did. In keeping such a journal, you might ask such questions as: What did I experience today? What happened to others sharing the experience? Were they talking about their feelings, ideas, or cultures? Was there "good communication" today or were people not communicating well? Did I learn more about myself or others? Did I learn new ways of communicating or about cultural dialogue? What did I learn about how to relate to people of other cultures, or about their culture? Did I gain any new ideas about nonverbal communication or about language? Did I act differently today than when everyone is from the same cultural grouping?*

*These questions are paraphrased from the instructions given us at the workshop for preparing a journal.

One of the most effective ways of understanding the opportunities and problems of intercultural communication is through role-playing. Perhaps you could undertake to role-play some of the dialogues which will be presented in these chapters. You will find the possibility of developing fairly detailed characteristics, both in terms of linguistic and nonverbal codes. Values and perceptions for the various participants in the group of eight participants (four Japanese and four Americans) are the focus of most of the dialogues in these chapters. If you decide to role-play dialogues or certain other aspects of interest in this part, you should be aware that it is important that you attempt to be as accurate as possible to cultural dimensions offered by the Japanese and American participants. This is more important than a simple mimic of the dialogues, and some very small incidents can be isolated for role-playing to provide a deeper understanding of the cultural similarities and contrasts.

CHAPTER 11

Some Japanese and American
Cultural Characteristics

Muneo Yoshikawa*

When I look back at my life cycle, I realize I have passed through several different stages: 1.) the stage of unawareness of my nationality conflicts; 2.) the stage of conciously experiencing the conflicts, identifying myself with the second culture (America) while rejecting my first culture (Japan); 3.) the stage of further identity crisis, during which period I felt out of place in either culture; and 4.) the well-adjusted stage.

I am now in the fourth stage in which I can identify with both cultures and appreciate my biculturality. Probably I can be classified a marginal man in the advanced stage, or a bicultural individual, who is often considered as a "man in the middle" or a "cultural middleman." How marginal I am, it is difficult to say; however, there is no doubt that I am a product of two cultures. I am now able to look at both cultures with objectivity as well as subjectivity; I am able to move in both cultures, back and forth without any apparent conflict; I am able to switch the linguistic and cultural code systems almost at will, as if there are two distinct individuals in me—one Japanese and the other American. However, it is more than a mere fusion of two "culture selves." I think that something beyond the sum of each identification took place, and that it

*Muneo Yoshikawa is a faculty member in the East Asian Language Department at the University of Hawaii. This essay was especially prepared for this book. It is used with his permission.

became something akin to the concept of "synergy"—when one adds 1 and 1, one gets three, or a little more. This something extra is not culture-specific but something unique of its own, probably the emergence of a new attitude or a new self-awareness, born out of an awareness of the relative nature of values and of the universal aspect of human nature. Now I feel I have arrived at the stage where I really am not concerned whether others take me as a Japanese or an American: I can accept myself as I am. I feel I am much freer than ever before, not only in the cognitive domain (perception, thoughts, etc.), but also in the affective (feeling, attitudes, etc.) and behavioral domains.

I find Hawaii an ideal place for me to live, for Hawaii permits and helps me to be what I am. In Hawaii I feel well-accepted as an emerging marginal man. However, if I were to be living outside of Hawaii, I do not think I would feel equally comfortable, free, and creative as now; I may expect adjustment problems. I feel I may have to make more adjustments if I were to live and work in Japan than in America. My marginality, therefore, is to a certain extent situational; depending upon the situational variables, especially that of place, whether Japan or mainland USA or Hawaii, my degree of marginality changes.

Comparing both Japanese and American cultural characteristics gives a better perspective of myself as a marginal man. Although I experience difficulties in responding, for many of my responses may differ depending upon situational and social variables such as time, place, role I play, persons involved, etc., I have tried my best to express my own general views on four main topics. In addition to my general comments under each topic, I have responded to specific cultural characteristics whenever I felt appropriate, just in order to make my views more specific.

Tangible Life Styles:

My tangible life style has been the product of two cultures. I have reached the stage (in terms of marginality) where I am open in adopting the desirable aspects of each culture without feeling guilt or conflict. For example, I consider the Japanese custom of bowing beautiful and so I still retain it, while using the handshaking American custom; I feel comfortable sitting on the floor as well as on a chair, but occasionally I find myself sitting Japanese style on a Western chair. My nonverbal behavior such as facial expressions, hand movements, and body language are also a mixture of both cultures, but my behavior is usually adjusted in accordance with the person to whom I am communicating.

I often observe that a shift from one language to the other results in a shift in content as well as the nonverbal behavior. That is, when I use the Japanese language as the medium of communication, my nonverbal communication is more like that of a Japanese, and when English is used, I behave more like an American; if I use English I can say things which I cannot in Japanese, and vice versa. The following are my responses to some specific cultural characteristics:

I feel quite comfortable walking down a street while eating popcorn, a hotdog, an ice-cream cone, etc. in America, but in Japan I am reluctant to do it. In fact, I have never done it before, the reason being that this is generally considered as bad manners in Japan.

In handling a Japanese saw, I pull because the teeth of the saw are made in such a way that it must be pulled. For the same reason, I push the American saw. Because of my earlier life style (sitting down on the floor and engaging in types of sports like Judo and Sumo), my back muscle or waist muscle as in the case of Japanese people, has been specially developed. Thus my physical makeup is well-suited for operating the Japanese saw. I think I still do better with a Japanese saw.

We first must make a distinction between kimono—formal wear—and yukata—informal wear which is usually worn during the summer time. Even in Hawaii where I live now, I often wear the yukata at home because it is very comfortable and it is well-suited for Hawaiian weather. However, I consider the yukata strictly as home-wear.

I usually take my shoes off before entering a house (in Hawaii). It is more comfortable that way; besides it keeps the house clean. This custom is in fact generally practiced even among Caucasian people in Hawaii.

I usually take a shower, especially after swimming, gardening, etc., just to clean up. But I still love to take a bath soaked up to my neck just for the enjoyment. My basic philosophy of bath-taking is still that of the Japanese—for enjoyment. I recognize and actually practice the basic idea of American bath or shower-taking—cleaning up (utilitarian purpose). At home we have what is called a "Roman bathtub" which is just like an ordinary Western bathtub but is greater in depth. One of my dreams is to have a bathroom with the Japanese-style bathtub.

In Hawaii, we sometimes invite friends to our home for both formal and informal dinner parties. If our guests desire, we show them around our house, even including our bedroom. This type of behavior is very rare among the Japanese people.

Whenever I address my Japanese superiors or elders, I call them by their last names no matter how close we may be. I still feel uncomfortable calling them by their first names even if I am communicating with them in English. In the case of American superiors, I feel quite at home calling them by their first names if our relationship is close enough.

Social and Human Relationships

My social and human relationships with others are—by Japanese standards—open, direct, informal, and horizontal, all of which are considered to be American. Unlike the American, however, I form a deep bond with another person although being selective in choosing such a friend; I often make personal commitments to others. Generally speaking, Japanese people are very timid toward people in high status, but I find it difficult to act that way. In my relationships with individuals, I do not make any real distinction based on social status. However, if I am in some organization in Japan, I will be more cautious in my choice of words and behavior. On the whole, my social interactions characterized by those terms as equality, informality, personal attachment, and permanence are the product of cultural traits of both cultures. My responses to the specific cultural characteristics relating to such relationships are as follows:

When I am talking with Japanese people in the Japanese language, I rarely express criticism of them openly; with Japanese people I am inclined to be concerned about the other person's feelings; I pay more attention to "how I say it" rather than "what to say." Generally with American people I am more open and direct in expressing my feelings and disagreements, and in giving my negative response to the requests and invitations. Since I realize that the impact of my being open and direct differs culturally, I consciously adjust my mode of communication, depending upon whom I am communicating with.

Although I am open and direct by Japanese standards, I am by far less assertive and insistent than the average American. I am often overwhelmed by both the eloquency and the verbal aggressiveness of American people.

Leadership roles, in my view, should be assigned on the basis of one's ability rather than on the basis of age or seniority. However, if I am in Japan, I will pay attention to age and seniority as well as one's ability and talent.

I ordinarily find it difficult to subordinate my will to the group's interest to the extent that Japanese people generally do. I am not fond of group activities, but once I decide to join the group, I place the group's interest first. I generally like to do things in my own way, at my own pace.

I can see merits in both consenus and majority vote in the decision-making process. I personally observe both systems working well in each respective culture. I have experienced both processes and am comfortable in both. However, if I have a choice, I prefer decision-making by consensus whose basic philosophy is based on the "give-and-take" principle. It generally takes time and effort to reach a consenus, but the effect is that no one really loses or wins, and that it can prevent power play, although I am well aware of the difficulties involved in the consensus approach in order for it to be readily accepted in such an efficient, competitive, achievement-oriented society as America. At least, in my view, I consider the decision-making process by consensus democratic as I understand it.

When I find myself in a difficult or a boring situation, I, like the average Japanese, will often try to endure the situation quietly, mainly for the sake of the speaker and the rest of the people involved. If, however, there may be any possibility of effecting change in the situation, I try to realize it in an acceptable way. In my teaching, I have devised a system to combat such a boring situation. At the very beginning of the class, the orientation period, I usually tell students that if they get bored in the process of learning, they are allowed to leave the classroom any time without seeking permission from me and that they do not need to please me just by enduring the boring learning situation. If they get sleepy, they are encouraged to step out to wash their faces, and come back or even to yawn in order to receive oxygen back into their blood system (yawning behavior in the classroom situation is considered very rude in

Japan). Learning is our business and we encourage whatever is necessary to facilitate learning. Likewise, we alter whatever impedes learning. This is usually accepted as one of our class rules for both teacher and students.

When I receive kindness or a special favor from another person, I would say "thank you" and feel indebtness. When the opportunity arises, I will repay not out of mere obligation, but out of gratitude for what has been done for me. If I were to make a living in Japan, of course I would be more sensitive to the gift-giving custom and follow the custom, for it still functions as an important lubrication for social relationships in Japan. While normally teachers in the American school system may construe their student's gift as a bribe or as an effort to seek special favors, thus not accepting the gift from their students, I accept such a gift if the student is from another culture like Japan where a different cultural meaning is assigned to the gift-giving, and where "face-saving" is of prime importance. It could be an embarrassing experience for the student if the teacher refuses the gift only on the basis of school policy. Such a face-losing experience often becomes injurious to the relationship between the teacher and the student. The point may be made that it would be better for the student in the long run if he or she is told that gift-giving is simply against the school policy so that the student and teacher may not be involved in such troubles in in the future. This may be so, and the student intellectually understands the explanation, but I wonder if he or she can accept it emotionally. For someone from a country like Japan, it is often better to be harmonious than to be right. The custom of gift-giving and receiving is simply one of the different modes of communication, and unless the silent cultural assumptions behind the gift-giving custom of each culture are recognized, miscommunication and misunderstanding are bound to happen.

Both "life-long employment" and a tenure system with a probationary period have their own merits and demerits. For Japanese people whose social virtue is to be humble and to be modest about their ability and talent, a probationary period or checking period, during which one must sell and prove one's capability, is indeed a trying period. At the university, I have observed Asian faculty members going through the agonizing probationary period. Japanese generally perceive that such an arbitrary probationary period gives rise to conflicts and

disharmony among colleagues because of the highly competitive nature of the situation, and thus impedes development.
On the other hand, American people generally perceive that
"life-long employment" or tenure system without a checking
period may yield many deadwoods, so to speak, thus impeding
development. Each system still seems to be functioning
relatively well, although I see some changes taking place in
Japan as well as in America. I have questions about the way in
which the present university "tenure system" is set up. Under
this system, a person seems to be perceived on the basis of
ability and achievement. On the contrary, under the "life-long
employment" system, a person is perceived as a total person;
not only by ability, special skills, or achievements, but also by
social relationships with others, cooperativeness, length of service, etc. are considered for any personal action. In a company
situation especially, even if a person fails in one area, he or she
feels accepted and finds a place in the system. This aspect of
the human-oriented system appeals to me.

Family and Male-Female Relations

My view on male-female relations is basically that of the
women's liberation movement. I do not accept the dominance of
either sex. I feel that both husband and wife should be responsible for child-rearing, cooking, shopping, house work, etc., at
least if both husband and wife are working. In the Japanese
culture, the practice of the wife working outside the home is
still considered unacceptable by social norms. In my own case,
both my wife and I are working by our own choice. At home,
therefore, both of us are responsible for almost anything,
although there is to some extent a division of labor among
ourselves because of our special abilities and talents. My wife
is methodical and organized, and so she has the responsiblity
for bookkeeping and taking care of all the bills, while I mainly
take care of manual work, such as maintenance of house and
yardwork; we take turns cooking and washing dishes, depending upon our physical condition; we go shopping together or
take turns; decisions are ordinarily shared by both of us. My
basic attitude toward male-female relationships extends to the
parent-child relationship. In my dealings with our five-year-old
son, I try my best not to place dominance or authority over him.
The mutual problem-solving approach is generally adopted.

That is, all of us participate in the decision-making process, if the matter is related to all of us. The child is thus motivated to carry out the decision; he is encouraged to decide for himself; he is encouraged to believe that he himself is the best judge of what he wants and what he should do. It is kind of basic belief that each unique parent and his unique child can solve each of their unique conflicts by finding their solutions acceptable to both. However, if our son were to live in Japan the rest of his life, I would have to make some adjustments to my basic thinking on child-rearing and education. It is obvious now that my basic underlying philosophy manifested in family and male-female relationships is more characteristically American.

Values and ethical orientations

My values and ethical orientation have been tinged by both Eastern and Western cultural orientations. I have been attracted and influenced especially by religious existentialists such as Martin Buber, Gabriel Marcel, Paul Tillich, Karl Jaspers, etc., within whom I can observe the elements of both Christianity and Zen Buddhism. The central idea is that existence is communication—that life is dialogue, centering around the I-Thou relationship. In other words, communication is dialogue, and dialogue, I-Thou meeting, is not just in the sense of two people talking, but of real efforts at mutual understanding, mutual acknowledgment, and mutual respect. This view of human communication as dialogue, not as monologue, is a central theme of my present course. "Foreign Language Learning Through Dialogical Approach." The basic objective of the course is to nurture a type of person who is an empathic, free, and open individual; such an individual is in a way a cultural middleman between East and West; he is basically a man of two selves—emphathic self generally encouraged in the East, and open self generally encouraged in the West. In order to express my basic values and ethical orientation, I have thus described what I am now doing with my basic philosophy. To be a little more specific, let me suggest some of the cultural characteristics relating to such values:

Ruth Benedict described the Japanese culture as a "shame culture" as distinct from the "sin culture" of America. It means that, for example, in Japan, parents admonish their children thus—"If you do that, people will laugh at you." In the process of this type of social control, children become more sensitive to what other people expect of them. On the contrary, parents in America generally appeal to the conscience of each individual child: "You should not do such and such, because it is bad, or it is not right." Ruth Benedict's concept can be looked at from different perspectives, David Riesman and others talk about "other-directed individual" and "inner-directed individual." In my view, both types of individual have merits. Empathic attitude toward others often demonstrated by the other-directed individual and the more autonomous self-motivated individual often seen in the inner-directed individual are, I think, good aspects of both types of individual. In order to be a whole being, I think we need those positive qualities in us. I, as a marginal man, aspire to be an empathic, open, free individual, who is the composite creation of East and West.

People who are good in language are not generally respected in Japanese society due to the different views on "verbal language." The psychocultural orientation (worldview) of Japanese people toward "verbal language" can be generalized as that of "mistrust." What is often verbally expressed and what is actually intended are two different things. What is verbally expressed is probably important enough to maintain friendship, and it is generally called *Tatemae* which means simply "in principle" but what is not verbalized counts most— *Honne* which means "true mind." Although it is not expressed verbally, you are supposed to know it by *kan*—"intuition."

This kind of intuitive understanding or psychic understanding between two individuals beyond the verbal expression is often known as *haragei*, which can be literally translated as "belly art or abdominal performance." This type translated as "belly art or abdominal performance." This type of tacit understanding has been working in a homogeneous country like Japan. Many Japanese proverbs remind us that "verbal language" is something not worthy of trust and in fact is even a dangerous thing. What is verbally expressed and what is actually intended are two different things. This is a basic principle of communication that Japanese people are supposed to be aware of. We are not surprised to find that most of the great leaders or heroes in Japanese history were known as men of few words.

On the other hand, in a highly heterogeneous country like

America, one must depend upon language as a means of communication, the basic philosophy being that one does not understand unless another speaks up. As it is written in the Bible: "At the beginning God expressed himself. That personal expression, that word, was with God and was God. . . ." Language has been valued in Western civilization.

Where do I stand as a marginal man?

I am aware of various dimensions and modes of communication which differ from culture to culture. At least, I have developed a keen awareness of silent cultural assumptions of each culture which affect the process of communication.

I am very fond of humor, and I often use humor in my speech, formal and informal. People generally laugh when they hear a funny story, but what people in one culture consider funny may not necessarily be funny at all. I often find American jokes not funny at all. Rather, humor generated from puns or a play on words which is very much characteristic of Japanese humor appeals to me. And I myself use an extensive play on words in my talk, especially in Japanese company. I acquired one American mode of communication (in terms of humor) but I find myself still very much Japanese in the content and form of my humor.

The act of "smiling" can be universal, but its connotation differs in each culture. There are times when a Japanese might announce the death of a member of the family to their friends with a smile. This may be easily misconstrued by Americans while this kind of behavior can be acceptable to Japanese: they smile to ease the particular situation; in other words, they want to be thoughtful to their friends by not letting their friends worry about their bereavement. They smile, therefore, not because they are insensitive, but mainly because they are sensitive to the other person's feelings. For the same reason, I sometimes find myself smiling unconsciously while reporting bad news concerning myself or my family to my American friends.

I am basically informal and generally am not fond of formal ceremonies. For example, I generally dress very casually even at the university; I dress like the students and it is difficult for anyone to spot me as a professor. Looking back, I realize that my dressing mode has been changed, as my marginality advanced to a more psychologically stable stage; I used to dress formally, and behaved like a professor at least consciously. However, I do respect formal ceremonies and am willing to participate if I deem them necessary.

I am fond of both the pompous grandeur of a Western palace and of the simple sober-looking Japanese temples and gardens, for example. At present, I am living in a Western-style house decorated both with things Western as well as Oriental, with a Japanese garden. I love both Western and Japanese art. On the whole, however, my aesthetic sense is basically that of the Japanese culture.

CHAPTER 12

A Journal of an American's Cultural
Dialogue in Japan: Preparing
for the Dialogue

July 2: The plane as medium and message

Departing from Los Angeles to Honolulu, I was struck by the
increased intercultural awareness provided through the
plane's decor, meals, and the dress of the flight attendants.
These dimensions were heightened when we transferred to
Air Siam, where the stewards and stewardesses were all
young Thais, who appeared to speak either English or
Japanese as well as their own language. In addition to the
Americans bound for Toyko, there were many Oriental
students and families returning to Japan, Singapore, and
Thailand. Their lack of fluent English was more than com-
pensated for by their unfailing good humor, and provided a
striking contrast to the louder and more brash Americans
aboard.

July 3: Upside down culturally through time and space

The thirty-five hour time difference demonstrated the impact
of our movement through time and space when the July 2
Japan Times headlined the grave illness of Juan Peron after
the July 3 Los Angeles newspaper had already announced his
death. At the Haneda Airport in Japan, I was met by a
Japanese professor friend who had not realized that a
chartered bus was awaiting the American group. After

discussing the merits of going with him, when he confessed that he didn't know where our Japanese hotel was, or taking the chartered bus, I chose the latter alternative. As the bus left, I decided that I had erred against the host-guest obligations of courtesy.

After settling into the small semi-Western hotel, four of us took a walking tour of the small winding streets nearby with modified shrine and templelike architecture rising above the tiny shops. It was about 5 A.M. Washington D.C. time, but we were nevertheless made hungry by the late afternoon restaurant aromas in Tokyo. The realistic "mihon" in glass cases outside the restaurants or plastic samples of each item on the menu aided us greatly in making our first choices. Being a "hashi" or chopstick-user in the past, my smugness evaporated after spilling the noodle soup which was offered us as a part of the supper.

July 4: A guest for the day at a Japanese university

One's sense of national pride on an independence day seems enlarged in a situation where no one else seems to recognize its importance. Since my Japanese professor colleague had invited me to visit his university, I arrived near our meeting spot by way of the subway with the Americans who were accompanying me. Spotting a bank, we determined to change dollars into yen. We were graciously provided tea while the bank manager appeared to be calling a downtown bank so that he could assist us. After a considerable delay and with much apology, he offered us a final "Tomorrow," which in terms of polite Japanese we learned later meant, "I am sorry that I cannot help you." Had we returned the next day as the invitation suggested, we probably would have received some other obliquely appropriate answer meaning "no."

When my Japanese professor colleague drove us to his university, I learned that I was to be the guest of honor for a visit with the dean and other administrators. We received first green and then black tea, and my colleague served as our interpretor while two ceremonial gifts were presented to me and my guests in the name of the university. An invitation was extended to me to be guest of honor that evening at a banquet hosted by the university. While the politely worded invitation would have also permitted me to include my American guests, it seemed directed essentially to me alone, and I perhaps correctly declined on their behalf. That evening I met my university hosts at the plush international Okura Hotel. I received my first multicourse Japanese dinner, served in many small individual dishes by a kimono-clad hostess, and bravely attempted to eat my first raw fish—a delicious treat, I learned. Engaging in a gift-giving ceremony, which assumes major significance in many international cultural communication situations, the Japanese rather typically depreciated their exquisite gifts, while in a fairly usual American fashion, I explained the symbolic importance of the copies of the original Jefferson cups which I had brought my hosts from Jefferson's home in Virginia.

We finished the lavish dinner and my hosts invited me to visit what I mistakenly perceived as a geisha house, which turned out instead to be a night club with 1,000 persons and 300 hostesses attending to all of our needs. A number of writers on Japan suggest that one small indication of a Japanese racism or xenophobia is the frequent turning away of unaccompanied foreign visitors from such establishments. With my Japanese hosts, I received a warm welcome as possibly the only American present and found our table surrounded by three lovely young ladies who constantly made business for their establishment by holding up lighted matches for the waiters to reorder liquor, beer, nuts, and pastries. They rotated around the table, inviting us to dance with them to the music of an excellent twenty-piece band, chatting with each of us, and constantly patting us on the knees, arms and shoulders, as they also shelled peanuts for us, poured drinks, lighted cigarettes, and seemed to suppress embarrassed or coy laughs. The young women hostesses seemed to exhibit a good sense of humor and dignity in their roles, and even if the event struck me as somewhat strange, it is probable that many other night-club settings throughout the world share many of the same characteristics. Learning that the two-hour visit to the night club alone had cost my hosts 22,000 yen or about $77.00, I received some feeling of the obligations incurred by the visit of a foreign friend to my hosts.

July 5: The public bath

On our first visit to the neighborhood around our hotel, we had seen several public baths, or "ofuro," and had talked about involving ourselves in such an experience. Finding no one to accompany me this evening, I started alone timidly from my hotel with its shower and bath in my room, carrying a large towel, soap, and the yukata (semi-house coat which I had seen being worn up and down the small streets to the bath) all under my raincoat. I had made the trip three times to and from the bath before I had enough courage to undertake the experience. Eventually, I entered the bath house, paid my fifty yen (about eighteen cents) to the woman cashier who had a view of the women's and men's dressing rooms, and began to feel the need for the relaxation that the bath was supposed to offer me.

I knew that one is not supposed to move directly into the bath after entering the bath room, both because people are expected to enter the actual bath clean, and because it is necessary to become adjusted gradually to the hot water before entering the otherwise scalding bath. Twenty or so men and boys were in various positions in the room, some in the large baths, one of which had circulating water and turned out to be the hotter bath. Some were in movement in and out of the bath, and most were sitting on low stools in front of low mirrors, either washing their hair, shaving, or brushing their teeth, or soaping themselves thoroughly and constantly pouring hot water all over themselves from the plastic pans filled from the faucets along the wall. There was a high level of modesty, with a number of the men and boys carefully covering themselves with the small hand towels about the size of a large washcloth. These towels were used for washing, covering themselves, and drying. I had never thought it possible to dry entirely from a full bath with one small washcloth-sized hand towel. Those who had reentered the dressing room and were drying used it like a sponge, wringing it out and reusing it until they were quite dry.

I squatted as ceremoniously and as unobtrusively as my six-foot six-inch frame would allow among the far smaller Japanese on one of the six-square inch stools in front of my own mirror and hot and cold water faucets, armed only with my soap and plastic pan for pouring water. Considering myself a "researcher," of course, I had to observe ethnographically what was being done and how it was being done so that I could follow it correctly. When I saw myself and this steaming room full of men and boys squatting on our stools, most of them turned entirely white because of their completely soaped bodies, I had a great urge to give out a laugh. Since a "researcher" should try not to show his subjective bias in such a project, I barely refrained from such a display of emotion. Fortunately, they too refrained from a similar display of laughter in my direction.

The soaping process with continued rinsing and resoaping seemed to consume the largest amount of time in the bath room itself. In the American shower, we usually use soap fairly functionally, but in the Japanese bath, it is both part of the ritual and appears to have a very relaxing effect on the person soaping himself. I found it relaxing too, especially after I noted that I was being allowed a certain invisibility, and since I couldn't speak any Japanese, even if people were speaking to me or about me, I couldn't respond. The hot water which I began to pour over myself was at first a shock, and I had to include cold water in each pan to temper it. Eventually, after twenty or thirty minutes of repeating the soaping and rinsing process, I thought that perhaps I was ready for the actual bath. I followed the bathers' lead in stopping at the edge of the bath and pouring many more pans full of water on myself from the bath itself.

The boys served as better models for me than the men, as I reasoned that my skin was probably more like theirs than the men who had been toughening their skins for a much longer period of time. I followed the boys to the step with only my feet and legs in the bath, repeated the rinsing several times, gradually moving down into the water to sit on the step, and then into the full bath. I finally moved in the same way to the hotter bath which had the circulating water. The whirlpool effect was very relaxing and became deceptively so, causing me to stay in longer than I should have. The bathers were going in and out of the baths, again soaping and rinsing, and returning to the hotter bath. Between their movement in and out of the bath, many of the bathers were dousing themselves entirely with cold water to close their pores, no doubt as in the Finnish sauna. I saw that after leaving the bath area to the dressing room, they would step outside to an enclosed area where cool air would

help them dry. After a cigarette or beer, they would return
to the dressing room, and put on their pajamas, as it was
now about 11 P.M.

Getting out of the circulating bath, I discovered that I
had indeed stayed longer than my conditioning had war-
ranted. My legs felt like rubber, I could scarcely walk, and I
felt waves of dizziness coming over me. This awkwardness
on my part caused the first smiling signs of recognition on
the faces of the small crowd still in the bath. Some of the
men made a gesture showing me that the bath had been too
hot, and I nodded assent. After stumbling to the dressing
room, I jumped on the scale as the other bathers did, but I
could hardly see my weight because of my lightheadedness
and at any rate, couldn't remember how to translate the
kilos into pounds. By the time that I had dried with my giant
towel while the others were sponging themselves with their
small hand towels, and dressed back in my clothes instead of
pajamas as everyone else was doing, I began to feel more
normal and had long since lost any sense of embarrassment.
If my clumsy attempts to imitate the model which the
Japanese had provided for me was a poor show, I am sure that
they understood. After all I was a "gaijin" or foreigner and
couldn't be expected to know any better. Later at the workshop
hotel where we had our own semi-public bath I could smugly
show some of the other inexperienced Americans how to do the
process correctly.

July 6: The intercultural communication workshop begins

Most of July 6 consisted of traveling by chartered bus from
Toyko to our workshop site. All of the Americans were asked
to select a Japanese participant so that we could immediately
begin a cultural dialogue. When we arrived at the spa
resort, a twenty-foot long sign stretching across the street
welcomed us. Although the town was a Japanese resort, it had
never before hosted an international conference. Many of the
shopkeepers came out of their shops to wave at us and make us
feel welcome. As we entered the hotel, we shifted from shoes to
slippers and there was a great flurry of excitement in helping
us get our luggage to our rooms. Where possible, every room
had two to three persons assigned with at least one Japanese
and one American sharing the room. Our three-room suite
overlooked a swimming pool and a beautiful Japanese garden.

It had a large Japanese-style sitting room, which could be turned into a sleeping room at night by putting down the sleeping mats, with low tables and tatami mats; a small sitting room with Western-style furniture, and an icebox filled with soft drinks and beer; a bedroom containing a Western-style bed; an area with a wash basin and separate Western-style toilets, and an enclosed small Japanese bath which could be filled by the residents whenever they wished. One Japanese and another American and I were assigned to the suite. Our Japanese colleague chose the Western-style bed and we chose the futan mats for sleeping. He hadn't slept in the Japanese-style for many years, he said, and besides he didn't want us to miss the opportunity to sleep in the more typical Japanese way.

After an early introductory group meeting with opening statements, we went to the dining room where we sat at individual low tables on the tatami mats for the formal opening of the conference. Each table had ten or twelve separate dishes of food including a heavy emphasis on fish, and its own supply of sake. At the beginning of the dinner, several welcome speeches were given both by the heads of the Japanese and American delegations, with attempts to offer both in Japanese and in English seventeen-syllable Japanese Haikus. The mayor of the larger town, Nihomnatsu, about twenty minutes away from this smaller resort area, spoke to us in Japanese, calling himself the happiest mayor in Japan, welcoming us, telling us about the area, and informing us that since the next day was the national elections, it therefore would be a very busy day for him. His interpreter was probably an official from his own office who read a translation into good English for us. Some of the Japanese participants told us later that when the mayor departed from the prepared text, the translator was not able to follow and said less than the mayor had initially said. Sake toasts and formal gift-giving were exchanged between the mayor and the head of the American delegation. As the meal progressed, some of the Japanese participants began to introduce us to the Japanese custom of sitting crosslegged in front of one of the other American or Japanese participants, and undertaking special sake toasts in which the host drinks down his sake, the guest pours sake in his cup, which he again drinks down, and then the host takes the same cup and pours the upraised cup full of sake for the guest. After the host's cup has been used twice, they proceed to do the same for the guest's cup. The Americans were eager learners and the nature of the exchange was intoxicatingly infectious. Unfortunately, one of the early American insensitivities occurred when an American delegation leader halted our exchange so that we could return to the scheduled evening meeting. The workshop might have begun better with no other meetings after the dinner that evening so that we could have time to know each other better as persons. At the end of the workshop, a chief Japanese criticism was that the American planners were not very flexible in adjusting the heavy procedural schedule when a changing situation seemed to dictate such a need.

In our opening sessions that evening, we learned a set of basic definitions for the workshop. The Japanese leaders informed us that their language has no precise term for culture separate from the nation, no concept for process, no term for communication separate from the language, and no term at all to describe intercultural communication which was to be the emphasis of the entire nine days. This lack of precise terms made it very difficult for the Japanese planners to understand or persuade others about the specific values of the workshop. It was to be partly goal-oriented with specific tasks to accomplish and partly process-oriented, letting things happen with attempts to analyze the process which was occurring.[1]

The central emphasis of the workshop was to be an exploration of who we were as individuals, as members of a culture, and as communicators with members of other cultures. One Japanese participant pointed out for us politely but strongly that he was willing to "play our game," but we should all recognize it as an American game, with American rules and not at all consistent with his Japanese sense of pro-

---

[1] If the Japanese had no terms for communication, culture, process and intercultural communication as separate identifiable terms, it must be assumed that the Japanese planners undertook a very courageous and somewhat risky act on their part. This courage mixed with some timidity about the adventure, was made clear both by Japanese leaders in the initial statements and speeches and by several other Japanese participants during the course of the nine-day dialogue. Some Japanese participants told us that they would have received more encouragement from their universities and companies for such a lengthy conference in the United States rather than at home. No doubt too, some of the Americans in attendance found it more appealing and pretigious to attend such a conference in Japan rather than in the United States. Some Japanese and Americans asked frequently what the planners wanted them to do in a specific fashion so that they could attempt to complete the task successfully. We could speculate that some participants were anxious about appearing to fail or lose face with other participants.

fessional information exchange.[2] This poignant warning served to make us all conscious of our own increased need for tolerence throughout the workshop toward the very different departure points from which the Japanese and Americans were starting in developing their dialogue. While we all failed at times to remember or accept some essential differences between the cultures, and although very serious strains were placed on both sets of participants, one success of the conference resulted in the fact that we did learn more about ourselves, and about others as members of a constructively communicating group within the cultural constraints that we were facing individually and together.

[2] The statement by the Japanese participant who indicated that we were playing an American game with American rules indicated his own anxiety. This anxiety may have accounted for the feeling on the part of some American participants that the Japanese had adopted a client attitude toward the workshop, with the feeling that they were responsible for learning a new set of methods so that they could later incorporate them into their own training efforts. Attempts had been made by both the Japanese and American planners to avoid such a client attitude, except that the Americans had recommended the workshop and had proposed early recommendations for conducting it, which the Japanese planners generally accepted. Some Japanese felt that they were forced to compromise more throughout the workshop than did the Americans.

CHAPTER 13

Beginning the Dialogue

July 8: Communicating just to communicate

Today we formed into small groups of eight, four Japanese and four Americans. Most groups included participants who could speak a fair amount of English; one group used professional interpreters when necessary; and one group spoke entirely in Japanese. Our chief purpose for the greater portion of the next several days was simply to communicate, in whatever way and about whatever topics our group decided upon. Our only restriction was that when we met for six hours daily as an official group, we were expected to meet in the same room so that the entire event could be videotaped and monitored, both for own own later partial viewing and analysis, and so that data would be available for research projects emerging from the workshop.

Certain hypotheses had been advanced about the comparative communicative styles of the Japanese and the Americans in relation to age and sex differences, different styles of facilitators and participants, in terms of the groups in which mostly English was spoken or in which a considerable amount of interpreting was necessary, or in the all-Japanese language group. One prediction which was made, correctly it turned out, was that the Japanese language group would have the greatest difficultly adapting to the process orientation of the workshop because of the tendency toward more formality in the Japanese language.

Within our own group of four Japanese and four Americans there was considerable diversity. Our American facilitator or leader was Mark, a twenty-seven-year old married staff member dealing with American students studying abroad in his own American university. He had lived in Japan for one year and spoke some Japanese. His Japanese co-facilitator was Mr. Osuzawa, age sixty-two, who had been involved extensively in various internationally and overseas assignments. Our youngest participant was Miss Takahashi, an undergraduate student in a Japanese university with plans to study in the United States. Other participants included an American married graduate student in the teaching of English as a foreign language. Rachel was in her mid-twenties. There was also a married Japanese professor in his mid-thirties who had received an American degree, Mr. Shirai, and Mrs. Nishihawa, a married Japanese professor in a woman's college in her early fifties. She also had obtained an American degree in teaching English as a second language.[1]

Our early dialogue was interesting primarily because it quickly involved us in discussing various interesting Japanese and American communicative and cultural tendencies, and interests among the group itself. Based upon my notes at the time, the following is a rough approximation of my perceptions of key aspects of our beginning dialogue. Comments made in the dialogue should not be taken as necessarily representative of the two cultures and must be seen as being filtered through my own subjective perceptions. For this reason, not to be further distracting, I have not included my own modest contributions to the dialogue itself, although I do occasionally offer my own value inferences. It should also be noted that the presence of the videotape machine aimed toward us during our entire dialogue, and the fact that I was taking notes during most of our discussions, may both have served to hamper free discussion at some points. Still, some very sensitive communication

---

[1] Names of members in our group have been changed. The Japanese generally preferred last names in our group, while the Americans preferred first names. These distinctions are maintained to demonstrate the relative differences in formality between the Japanese and Americans throughout our discussions. Within the dialogue itself, *san* is often added to names by the speakers as a mark of respect both to male and female surnames. Some few details have been changed.

breakdowns within the group itself, which are not included directly since real persons are involved in the dialogue, did occur and were fairly accurately recorded by the videotape which was constantly in action.

Mr. Osuzawa   The first intercultural difference is in the forms of address. You Americans typically use first names and the Japanese like to be called by the family name, either with or without Mr. or *san*, for example Kato-san. The Americans also tend to use names in conversation: "Paul, what do you think?" The Japanese rarely do.

Mr. Shirai   I feel more comfortable being called by my first name in an American setting, but I would expect a Japanese to call me by my last name.

Mrs. Nishikawa   An American woman friend twenty years older than I insists that I call her Helen. It is difficult for me to do so as I would never do it in Japanese society. I solved the problem eventually by calling her Helen-san. She accepts this in lieu of being called totally by her first name, and I have compromised by not calling her by her last name, as I would prefer.

Mr. Osuzawa   While I am older, I also consider myself romantic. Don't worry if I appear to be formal and older. I may appear so because of my background and age, but I am young at heart or romantic. So you may call me what you wish.[2]

---

[2] The concepts of naming and forms of address, both formal and informal, are important to most cultures, including both Japanese and American societies. Problems relating to naming and forms of address played a large part in our discussions. One group made the subject of nicknaming the emphasis of a final ten minute video tape prepared by their group, and one American in our group tried unsuccessfully to get us to give nicknames to each other. Most Americans have given names which tend to lend themselves to nicknaming, though different Americans enjoy or permit the use of nicknaming with varying degrees of acceptability. We also like to provide persons like the Japanese with nicknames because often their actual names are difficult to pronounce and we feel awkard not being able to pronounce their given or family names. The Japanese male, Mr. Shirai, could feel comfortable being called by his first name by an American but not by a Japanese partly because the Japanese language is fundamentally more formal and English is more informal. In some American college and university settings, students are almost always called by their first names, but in other more rare cases they are called by their last names. How do you react to being called by your last name by student friends in class, by your instructors, by children, by the parents of your friends? How would you react if an acquaintance selected a nickname for you which you didn't feel particularly complimentary? How do you feel about calling adults considerably older than yourself by their first names? If you were in a totally Japanese setting, how would you feel about the more formal approach in terms of naming and forms of address? If you are a woman, do you choose to be addressed formally as Miss, Mrs., or Ms? If you are a man, how do you choose to call women among these categories? The Japanese solve this dilemna by addressing both men and women with the added *san* to the name.

Rachel   I feel isolated because of my inability to communicate through language. Everytime I walk down the hall I can't speak to the employees.

Mr. Shirai   How do you communicate, nonverbally?

Rachel   I bow and smile, but I feel a little silly being able to do only that.

Mark   I feel uncomfortable even though I speak Japanese. Even the nature of the bow was hard for me to get used to. Then my family laughed when I came home because I bowed so much. This offended me as the bow had started to become second nature to me.

Mrs. Nishikawa   The simple fact that Americans bow is strange to us. We would expect to shake hands in America, but don't expect the Americans to bow here. I was surprised recently by an American who said that Japan was the most racist society. We didn't expect him to do like we do. We don't expect Americans to be able to authentically duplicate our language, customs, culture, etc. He thought that these attitudes made us seem racist.

Mr. Osuzawa   Above all, the Japanese want to remain Japanese. (Here a lengthy discussion occurred about the relations concerning ritual, bowing, touching, and gift-giving and receiving).

Mr. Shirai   I have taught in a girls' high school and now in a women's university and I notice that many of the girls and women walk arm in arm and hand in hand. Boys would not do it much.

Mrs. Nishikawa   We seek for a unisexual emphasis in Japan. The U.S. appears to be more bisexual. The members of the same sex touch each other for a longer period in Japan perhaps than in the U.S. American friends start to worry if members of the same sex stay together much longer. I think that your society looks at man and woman as a unit.[3]

[3] How do you feel about being touched and touching, apart from contact sports and accidental contacts, between yourself and other members of your sex, between yourself and members of the opposite sex, and between yourself and your parents? In each of these categories, would you say that you touch and are touched, frequently, occasionally, or infrequently? Are there certain parts of the body for persons in these categories which you feel very comfortable, or uncomfortable about touching or having touched? How do you feel about holding hands or embracing with members of the same sex, members of the

Mark   Couples are always invited as a unit.

Mr. Osuzawa   In Japan the professional gets the formal invitation by himself or herself, almost never as a couple. (A discussion about role reversal followed.)

Florence   My husband had some dissonance with me coming from home to attend this conference without bringing him along. He is used to going to conferences alone, or taking me, but this is the first foreign conference that I have come to by myself.

Mr. Shirai   When I was at my American university I was completely free from the bondage of my family.

Rachel   I feel myself bristling at that statement.

Mark   That is a terrible thing to say.

Mr. Shirai   My freedom from the bondage of the family is entirely necessary. I wouldn't think of taking my wife or children to a conference or out for an evening with my professional friends. My wife wouldn't expect it. I'll be in the states for three weeks this summer, and I wouldn't think of taking her along and she wouldn't think of asking to go. It's O.K. for Rachel as an American married woman to be here with or without her husband if she chooses. Nishikawa-san is not exactly a typical Japanese woman or she would be at home and her husband would be here.

Mr. Osuzawa   I prefer having the sex mix about half women and half men. For one thing, the Japanese women professionals speak better English than the men. I would have encouraged students to come because intercultural communication is such a new experience for Japanese students. Among your delegation there is a wide variety of students, professionals, professors, all of whom have wide experiences in intercultural communication. Our students need this experience. I welcome more committed students.

---

opposite sex, and with parents? Why do American girls and women often dance with members of the same sex, but American boys and men rarely do so? Do you agree with the statement by Mrs. Nishikawa that in the United States there appears to be a greater emphasis on bisexuality? She stressed that in Japan there is a greater emphasis on unisexuality. Is there evidence to show that American youth are becoming more unisexually oriented?

Mr. Shirai   The women essentially are still expected to stay at home, or shop in Japan.

Mr. Osuzawa   Volunteer community service is very evident in the U.S., especially among women. In Japan, this role is almost nonexistent. There is no awareness of such possiblities for women here.

Rachel   In the United States, women are wanting to start moving beyond that phrase.

Mrs. Nishikawa   Some active women here need to start things and get others to follow.

Mr. Osuzawa   Some women, wives of professionals here, are starting to take side jobs, as the Germans say "Arbeit." They could take up community service instead of the side-jobs.

Mark   The women in the U.S. still have trouble being taken seriously. American men expect them to have their outlet through the community service rather than through more serious outlets.

Rachel   In a sense this outlet is a trap for American women.[4]

July 9: Discussing the role of sexism

The aspects selected here for rough approximation of our dialogue demonstrate our group's increasing concern with sexism as an important aspect of communication breakdowns.

Mark   I have a hard time communicating with Japanese and American men, less trouble with Japanese and American women. You, Osuzawa-san, as my cofacilitator and an older Japanese male, are hard to get to know. Japanese males seem to me to be superior, sexist—and I need to generalize on other Japanese men from the Japanese men whom I meet here.

Mr. Shirai   We all bow to an older experienced person such as Osuzawa-san.

---

[4] Two of the Americans became somewhat disturbed at the statement by the Japanese male, Mr. Shirai, that he needed to be free from the bondage of his family. How would you react to such a statement? How do you feel about the Japanese attitudes toward women expressed in this dialogue? Would you agree with the statement by the American facilitator (Mark) that in the United States women still have difficulty being taken seriously? Rachel called emphasis on volunteer service a trap for American women, but a way in which Japanese women could be expected to move. Is it?

Mrs. Nishikawa   We try to be in top form in front of a person of Osuzawa-san's experiences.

Mr. Osuzawa   That is disappointing that you would not feel free to discuss topics freely and that you must feel reserved with me. My young women friends are very relaxed with me.

Mrs. Nishikawa   I am more traditionally bound—despite my Westernized appearance. I would use different language and linguistic tone with older and younger Japanese males. When Osuzawa-san addresses me formally, with the *san*, I automatically feel myself and my body moving in a more traditional style and saying "hai" with a quick bow.

Florence   Older Americans often are flattered by more informality in name-calling.

Mr. Osuzawa   English has only one first personal pronoun for the singular and one for plural. Japanese has perhaps fifteen different situations. To express "me" there are many words. One "me" is only for the male, another is for the female.

Mrs. Nishikawa   We don't use the "you" pronoun. We use the more formal titles. You can use "you" pronouns to your spouse or inferiors, but not to others.

Mr. Osuzawa   Until recently, there has been no word for the singular third-person pronoun in Japanese.

Mrs. Nishikawa   You can't use the language of the Japanese without knowing to whom you are speaking.

Miss Takahashi   People say that I am very expressive nonverbally. This is unusual for a Japanese woman.

Mr. Shirai   Japanese students often become very Westernized here and then when they go to the U.S. they find that they become more Japanese than they were at home. I never wear Japanese-style clothes at home, but when I went to study in the U.S. I found that I was wearing the Japanese-style clothes more.

Mrs. Nishikawa   When I was at my American university, the International Center was always asking us to wear our kimono and do traditional dances. Normally, I wouldn't emphasize my Japanese character unless asked to do so, as I wanted to fit in quietly. Even in Japan, I don't often wear traditional clothing and have never done traditional Japanese dancing.

Florence   Were you insulted in the U.S. by being asked to wear the kimono?

Mrs. Nishikawa   The Fulbright office asked us to bring along at least one kimono to the U.S. I had to learn how to wear one as I had never worn one before. My mother was horrified when she saw a picture of me in the U.S. wearing the kimono wrong. She felt that I had embarrassed our family and Japan. Americans are very imaginative in using our clothing. It is something that I like, but sometimes I giggle and hide my face.

Rachel   I felt that Michael's putting the tea just now in front of Nishikawa-san to pour was sexist and that he was unaware of this sexist role, but that he can deal with this revelation. I wouldn't think of pointing this out to one of the Japanese men in our group if he had done the same thing.

Mr. Shirai   The psychology of Japanese who buy a new kimono before taking a trip abroad is very interesting.

Mark   We have a critical incident here (or a potential communication breakdown). We were off on a subject in which a "fishbowl" analysis (a process observation of an ongoing communication event) was just being made about a sexist action which could be corrected, and here is Shirai-san changing the subject back to buying kimonos for traveling abroad. His avoidance is sexist too. Perhaps we should talk about it.

Mr. Osuzawa   I don't frankly feel willing to open the subject on sexism which you seem to want to move to. I am not so liberated that I want to talk about sex. I have never been in a coed situation. Sex is generally not a topic to be discussed either at home or at school. If such a discussion is initiated by my daughter and my wife, I withdraw myself and I try to turn the discussion to another subject immediately or I leave the room.

Miss Takahashi   I wouldn't initiate such a discussion myself. I try to shut my ears or turn away the subject. I would not talk about sex with my girlfriends.

Mrs. Nishikawa   Sociologically, I can discuss sex trends, but my personal views about sex would never be mentioned. Love on a personal level between man and woman would never be discussed at home, or with my friends, or with my students. After the war, American movies with kissing were shocking to us. We couldn't watch them. Belafonte gave a performance and the Japanese teenage girls ran up and hugged him, and we had to turn away, sick at our stomachs. My built-in system doesn't allow a very vivid display of affection. Our body language is very subtle.

Mr. Shirai   I am very much more liberated on this subject than the average Japanese male. I speak freely in front of my friends about sex or even in front of my women students. Sometimes my women students are embarrassed and I don't discuss sex to embarrass them, but to make an important point in the discussion.

Mr. Osuzawa   The Japanese males in private are very fond of pornography and in a teachers' room eventually all the men might move into dirty sex talk, but if a woman comes in, they would not continue it. I wouldn't stay myself in such a conversation. The men are much more frank among men, especially when alcohol loosens their inhibitions. Intellectually, I would encourage more frank discussion about sex, but emotionally I am not able.

Mrs. Nishikawa   In my women's college, the women are totally unprepared, but no one would discuss basic sex essentials, either in the classroom, or in a private counseling session or at home by the parents or older girls.[5]

July 10: The field trip and the mayor's luncheon

Today, we were scheduled to break from our group discussions, which was happy news for our group and others too, I am sure. By this time in the workshop, there were rumors of com-

---

[5] When the topic in the dialogue turned toward sexism and sex, three of the Japanese members of the group, the Japanese woman student, Miss Takahashi, the middle-aged woman, Mrs. Nishikawa, and the older man, Mr. Osuzawa, all expressed their aversion to discussing either sexism or sex. Only the male, Mr. Shirai, indicated his willingness to talk about these subjects, and especially in front of members of the opposite sex. In a mixed group of four of your American friends or family ranging in age from twenty-two to sixty-two, would the responses be generally similar to those of the four Japanese in relation to their willingness to speak freely about such subjects as sexism and sex? In a mixed group all your age or in a group of your own sex, how would these attitudes be similar or different? Do you feel free to discuss such subjects on a personal level in a college class? Is your body language in relation to such subjects similar or different than the statement made by the Japanese woman, Mrs. Nishikawa, "Our body language is very subtle"? Do you feel free or restricted to make an open display of affection with your parents and family, members of the opposite sex, and members of the same sex?

munication breakdowns occurring in several groups and strong personality clashes had occurred in our own group between two of the Americans. Without specific task orientation the last two days, a number of the groups had been suffering the frustration of aimlessness. A morning tour was planned of Nihommatsu, the larger town about twenty minutes from our little resort area so that we could briefly see an elementary school, an English-language class in a secondary school, a silkworm farm, a silk factory, a company making wooden chests of drawers, a footware-producing factory and outlet, and a pottery factory to get some sense of how others worked and lived here. At noon the official mayor's luncheon was being given, and the afternoon was free for individual projects. Although the day had been billed by the conference leaders as a day for collecting extra data for our discussions and journals, it seemed a subtle recognition early in the planning that by this time in the workshop the intensity of our projects and discussions would need some relief, though our leaders couldn't quite bring themselves simply to give us the day off for fear that our entire nine days would not be spent eventfully.

The mayor's luncheon was a curious mixture of Japanese and Western cuisine. There were cold fish cakes, and Japanese-style fruits and vegetables on separate plates, and in addition, a bottle of Coke, a carton of milk, and a plate of small American-style sandwiches for each guest. As had happened at our opening banquet, speeches were given at the beginning of the meal with toasts being exchanged between the mayor and the head of the American delegation. Various heads of the city government were introduced, as well as the presidents of the local Junior Chamber of Commerce, the Lions, and the Rotary, all American-type organizations. Several smaller tables flanked the main one for the local dignitaries, and a special small table had been set for our two professional interpreters who were to assist in simultaneous translation, but the mayor decided to make a spot for them at his left and right, which apparently was an unusually gracious act on his part, since interpreters normally receive a much lower spot in such an event in Japan.

After the luncheon, the mayor consented to respond to our questions and promised to try to answer as fairly as possible. No one at the workshop had expected this opportunity, and it took a little time before people started asking questions. One member of the Japanese delegation began asking a series of politically sensitive questions, especially since the national election had just been held three days before and the mayor's party had done less well at the polls than had been expected. The "happiest mayor in all of Japan" was less happy with the election results and the relative loss of strength for his party, but did proceed to answer the questions. With the usual Japanese dexterity for moving around difficult questions without being directly insulting, but still more open than we would have predicted for a politician, the mayor seemed to hold his own very well.

Previously, the Japanese members of our small group had taught us the art of gift-wrapping and gift-giving with the appropriate ceremony of how to present such a gift, saying at the same time, "What an insignificant gift this is, and I feel ashamed to offer you such a worthless token, but I hope that you will accept it." When most of the questioning had ended, one of the American participants in our group practiced the newly learned art by presenting the mayor a small gift. The mayor accepted it in the appropriate fashion and ended his dialogue unexpectedly by asking the Americans present what we thought about the Japanese-style democracy. After a long pause, an American struggled to his feet and offered some vaguely polite response which effectively provided a sense of closure for the event. As in so many Japanese situations, as our Japanese colleagues later informed us, the type of response was less important than the fact that a response had been made on our behalf.

When the luncheon ended, we all departed. Unfortunately, from the point of view of some of our group's participants, there had been considerable tension in our group the day before and an actual serious communication breakdown had occurred there, but our group decided to remain together for the afternoon so that we would have similar experiences for our discussions the next day. Japanese and American friends from other small groups had invited us to join them for the afternoon on their own excursions, but although we were tempted to leave our group, we felt constrained to remain with the group because of our collective decision. Part of our afternoon was spent in an out-of-the-way coffee shop in which the proprietor and his wife were delighted with our presence and requested permission to take several photos of us to hang on their walls. Later, the women in the group spent time in a kimono shop. We returned to the spa by a public bus during the rush hour. Since we were standing, our large frames caused much smiling from the secondary school students on board the bus.[6]

[6] Would you have remained with the small group in its movement around the town if you were frustrated at staying together (as several members of the group were), or would you have joined your other friends who invited you to accompany them on their excursions? Without breaking group solidarity, were there other alternatives which individuals in the group could have taken to relieve the frustration of feeling that we had to remain together?

CHAPTER 14

Communication Breakdowns

July 11: Processing communication breakdowns in general and our own communication breakdowns specifically

As our discussions resumed as a group, we talked about various aspects of intercultural communication, conflict resolution within a culture, and we eventually returned to a discussion of sexism with an exploration of the women's movement in Japan and the United States. The dialogue which follows again continues to be an approximation of our discussion.

Mr. Shirai   In Japanese culture, what not to say is more important than what to say. In terms of my expectations for the workshop, I would rather learn about intercultural communication gaps, rather than about interpersonal gaps within a culture—even though these gaps may be closer to us than we expect. I would like to talk about Japanese-American cultural communication programs and problems.

Florence   My ideas agree with those of Shirai-san. I deal with about 200 Japanese a year, many students, and more visitors.

Miss Takahashi   I began to learn English when I was about thirteen. When I entered the university, I wanted to learn not only English, but American culture, too. I found that the more that I learned about American culture, the more I learned about my own Japanese culture. Communication as a major seems to tie in to my own daily life better than such subjects as anthropology or sociology. After college, I don't know what I will do. I am certified to teach Japanese as a second language and may be interested in becoming a simultaneous interpreter. I will study in the U.S. next year.

Mark I advise students in helping them prepare for an overseas experience—working, traveling, and seeking funding. I administer the predoctoral Fulbright, Marshall, and Rhodes scholarship competitions. I am always working with American students. Intercultural communication experiences are not always happy or successful experiences. I find it impossible to isolate the academic from the interpersonal experiences.

Rachel About 20 percent of the students in our English as second language classes are Japanese. I find it hard to talk with them and to understand their behavioral patterns and problems. As their American teacher, I find it hard to relate to them. I'm interested in teaching American culture and literature to foreign students. Advising foreign students is an interest of mine, but at my university the foreign student advisor is essentially a clerk and worries about my interest in advising for fear that I may be after the job. I'd like to learn how to attribute meaning to behavior. I was a Peace Corps worker in the Philippines. I had lots of culture shock, but eventually I hated to leave. Lots of the Peace Corps workers there became hostile and bitter, and sustained almost total communication breakdown. This gave me considerable insights. I had another cultural shock again when I returned to the U.S. My family and friends seemed hostile, greedy, and self-interested. I married a few months later and had to work out my relationship with my husband. He had been a Peace Corps member too. We had a hard time accepting the materialism and superficiality of American life.

Mrs. Nishikawa Shirai-san has summed up my feelings. I also teach English as a second language. I thought that learning English well was all that was necessary, but I now realize that learning the English was the simplest part. When one is aware of the complexities of the culture, more comes into the understanding of the culture. I've never attended an international workshop of this sort. There are no formal lectures to talk about which provide a conversation topic without fully exposing ourselves. Here we are all openly exposed. Some of you have certainly exposed yourselves and your emotions.

Mr. Osuzawa I was almost forced to be involved in the workshop very early without wanting to be involved or taking the initiative. Nevertheless, I took responsiblity in the joint committee. As intercultural communication simply cannot be translated into Japanese, we just had to take it on good faith and go with it. I was always aware that there were problems in intercultural communication, without knowing the term. The Japan Planning Committee for this workshop took almost no initiative and responded mostly on the basis of the American suggestions. This workshop probably is not applicable to third world situations and we are not interested in sending volunteers to the U.S. I already knew many friends from the U.S. and did not find the workshop necessary simply to develop new friends. I began practicing my English in Afghanistan at the age of forty-two and found that it isn't so hard to learn well if there is a practical necessity for it.[1]

---

[1] Would you agree with the statement by Miss Takahashi that when you begin to attempt to learn about another culture, you also find yourself learning more about your own culture? If so, why would this occur? Would you agree with the American facilitator, Mark, when he commented that intercultural communication experiences are not always happy or successful? Why? If you have found yourself in unhappy or unsuccessful intercultural communication experiences, how have you tried to resolve them? Have others in the situation helped or hindered the solution of these problems? Why is it likely that the Peace Corps workers in the Philippines faced such serious and sustained communication breakdown that they had to return home? Rachel faced a cultural shock when she returned home because she found her family and friends hostile, greedy, and self-interested. What had happened to her own value system, which probably had been similar to that of her family and friends as she knew them before going to the Philippines? From her comments, we can assume that her return culture shock lasted a long time. What steps would seem necessary to overcome this culture shock? How would you handle such a culture shock after a two-year period working with a proud culture whose values were consistently opposite those which you had developed before undertaking the assignment?

Mrs. Nishikawa's statement about the extensive self-exposure to which the workshop participants were subjected was somewhat representative of the comments of many of the Japanese participants and some of the American participants at the workshop. It seems unfair of the American planners to force the Japanese to involve themselves in such a potentially dangerous hostile environment for a sustained period. I wonder whether the benefits of such a situation outweighed the disadvantages which it caused for the Japanese concept of harmony and the avoidance of wounding human feelings. It is obvious from Mr. Osuzawa's remarks that he perceived the Japanese planning team as taking little initiative. On the other hand, the American members of the planning team attempted to involve the Japanese heavily at every step. Does this simply appear to be a fundamental difference between the two value systems? Or did the American team simply appear to approach the problem from the wrong direction? How could such a difference be resolved?

Mark   Rachel, you look as though you are sitting on something.

Rachel   I am. I'd like to talk about our experiences yesterday. It didn't sit well.

Mark   It was a pleasant day, but superficial.

Florence   The morning was more valuable but it was superficial too. In the coffee shop, the proprietor said that we were his first foreign guests. He took lots of pictures of us, but we never thought to have him and his wife sit down with us and engage in a real intercultural communication. We even had interpreters present.

Mrs. Nishikawa   We went to meet a "go-between" for marriages yesterday. He never met his wife until his wedding day. He tries not to allow this to happen now. When he got married he couldn't look at her closely because of her traditional veil and he didn't know what she looked like until after the wedding. This is typical of the old arranged marriages. Such couples, if they feel happily married themselves, feel obligated to arrange at least three marriages in the same way.

Mr. Osuzawa   My marriage was arranged like this during the war.

Mrs. Nishikawa   In this community (Niohmmmatsu) before the war, 99 percent of all the marriages were arranged, but now only about 50 percent are. In the prewar periods only the two sets of parents met, and the children would simply follow if the parents were acceptable to each other. Now it is much different. The "go-between" checks around to find out about different marriageable persons, receives documents on their background, and exchanges pictures between the bride and groom.

Rachel   This makes me shiver all over.

Mark   My wife and I had known each other for twelve years before we married. When we decided to get married, it only took a week. When the Japanese arranged marriage fails to take place, everyone is very evasive. The way the "go-between" shows the parents the unfavorable decision is to say that the fortune teller has said it is unfavorable, and then the fortune teller can be the scapegoat and take the blame. People have to be able to trust the "go-between," and he is usually a member of a higher class than those for whom he is arranging the marriage. The "go-between" in Japan is always a couple. The man is not so interested in match-making, but his wife is.[2]

Rachel   Why weren't we able to say yesterday that we wanted to break the group loyalty if we were all so frustrated?

Florence   Even in an American group, if I had made the commitment to stay together, even if I didn't like it, I would have stayed with the group.

Mr. Osuzawa   Using a conflict that we have seen here at the workshop, can we generalize to a situation like that in a company? A couple of years ago there was a bitter confrontation between me and my boss. Under normal circumstances, I would have been forced to quit my job. I didn't. We would pass in the corridor and not speak for more than a year. He was forced to retire before retirement age. I passed the official retirement age of fifty-five and stayed on. This critical incident had an exceptional solution. The confrontation was bitter and well-known. Though a retiree often comes back to visit with the office staff, my boss never did.

Mr. Shirai   Such a thing has never happened to me. I don't have that much courage of my convictions. I would probably resign. I am easy-going. I drink to have fun, but not to let off steam.

Mr. Osuzawa   A lot of Japanese males would go to a sake shop and try to work it out by drinking. To generalize—whether the

---

[2] Since our group members were essentially the only visitors in the coffee shop when the proprietor took many photographs of us and told us that we were his first foreign visitors, it was a shame that we failed to invite him and his wife to join us to discuss ideas which might seem important to them, especially because there were Japanese among our group. Our discussion about the "go-between" for marriages demonstrated a strong difference in values between the Japanese and American societies. The one comment by Rachel, "This makes me shiver all over," probably summed up the American group's attitude toward such marriages. The earlier communicative style of having only the parents meet each other before the marriage was arranged also suggests a strong difference in the communication patterns of the two societies. As an American, how would you respond if a friend or member of the family tried to "fix you up" with an available person interested in marriage? How do you respond to the blind date which your friend may try to arrange for you? If you are on a blind date, and you feel uncomfortable or think that it isn't working well, how do you respond? If you lived in an area where there were a number of Japanese, and a very traditional Japanese asked you to serve as a "go-between" for arranging a marriage with a Japanese woman, how would you respond?

matter is wrong or right is not so important in Japan as not to wound human relationships.

Rachel Feeling that you are right in the American situation would probably carry more weight than people's feelings.

Mr. Osuzawa In Japan, there is a big risk in fighting a superior. A subtle pressure would exist thereafter. In Japan a person is in a narrow situation always with his social relationships.

Mrs. Nishikawa Just a little deviation from the norm would win the stamp of troublemaker in Japan.

Rachel I had a serious confrontation with my library boss. I was being paid the lowest salary but I was working at two levels higher. I didn't lose my job but the superior never spoke to me again after I had made a big complaint. I had a sort of cowardly satisfaction after I quit later, as my job was raised two pay levels which I had felt I deserved.

Mr. Osuzawa Looking at my case, how would Shirai-san solve it?

Mrs. Nishikawa Osuzawa-san, you were not working in your company alone. Were there others supporting you which would encourage you to take the strong action against your boss? Without knowing the context, I don't know whether you were deserting those who were working with you or whether you were being foolhardy.

Mr. Osuzawa I decided to fight alone. I knew that there were many supporters in the beginning but that they would drop away.

Mr. Shirai In my case, if there were a problem in teaching, the students would remain mutual friends with me. The students would not take sides, whereas in a commercial situation with their livelihood at stake, they might have to take sides.

Mr. Osuzawa No. They didn't want to take sides in my case. I didn't want to take supporters down with me.

Florence Many Americans would try to create a power struggle at such a point.

Mr. Osuzawa If I lose, I haven't carried others down with me.

This tendency to fight back is disappearing among the younger Japanese generations.

Rachel   After I quit my job, when my job was reclassified, I got an extra paycheck. The women's group here that we had—the Japanese women spoke up a lot. There was an immediate sense of trust among us.

Florence   Not much happened there, but something happened.

Mr. Osuzawa   I want to say something nasty about the women's meeting: the weak band together.

Rachel   I would expect that from you. We are the powerless who are strong.

Mr. Osuzawa   The unions are getting stronger here in Japan—but it was the weak who began to band together. There was always a small core, intelligent and aggressive who started to make the unions popular and acceptable. The weakest have no power, but they join the unions and that gives them the power which they are unable to achieve alone.

Mark   In the women's movement—it isn't always clear who are the strong and who are the weak. Perhaps if the women are weak, they find some courage together.

Rachel   My gut reaction is that not everybody can have power. If a society creates weak people, how can you despise them? It is infuriating to hear men talking condescendingly that way. Osuzawa-san, you don't even recognize that you are being sexist. Mark at least recognizes when he is sexist.[3]

Mr. Osuzawa   I am one of the few Japanese men of my age who understands this issue better than others. I understand how the women have been forced to stay at home. I am a supporter of women's liberation in this country. Thus I don't understand forming a separate women's club within a labor union. Usually there is a special women's group anyway. This

---

[3] Rachel stressed her feeling that Mr. Osuzawa was highly sexist, which he himself contradicted. In the continuing discussion, the Americans and Mr. Osuzawa perceived the role of sexism very differently, based on their own cultural biases. As an American woman, would you identify more strongly with the views of the American or the Japanese women? As an American man, do you consider the Japanese males, Mr. Osuzawa and Mr. Shirai, as sexists as they are portrayed in the available dialogue? Do you identify more strongly with the American or Japanese position on the subject?

seems to suggest a reverse sexism. They are saying that women are special and too good to allow men in their group—like the dinner table here, where all the women wanted to keep the men away from their table. Some of the men had their feelings hurt. That was really sexist.

Florence   You still don't seem to understand, Osuzawa-san.

Mrs. Nishikawa   Osuzawa-san has exposed his philosophy of fighting it alone. His view of the women's group is to let each individual make it alone.

Rachel   We have tried to do it on our own—as a few in Japan have also done. The women's rights issues are good to provide an analogy with the American labor unions fifty years ago. Any worker who said then "I'll fight alone" would be rubbed out. There is no way to make it alone. The American women are now where the American labor unions were fifty years ago.

Mark   I think that men can make it alone better than women. The women have to come twice as far to catch up. In the U.S. they have begun to use the law through law suits, to win their rights. We men need to help them.

Rachel   Osuzawa-san, it is easy for you to say that you ought to pull yourself up. You are in the top strata of Japanese society. We have to fight battles that you don't even have to fight. You are really a special kind of man.

Florence   The Japanese woman would still start behind you no matter how competent she was.

Mark   If a Japanese woman doesn't marry, she will have certain problems, and if she does marry, she will have other problems.

Mr. Osuzawa   Nishikawa-san, were you aware of this difficulty of American women when you studied in the states?

Mrs. Nishikawa   No. I wasn't aware of such social difficulties. In Japanese society the American sort of approach would not work. Rachel says how they divide up their work, she and her husband. I say, "Wow! Really! I wish it would work for me."

Florence   My husband is about the age of Osuzawa-san. He wouldn't prepare the meal, but he does the dishes, which he feels competent to do. Would this happen in your society?

Mrs. Nishikawa   No. Certainly not. I consider myself lucky to have a husband who allows me to pursue my own interests. I don't want to put extra burdens on him. What Florence's husband did could never happen in my own home.

Mark   But how do you feel about it?

Mrs. Nishikawa   It is my life—and I can't change that.

Mr. Osuzawa   Were you, Takahashi-san, aware of the women's liberation in the U.S.? How do you feel about it?

Miss Takahashi   I have two personalities. I think women should take care of all the household things. I don't mind. If my father helps, I don't mind, but I'd just as soon do it myself. I was asked to marry a very typical Japanese man who is a good man. He would allow me to do whatever I would want after marriage. But if I would concentrate on my household work, I wouldn't be able to do what I want. Two weeks ago I told his mother that I couldn't marry him. I don't know which personality in me is stronger.

Mrs. Nishikawa   I don't feel any injustice in my case. I feel so tired sometimes and I have papers to grade. I know that my husband would say, "That's your calling."

Florence   That would infuriate me.

Rachel   Me, too—he makes me mad just thinking about it.

Mr. Osuzawa   Shirai-san, were you aware in the U.S. of the discrimination against women?

Mr. Shirai   I was very glad that I was married to a Japanese woman, and as I said before, I was glad to be free from the bondage of my family. At the same time, I wished that our women would have a chance to do useful activities.

Mark   If your wife had been along in the U.S. and you were to respond to these favorable responses, how would you?

Mr. Shirai   I think that I would stay in my present situation. It is a matter of value and happiness. My wife is very happy at home with the children. If I tried to press her to go out she would be frustrated.

Rachel   That's what they were saying about the American slaves—"They will be frustrated if they leave their plantations."

Mr. Shirai   American women are kind and stimulating to be with, but not the ideal type of woman for me. I like my wife the way she is. She is kind, obedient, and satisfied.

Mark   What if your wife became disobedient or dissatisfied?

Mr. Shirai   I've never thought of it. Why would she? She is Japanese.

Florence   What about when your children are grown up and gone?

Mrs. Nishikawa   That will be very difficult. The matchmaker said that those girls with special talents like woodcarving and music are lovely to look at but very hard to find promising young husbands for. They say, "No, sir, that's not the type of wife I want."

Florence   That is still occurring in the U.S. My daughter likes her single freedom and she doubts that men will find her satisfactory.

Mr. Osuzawa   Let me express my total ignorance that women are suffering so much in the U.S. In my experiences in the U.S., the couple always seems equal. The lady-first syndrome makes me think that at least the women were doing all right there.

Mrs. Nishikawa   The American women stay in the conversation and can keep up with the conversation. I thought they were equal there too.

Rachel   Pretty soon in a conversation here in Japan, the men realize that I am still a woman and begin to ignore me.

Mr. Osuzawa   One consoling fact—when I heard that the women participants were getting together, I didn't like it—but at least the women calling the meeting were good-looking.

Rachel   That is very frustrating. Why must our leaders be good-looking? Men leaders don't have to be good-looking. Older men are not considered past their prime—but older women are. It makes us younger women in the movement appreciate the older women more.

Mr. Osuzawa   My last nasty thing—when women are more interested in kimonos—

Rachel   As long as men think only about our beauty, there is no liberation and no equality.

Mr. Osuzawa   In Japan, men usually talk about four things: jobs, economics, politics and the arts. The women talk about their kimonos.

Mark   The women are being asked to be superhuman. How can they be expected to do everything? How can they talk about male subjects with us if they are kept only as housewives? Being a housewife is a full-time job.

Mr. Osuzawa   I'm thinking of college students or those who claim to be women's liberation fighters.

Mark   Those don't seem to be the issues. Aren't the issues whether women deserve the same respect and dignity in your culture and ours and between cultures?

CHAPTER 15

Concluding the Dialogue

July 12: More potential communication breakdowns

This was our last day to meet as a group to continue our dialogue. We again discussed titles, then moved to a discussion about the Japanese educational system and changing morals in Japan, with some comparisons to American education and morals, and finally ended our dialogue with a criticism of the dialogue itself, its potential assets and problems as a cultural dialogue, and its usefulness for better understanding of the members of the other culture.

Mr. Osuzawa   There are three meanings in *sensei,* especially teacher. It is more respectable than *san.* I don't feel uncomfortable in being called Osuzawa-sensei, as I have been a real teacher in the past. The literal meaning is doctor, lawyer, teacher. Other persons called *sensei* are in a higher position of great respect. The Diet members like to be called *sensei.* It could also be used in a somewhat derogatory way—looking down on someone who is older. Usually it honors any older person. If it is pronounced incorrectly, it means "your first wife" and can be embarrassing.

Mr. Shirai   I wouldn't feel comfortable calling you anything without the *san* or *sensei* added, but I wouldn't feel strange calling Prosser-san by his first name, Michael.

Mr. Osuzawa   How do you call your ambassador? In the Southeast Asian countries you must always put "excellency" in front of the name. We just call him ambassador.

Miss Takahashi   I call my father "honorable father," or my older brother, "elder brother." I call the second oldest brother "second son" but never his actual name.

Mr. Osuzawa   The treatment of children—I am an older man and I am fed up with the way our children are brought up in postwar Japan.

Mrs. Nishikawa   In Japan, childhood is the glorious golden time—children are considered unstained. As the child grows older, he or she is considered stained by exposure to society and its problems. In the U.S. you are very much more controlled at the early stages, and ease up later.

Florence   At the elementary school that we visited, the children seemed much more controlled than in the American schools. The Europeans think that American children are bratty, uncontrolled.

Mr. Shirai   At the elementary school, the Japanese visitors were saying, "Oh, how nostalgic, wouldn't it be nice to be children again?"

Mark   The controlled and respected child seems to return the respect of adults. In privacy the American values are very different from the Japanese values.

Miss Takahashi   When I was ten to fifteen years old, I wanted a separate spot to just keep my diary in; only that.

Mrs. Nishikawa   In my family with nine children, three rooms were preserved for study. At night, we all slept in the same space. I learned a great deal from observing my brothers and sisters in such situations.

Mr. Shirai   Western society is a "key" culture. The average American has five or six keys. I have no keys and have never owned a key. I don't drive, so I don't need any keys. My wife is at home when I come home so I don't need a house key.

Rachel   My husband's family is a "lock-the-bathroom-door" type, but my family is much more open, with women showering together and laughing and talking.

Mr. Shirai The cool monster named TV causes the children in my family to never want to go to bed. I have to drive them out of the room by 9:00 P.M.

Mr. Osuzawa For extra study, which naturally makes a group, and we Japanese are very concerned about groups, children are involved heavily in extracurricular activities. The principal of the elementary school that we visited said with pride that the children here have no need to go to *juku* (the extra curricular exercises of an academic nature in Japan). In Toyko, 90 percent of the school children go to *juku* classes. Often teachers do this extra teaching on a part-time basis and charge large fees.

Mrs. Nishikawa I took a group of Japanese students to Europe. Each one had to pay a substantial amount for the trip. Their families paid. The Danish students were astonished that the Japanese students' families would pay for such a trip. It is important to keep up with other families and give the same opportunities. Generally, the families are not affluent, but they feel they must manage somehow to give their children the same benefits that their friends are receiving. The children are taught to be dependent upon their families, and later when the parents become old, they can be dependent upon their children. When their parents give them as much as their friends get, they feel that the children can get into good schools later. We don't have the 11 + exam like the British, but some universities are more prestigious than others and harder to get into, like the University of Tokyo.

Mark Sometimes the Japanese students work two years to get into prestigious universities like the University of Tokyo.

Florence When my children were in the American high schools, many of their friends were very competitive, trying to get into the prestigious Eastern schools. There seemed to be a later trend to downgrade the prestigious schools, and to drop out or to enter the large state universities.

Mr. Osuzawa There is a trend to view the university education as nonsense. These are generally boys who take on a hippie lifestyle.

Mr. Shirai These students are frustrated and disappointed at the life style of the universities and what they consider irrelevant course offerings.

Mark   Now in the U.S. it is harder to get a job even with a Ph.D. This is causing a big reevaluation of higher education there. Employers were impressed that I had a master's degree, but didn't care about what it was in. I wish they would repossess my master's degree, since it cost me more than it was worth.

Florence   Coming back to the Japanese situation and the Japanese child: if children go to the *juku*, how much free time do they have?

Mr. Osuzawa   Practically none. They leave school at 3:00. They may go to *juku* for two hours, and possibly to another *juku*, and then come home to eat supper, take a bath, and go to bed. The children are grouped like sheep, and their life becomes rather regimented. There is no time for children to think or digest information. It starts at about the third grade, and may begin as early as kindergarten.

Mrs. Nishikawa   How many hours in school? We have Saturday morning classes, and school lasts a month or so longer in the summer than in the U.S. Summer vacation is about forty days; the winter vacation is two weeks, and spring vacation is one week.

Mr. Osuzawa   Why are the Japanese parents so interested in sending their children to *juku*?

Mrs. Nishikawa   They want to keep up with the Suzukis or Joneses. They would lack the courage not to send their children if their friends were sending their children.

Miss Takahashi   My mother's friends initially resisted sending their children to *juku*, but finally couldn't resist the social pressure.

Mr. Osuzawa   Before the war, children had more time to play, but not anymore.

Mrs. Nishikawa   I get invited to a lot of my former students' weddings and I'm always invited to give a speech, March to May, and October and November. If I don't give a speech in honor of the bride, then I offend the bride, and her friends think that she did not do well in college. So, I run from banquet hall to banquet hall giving speeches. The groom's guests talk about the glorious future expected for him in business. These speeches are all formalized and stereotyped. The content of the speeches is not important and no one listens—but the point of giving the speeches is important.

Mr. Osuzawa   We are always waiting until the speeches are done. Yesterday's speeches at the party given us by the townspeople were remarkable in terms of their brevity. Prosser-san, when you gave your little speech yesterday to the hotel manager to present him the goose-quill pens at the party, did you notice that no one listened? At least not the Japanese? But, everyone was impressed that you gave the speech and gave him the gift, and afterwards some of the townspeople were congratulating him. Perhaps the brevity of these speeches means the people here were more enlightened.[1]

Mr. Osuzawa   In terms of the education for the boy, the parents will try to provide as much as possible for him, less for the girl. Since the war, a misinterpreted freedom and democracy has set up the idea of providing everything for the children.

---

[1] Are there parallel pressures on American school children like the *juku* in which large numbers of Japanese children are enrolled after school? In your own family, what are the pressures which you faced after school while you were growing up? How are members from different cultures likely to face these pressures? What do such activities say about the value orientations of different cultural groups? The point was made about the differences between the Japanese and American values of privacy, with Miss Takahashi saying that her greatest concern for privacy was just to have a place to keep her diary. What are your attitudes on the importance of privacy? How much privacy do you personally need now as a student? I noted in the schools that I visited in Japan very little privacy available in the toilets, even between the sexes, though considerable modesty still seemed evident. How would this lack of privacy affect you? In Japanese society, many families are extended, with married children and their spouses and grandparents all living in the same house, while in American society, there is a growing trend toward the nuclear family with just the parents and children living in one house, and grandparents and other relatives living far away. How do you respond to the contrasting value of the extended family versus the nuclear family? Under normal circumstances, how would you feel about moving back in with your family after you are married, or about your parents moving in with you when they become older? As a college student, you place a value on college education and reject the view of some Japanese and American youth that attending college or university is nonsense. What is the reasoning for the argument that a college education is important or essential for you versus the view that it is nonsense? The lack of attention which Japanese pay to speeches, while at the same time feeling that it is important that the speeches be given, suggests that the Japanese may distrust language and verbal communication as indicative of real human values. Why?

Mrs. Nishikawa   We went overboard after the war. Our whole traditional system of values was shaken up. Our old values were lost. The young people wanted to have everything American and to shut out all of their past, even the good features.

Florence   There was also a phase of extreme permissiveness in the U.S. too. Dr. Spock helped this trend, as he was read almost like a Bible by young parents.

Mr. Osuzawa   After the war, we grabbed at everything American. We rejected everything traditional. Parents practically lost their authority.

Rachel   There is a current attempt in the American schools to reinstate the old traditions.

Mr. Osuzawa   When I was young, we ate grass boiled in water once a day to flavor the water, or we might have a bowl of rice, or a sweet potato. Everyone was always very thin, nearly starving. Our parents didn't want us to repeat this experience. When Nishikawa-san was small, this extreme poverty was not so great, then when Takahashi-san was a child the situation had improved greatly. Today, our per capita income is better than $2,000, perhaps the highest in Asia. These achievements caused by better material life helped us to lose our guiding principles for our Japanese young people.

Florence   In the U.S. this materialism has caused a rather radical reaction among the young.

Rachel   The change has been more to the joy of working, not for material things. How worthwhile one's life is is becoming more important for some of our young people.

Mr. Osuzawa   Many Japanese youngsters are beginning to say: "What is the worth of life? Is all this what our parents have worked for? Is it useful?" This subtle difference is just starting to occur. A good indication of the change is that some are beginning to want to share their wealth with less privileged people of the world. The Japanese Overseas Corporation Volunteers organization is a good example, though this is still a very small number of persons involved.

Florence   This is a parallel to the situation in the United States. Others are looking for new ways of providing service.

There is a certain religious fanaticism in the U.S. Those who were interested in service through seminaries and religious ministry now seem to be going into social action types of service.

Mr. Osuzawa   But the Japanese aren't even going into social service yet inside Japan. It is more romantic to go to an underprivileged country. As a junior high school teacher, I would punish my students when they needed it. Other teachers and parents would simply give in. Students said on the surface that they didn't like adults who punished them when they were bad, but inwardly they seemed to like it and had more respect for the teachers and parents who made them obey.

Miss Takahashi   On our TV programs, if children are asked if they like being scolded, they say they do when they need it.

Mr. Shirai   When I taught high school, parents came to me and asked me to be strict with their girls as they weren't able to control them at home.

Mr. Osuzawa   The boys are better tolerated in Japan than girls.

Rachel   In the U.S. also, the boy's misconduct is more tolerated too—"Boys will be boys."

Mr. Osuzawa   Here there are severe entrance exams for college and the university, and severe preparation is required. Students must study four to six hours extra at home to be able to compete for these exams. The boy is often given a special room to study in so that he will not be interrupted.

Mr. Shirai   Girls in my university have not studied so hard.

Mr. Osuzawa   My girls always enrolled in international-type schools. They had no problems getting into their university here, though the entrance exams are hard. The student enrolled in the University of Tokyo doesn't have to study hard after he gets in, but he might have to spend an extra two years after high school studying to get in. This is why Japanese students are often two years older than American students when they graduate from the university. They probably aren't any better students than those in many of the other universities and colleges. Suicide occurs sometimes because the students can't get into the university of their choice, and then their families lose face. It is a mistake for Japanese students to be forced to study so hard. It's a period when they should be developing their own interests as young adults. They are educated very narrowly, just to pass the entrance exams, and not about anything else.

Mrs. Nishikawa   We have a mass production of human beings in our colleges and schools.

Mr. Osuzawa   I'm being dogmatic here, but I have noticed that Japanese students are rarely extraordinarily bright; most are simply mediocre. Of course there are many dull American students, but there are proportionately many more extraordinarily bright American students. The bright ones there are much better and more broadly educated than our bright ones.

Rachel   Perhaps the Japanese system doesn't allow non-comformity and thus doesn't encourage the very extraordinary students.

Miss Takahashi   My father didn't want me to go to my university. He said I didn't need to be so intelligent to be a good wife. My mother said I could be whatever I wanted, even if it meant being intelligent too.

Rachel   In my high school, being on the cheering team and dating key athletic figures were the greatest achievements for the girls.

Mrs. Nishikawa   I was so happy that I didn't have to work hard at being popular in my American university because I was Japanese.

Rachel   In college, I was in one of the new coed dorms. There were many disadvantages, but we started to get to know men as people rather than on the usual artificial dating basis.

Florence   What about divorced women in Japan?

Mrs. Nishikawa   The woman is unable to remarry usually, but she generally keeps the children on a very low-support basis.

Mr. Shirai   Men here can divorce easier.

Mr. Osuzawa   The wife usually goes to her parents' home and doesn't leave again. The lawsuits may follow after an actual divorce in terms of getting maintenance for her and the children.

Rachel Why do women leave their husbands in Japan?

Mr. Osuzawa The husband probably is too fond of gambling, or he likes horse-racing better than his wife, or he comes home too often under the heavy influence of sake and is abusive to the wife or children, or he has a mistress, who existed sometimes even before the marriage. Total drunkenness will often lead a woman to leave her husband. There are few Japanese women alcoholics.

Mrs. Nishikawa An American woman not long ago divorced a very high government official. We were all shocked.

Mark He probably deserved it.

Mr. Osuzawa One of the high division chiefs of the party here ran for the presidency and lost but is still a powerful figure. He has had for years a very famous actress mistress. He is too intelligent to be the prime minister. He spent all his money for the Liberal Democratic Party and raised no extra money for the Party. But still he is well liked and people seem not to mind his mistress in the background.[2]

Mark Well, we have a half hour to go. I have the feeling that I have learned nothing new here today. I don't think that we need a critical incident for the sake of a critical incident, but we don't need to be afraid to communicate. Today, we have just talked politely around issues.

---

[2] The point was made that the whole Japanese value system was overturned after World War II, and Florence indicated that the American society had undergone a phase of extreme permissiveness as well. Would you agree about the development of such a phase in American society?

Reflect on major social, religious, or moral values which have changed considerably within your own experience as a member of your own family, in your own specific cultural group, or in your larger society. What types of cultural maximizers help to bring about such changes in society? Two Japanese participants suggested that the Japanese educational system has mass-produced human beings, and that Japanese students essentially are typically more mediocre than American students. Is this potentially a form of stereotyping about Japanese young people by a member of their own culture? How do you feel about the North American educational system in relation to the same question? How much creativity do you think is possible in helping to shift values, beliefs, and assumptions within a culture such as your own? If you feel that the North American system allows more such freedom, does this suggest a perception about American cultural superiority or is it based on facts?

Florence   I brought a task-oriented function to the conference—not a process-orientation for the sake of process-orientation to the group. I'm not frustrated. Why are you?

Mark   I would probably learn more by reading or taking a course.

Florence   But we do have four Japanese—representing different ages and backgrounds. We can all read the printed page but we don't get the interactions that way.

Mark   Here is an observation: only Takahashi-san talked about how she felt about her mother's desire for her to go to a university where she could be intelligent as well as be a good wife.

Florence   You say that we haven't dealt with anything personal. Should we?

Mark   I hoped for much more.

Mr. Osuzawa   What do you want? Actual cultural confrontation?

Mark   There really was very little negative confrontation, which was good. I wanted more personal interaction.

Mr. Shirai   I've been frustrated for two or three reasons. Why I am here? Where am I going? Being confined in the small room, sitting all day for several days in the same position, discussing and discussing, was all very frustrating. The whole workshop seemed to have only the vaguest purpose. Why did they spend so much money for us to sit in such a small group for so long with no real purpose?

Mrs. Nishikawa   We use words to work out something. Here communication is the goal itself—not a task-orientation as I am used to. There must be a motivation for communication. Here, after the first couple of days, we had no goal beyond just communicating. When we have no task-orientation, we Japanese just keep silent. Here, we kept communicating just to keep the flow of conversation going.

Rachel   People are not just what they say. We have had little chance to see each other in real situations, just sitting here on our buns. We haven't had a chance to see each other in changing moods and circumstances.

Miss Takahashi It doesn't mean that we don't get anything out of the communication. Behavior is communicated.

Mrs. Nishikawa I've never been exposed to this type of workshop before. Usually there is a plan. Here there is deliberately nothing to do.

Florence We aren't meeting your expectations, Mark, and perhaps not that of the researchers.

Rachel They want us to do something, but won't tell us what they want us to do.

Mark But, we made a statement here, which should be the goal of the workshop—a task-orientation instead of a process-orientation.

Florence The whole workshop and our purpose were very amorphous. In our group, when Osuzawa-san takes charge and says, "Let's discuss such-and-such an item," I am happier, as we know where we are going. You seem, Mark, to offer us no direction. His way is the more standard procedure that I am used to.

Rachel My workshop that I held with four American women, two Japanese-American women, and four Japanese women at my apartment was entirely process-oriented, but it was much more successful. We did three exercises, a breathing exercise, a touching exercise, which caused us some problems, and an exercise to find an object in the room to show how we felt about every other member in the room. That exercise was like the one we did here, but that people felt uncomfortable with. We put a notice in the paper and two of the women here at the workshop were in the group. The youngest was eighteen and the oldest was thirty-six. I felt much closer to that group than to this one. A couple of them I don't have much in common with; still we will be friends later.

Florence We are sorry that we let you down as a group.

Mark You haven't let yourselves down. That is important.

Mr. Osuzawa The basic assumption on which the whole workshop was planned was that there were serious cultural differences between the U.S. and Japanese cultures. We have seen some of these differences, but we have also seen many similarities between our cultures that we didn't expect: for example, in our attitudes about raising children, some of the problems of women, some of our expectations out of life. If the conference is to have an after-effect, one of our accomplishments may be that we can explain American culture better, and you can explain Japanese culture better at home. Since we have no term for "communication" separate from "language" and no term for "culture" separate from "nation," and no term at all for "intercultural communication," we may have learned a great deal, and much of the learning, despite our frustration, may have taken place for us in this room.

Mrs. Nishikawa   We have received cultural conditioning in new ways that we didn't expect. We thought that only the Japanese are indirect and politely work around the issues, and that Americans always face issues head-on and in public, and without sensitivity for the feelings of others. While two of the Americans had what we consider a very serious problem in which the sensitivities of both were hurt, we were amazed to see how well both of you worked to lessen the impact of the event. When another American was so frustrated with the group, we were interested to see how all the American members as well as the Japanese members worked to help bring her back quietly into the group. We expected the Americans to be such individuals that when you didn't like something like the field trip, you would have said so and left the group. We expected to stay with the group even if we didn't like it, but you all stayed too. I have learned many things about American culture that I thought were only Japanese cultural traits.

Florence   Mark, I think that you are so much ahead of us in some ways that you don't see the tremendous distance that each of us has come in these last few days. Even if I did find out that I was motherly, it has been a growing experience for me. I hope that even though you don't see it now, it was a growing experience for you too.

Mark   Perhaps it was in different ways than I expected.[3]

---

[3] In the final phase of the dialogue, we returned to a sort of unintended evaluation about the several days together, caused by Mark's comment that we had nearly finished our dialogue, but had not accomplished much. Would you share the expressed frustrations of both Japanese and Americans about having to sit in the same room for several days with no

Since a lingering tension seemed apparent in the group, one participant suggested ending our session by relating the details of an experience in Japan before the workshop began. The humorous nature of the experience seemed to relieve the group's anxiety. Someone suggested singing in Japanese and English, "When you're happy and you know it, clap your hands." The group laughed about their efforts at bilingual harmony as the formal aspects of this part of the workshop ended.

---

goals? If you had an opportunity to develop your own intercultural communication workshop, what features would you insist upon? Was the technology of having all the sessions videotaped for later playback a hindrance or a help? How could technology be utilized to develop such an intercultural workshop?

In reading the various dialogues in the journal, what are the likely insights that can be drawn to the first three parts of this book? How does the journal assist in linking key issues discussed earlier in the book, aside from the principle of similarities and differences to your own understanding of intercultural communication? How do the communication components fit into an understanding of the participants, messages, channels, and the event itself as it occurred in the dialogue? In what ways do you see key concepts of culture linking into key aspects of communication through the dialogue? Would it be possible to draw any values and value orientations from each participant in the dialogue as you perceive him or her interacting with others? In what ways could you tie the dialogues into applications for your own lives, especially in your intercultural contacts?

CHAPTER 16

Evaluating the Dialogue

July 13: The special women's group reports

When the entire workshop reconvened, we heard first from an American representative of the special women's group which had met spontaneously during the workshop. A female Japanese interpreter sequentially interpreted the entire message so that the full impact of the statement would be received equally by all of the participants. The American representative stressed that the group had two goals, to bridge the bicultural gap between the Japanese and American women who shared certain similar outlooks despite the cultural boundaries, and to understand themselves and others in the workshop better. They considered the fact that they had met three times as a group an accomplishment despite the fact that the workshop planners had provided virtually no time in the busy schedule for such extra meetings. [1] In relation to the communicative process which had taken place among the women's group, the American representative said that there were four

[1] The women's group decision to hold one of their meetings at dinner and to exclude males was offensive to a number of the workshop participants, including both men and women. Some men tried to join their friends unwittingly for dinner but were rebuffed. Some of the American men wanted to insert themselves deliberately into the group, but were dissuaded. The first meeting had included most of the women at the conference, but by the third meeting only about half were present, largely because of time pressures. Later when a representative of the Japanese women reported the evaluation session which they had

examples of effective interaction which occurred in their group rather than in the mixed male-female groups: they were more personal with each other, particularly because of the older Japanese men in the other groups; they were more honest and open with each other; they offered a safer physical and nonverbal environment for each other; and they were more supportive of each other. As for content, she said they were seeking an understanding of similarities and differences among the women, with their personal feelings as a basis for the analysis. The women discussed three topics: How would this conference have been different if more women had been present and if time had been provided officially for the meetings of the spontaneous women's group? What were their personal relations with their own mothers and children? How did personal touching help to support or nonsupport each other?

July 13: The American men react

The last activity scheduled for the last afternoon of the conference, before our final dinner and talent show, were separate evaluative discussions for the American men, the American women, the Japanese men, and the Japanese women. These groups were to report the next morning on evaluations and recommendations for the future of such joint projects. Tired, but glad to be able to relax as American men alone, sharing a round of beer, we had a useful and provocative discussion about the workshop. The dialogue which follows is condensed and based on a rough approximation of my notes taken at the time. I have supplied the American men with fictional first names. About fifteen men were present. There was no assigned leader for the group.

---

held alone, she indicated carefully, politely, and indirectly that while they were very happy about the women's group which formed, it had also caused them some difficulties, since they had to return to Japanese society in a different role than that promoted by the special women's group. Some of them additionally had been embarrassed to have to turn away their male friends from the women's meeting held at dinner.

As an American woman, do you feel that the American representative's generalization that despite cultural characteristics, it is possible for women working together to be more personal with each other, to be more honest and open with each other, to offer a safer physical and nonverbal environment for each other, and to be more supportive of each other than would be possible working with men? As an American man, do you agree that these generalizations could be applied to women working together separately and men working together separately?

Lawrence   Basically, our whole question is one of motivation and cognitive approaches to intercultural communication. One way to do it is to talk about ideas, data, and results. In our group, the Japanese-language group, there were impossibly different perceptions about how to incorporate these approaches. We got almost nothing done because we could never agree on what should be the group's collective attitudes on which approaches to use. My Japanese was only fair and I wasn't much help. Perhaps one part of the conference should be structured and other parts nonstructured.

John   Another dimension which has to be considered besides whether the conference should be largely academic or experiential is how the group is loaded with Japanese men. You have to give Japanese men time to discover their relationships before they are even able to move onto any sort of content dimension. The Japanese-language group seemed stuck on process from the very beginning, and we never got off that problem. If some don't want to move into experiential dimensions, which is against their nature in a professional meeting, there needs to be a set of older Japanese men who are very openminded. All the other Japanese men tend to follow the example set by the older males. If the older Japanese males in the group are dogmatic and set in their ways, there is no way to get the younger Japanese men to take the lead into more flexible approaches.

Lawrence   We aren't so worried about what we say here affecting us professionally or socially afterwards. The Japanese men are so worried about their social obligations, that a few were practically paralyzed in some cases at the conference. They are probably worrying right now as a group about what things they ought to agree upon, instead of having an open discussion where each one expresses his opinions.[2]

Jim   We had a very sharp division between those who wanted a problem-solving versus a feeling approach. The older participants, especially the men, were much more problem-solving oriented whether Japanese or American, while the younger

---

[2] This turned out to be a very accurate prediction; however, the final Japanese male report turned out to be short but very carefully thought out and stated. While the American men's report consisted only of a variety of individual statements with little group agreement, the Japanese men's report demonstrated considerable group consensus.

Japanese and Americans liked the intense emotional feeling approach. I believe that we have seen that cognitive styles transcend nationality, though I had been led to believe that they were shaped by nationality. The women's group talked about the importance of some great similarities between groups that other groups within the same culture cannot even share.

Ralph By some luck, we used our mornings on the interpersonal levels and the afternoons on the more abstract levels. We may want to consider strictly dividing the day, with experiential in the morning, and abstract in the afternoon, satisfying both groups and allowing generalizations to be based on the morning experiences.

Bill This isn't the real world, with experiential in the morning and cognitive in the afternoon. It all blends together. This idea destroys the flexibility of the individual groups which are to develop at their own pace. I wonder about our grouping procedures. They did not always seem so well planned. The key issue is why people are here and what they expected to get out of it.

John There is a certain critical mass for an effective group. The older people, Japanese and American, are more resistant to change. Perhaps they need more support. The younger people may already have had more affective experiences—but haven't thought about how to give support to the older participants who have never been involved in such experiences. Some of the Japanese men feel that the American men, and especially the workshop leaders, were very rigid. No matter what the changing climate, we proceeded doggedly with the program. This was symbolized at the beginning when they were teaching us the custom of exchanging the sake at the first dinner but we had to stop so that we could go on with the evening meetings. Some of the Japanese men feel that this has been a dominant and negative characteristic of the conference.

Tom There is also the problem of expert perception. The Japanese conference is very structured and every one knows his place and how he is to operate in the context of that situation. They view us as high-status experts coming to teach them the correct way to handle new ideas. The opening night speeches that the conference would take us to a very important goal or find us in an embarrassed position were indicative of that attitude. Perhaps we need to develop less high expectations for such a workshop, but it is difficult when so much foundation money is involved. The Japanese all expected that we were experts in small group leadership and experience, and were surprised to find that the level of expertise varies greatly among Americans, even among the older Americans.

Jim   In our group, the more we used language, the more problems we encountered. The language was really a serious barrier, even in groups that mostly used English. The vagueness of our own language perceptions surprised them, as they expected the precision of their language to have the same meanings when transferred to our language. The Japanese took each other and us far too seriously, and the Americans took each other for granted.

John   One Japanese man said that the Americans talk far too rapidly and don't give him time to select the best possible answer. He said that he doesn't reply unless he can give the best answer. We say it is OK to make a mistake, have it corrected by someone else, and reply. The Japanese often go into a phase of definition, like constantly defining what the purpose of the workshop was to be, and the different possible approaches give them time to develop a consensus of opinion. In a way, the workshop was like trying to mix oil and water.

Paul   Coming back to our different processes of learning. There is a dichotomy between cognitive and affective learning. We need to understand the individual people both as individuals and as typical of their culture. There has to be a mixing of the cultures and the cognitive styles if we are to be able to deal interculturally with each other.

Ralph   We need to understand the human beings first as human beings.

Tom   Is this the best setting? It is not fully a real Japanese setting. Even though we are in a much more traditional area than Tokyo, it is still a resort area for Japanese. Our visit to Nihommatsu was superficial. We should have had real tasks that teams of Japanese and Americans were to accomplish. Some of us should have gotten permission to spend a full day in a school, with some possibility for trying to teach a class, or a day in the mayor's office, or working for a day with a clerk in a store, or visiting homes. The Japanese are hospitable enough that such real experiences could have been arranged, and a lot more learning might have taken place.

John   This was really and primarily an American workshop transplanted into a Japanese setting to give it an extra dimension. Some of the Japanese men kept saying this over and over.

Ralph   In any future conference we must exploit the medium instead of misusing it as happened here. This requires more money to hire a professional taping team. There should be a camera in every room and a "mike" on every person. There should have been cameras in the dining room where a substantial portion of our activities took place, and every meeting such as this one now should be videotaped for future research purposes. The workshop leaders tended to think that all of our data would come out of the group sessions in the rooms. What about the bar? Here we could have mixed with Japanese who were not part of the workshop. The damage done to this workshop by the misuse of the medium is almost incalculable. We were amateurs playing with very expensive equipment. We allowed almost a full day's videotaping to be lost by overloading the equipment. Then we didn't have enough videotape to preserve everything that was videotaped, so we lost more.

Tom   In watching our group's tapes, and the tape episodes, I wondered how much of the verbal was needed.

Arnold   But a zoom lens would have made the professional competence of all our videotaping much better.

Ralph   I simply can't understand our expenditure of money, the loss of tapes, the overloading of equipment and staff, and all of the intended research which can't be done now.

John   We essentially got sound recordings with poor quality video. It was an experimental conference, and perhaps the next time we can do better.

Ralph   We had better not overload the staff so seriously as we did here.

Paul   Was the videotaping for evaluation or for client orientation? If you take the equipment out of the hands of the group dynamics people and put it in the hands of technicians, you have lost a great deal. They wouldn't know what to look for.

Douglas I very much would liked to have had effective videotaping both for good evaluation and for client preparation. Certainly a workshop this size with eight videotape cameras and monitors at our fingertips should have been able to save more of the videotaping that was done, videotape other events, and have at least two or three good hours of video tapes which could be sold to interested persons either to use in their own research, or to use for teaching and training.

Arnold At our human relations programs here in Japan, we use videotape equipment one way or another two or three times a week. We train people, who are essentially amateurs, in one day to handle the equipment effectively, and to help make them sensitive to what can be done by effective use of the cameras. This could have been done here. The control room monitors could have spent some time in the discussion rooms working with equipment, or could have taught the members of the group how to use it more effectively themselves. There were many times when some people weren't being picked up properly either by sound or by the video for as long as a whole morning.

Bernard Perhaps we have not yet talked about what we learned from this workshop.

Ralph I learned that it's easy to mess up television.

John The people should be more important than the equipment.

Ed Goals need to be stated more clearly within the context of freedom of alternatives. Perhaps one group should be goal-oriented and another process-oriented. People who like the one type can sign up for that and vice versa, then a selection can be made to obtain enough diversity out of those who sign up. Our first day was goal-oriented and we had a lot of good communication going on, which could also be effectively processed. The end product should be an increased personal awareness, plus the ability to work better with our own clients, and being able to help them work better with their clients. For those interested in teaching, a goal-orientation would have been how to prepare certain effective educational materials. For those who have business clients who must work with people of the other culture, it would be useful to be able to prepare a certain amount of effective training materials. It is good to know people of other cultures, but it might be more effective for us to understand stereotypes we are likely to meet. This would be helpful for a better understanding by our own clients, whether they are students going overseas or meeting overseas students, or businessmen engaged in international trade, or military personnel suddenly going to a foreign culture. How can we, who are fairly sophisticated, learn better how to deal with the less sophisticated kinds of clients who are more likely to be placed in these situations, situations where they run up against the stereotypes and don't know how to handle them or find them reinforced by the small amount of contact? If we know what the stereotypes are, which ones are totally accurate, or somewhat accurate, or misleading, or wrong, such a workshop should help us do a better job for our clients in helping them to handle such problems. Perhaps this would mean a more structured selection process. Our group had all the variations which made it difficult to work with, but also gave us the fuller range of types. We need as much latitude as possible. We have to maximize various desires and potentials, and eliminate the problem of sitting down for six days and having people saying every hour, Why are we here?

Lawrence   It would be interesting to take the notes from these four groups, the two sets of men and the two sets of women, and compare them in terms of our cognitive approaches to evaluation and recommendations. Our cognitive styles will be very different.

Tom   We have to be careful about how we phrase our final report, or for the Japanese men, it will reinforce their ideas that all we want to do is learn how to do bigger and better workshops, not what is supposed to happen to the individuals at the workshops.

Mark   Are we agreed on any specific ideas for our report?

Douglas   No. I suspect that the report should say that these were observations and recommendations which individuals offered, and tie those which fit well together into the same sets of observations and recommendations, and where there is conflict, tie the appropriate conflicting opinions together too. This seems to typify our own individuality best.

(This approach was generally accepted by the group).[3]

Evaluating our group experience

In general, though others and I had expected cognitive styles to differ markedly between the Japanese and American participants in the workshop, it also seemed clear in our group and in certain other groups that the task-orientation, problem-solving communicative style was more generally accepted by the older Japanese and Americans at the workshop, while a process-orientation approach stressed by our American group facilitator seemed generallly more acceptable to younger Japanese and American participants. As one of the American men later commented in the men's group, affective or process-oriented versus more theoretical and conceptual cognitive styles may have been more related to age and sex than to the two cultures as we saw them.

Within our group, our major frustrations seemed to center upon this dichotomy. There was no workshop regulation that we couldn't have shifted entirely to the task-orientation throughout our discussion, and there were attempts by Mr. Osuzawa and others in our group to move us in that fashion. For some reason or another, we were unable or unwilling to move as far along the "feeling" level as might have been appropriate if we had been more clearly attuned to the affective or process-orientation approach advocated by our American facilitator.

---

[3] Based on the reactions of the American men with their cultural biases, what would you see as their most importantly perceived issues at the workshop? Which do you consider more relevant for learning about intercultural communication, the cognitive and theoretical levels of learning, or learning by affective and experiential means? Based on the discussions of the American men, how could the media have been utilized more effectively for this particular workshop or for other workshops including two or more major cultural groups? What should be the end products of such a workshop? If you had a chance to participate in such a workshop, what would be your goals for a successful personal involvement? If teaching or training materials were to be a goal of such a workshop, what sort of materials would you want to help you become a more effective intercultural communicator? What kinds of materials could be developed for the less sophisticated types of clients than those who were at the workshop? If the Japanese were to decide to hold their own workshop with South East Asians, what considerations would have to be made so that the Japanese would not appear to repeat the same mistakes which seem to have been made by the American planners and participants?

Evaluating the workshop

By the time the actual workshop took place, several planning sessions occurred and both the Japanese and Americans had received significant foundation support in their own countries. Generally speaking, the participants were very carefully selected to provide considerable diversity in membership, and every effort was made to set up the best possible conditions for its success as an intercultural communication experience, both for the research and for the future impact which the workshop was intended to produce in terms of individual and more general benefits.

Despite the precautions, of course, it was simply not possible to overcome all the obstacles. The workshop had been proposed by Americans and followed a basic design established by the Americans, and as some Japanese argued it may simply have been an American-style conference transplanted to a Japanese setting. Too much was attempted in the workshop, causing serious overload on the staff, participants, and especially on the technology in use at the conference. At one point, all eight videotape machines in constant operation completely lost the sound portion for a large part of the day, and caused serious difficulties for the workshop staff who were trying to cope with such a situation. Expectations were too high, particularly since Japanese and American foundations had committed the major funds for its success. With the best intentions on the part of its planners and participants, certain communication breakdown was inevitable by the very nature of the differences in patterns of linguistic, nonverbal, attitudinal, and cognitive dimensions between the Japanese and Americans, and between the younger and older, or male and female participants. The workshop was neither an unqualified success nor a failure. As in most human encounters, there was a good share of effective communication which took place, setting the base for a variety of continuing joint friendships and projects, as well as a certain amount of communication breakdown among participants. As a final widespread view of the participants, I would suspect that it was generally considered a success. At the same time, as the workshop ended there was still confusion among many participants as to its real goals, and some generalized frustration at the procedure that the actual workshop moved toward in its conclusions.

The final comments of the American participants reflect a certain giddiness after the intense nine-day cultural dialogue, and the most serious criticisms which they wished to make of the workshop. Examples of their responses to a workshop evaluation question, "What disturbed you most about the workshop?" included: "I tripped over my yucata," "My slippers fell off all the time," "I couldn't remember to take my slippers off when I went into a room," "I couldn't remember to change into the bathroom slippers when I went into the toilet," "I couldn't learn how to squat on the Japanese-style toilets," "I kept bumping my head on all the doors," "My legs got all cramped up sitting on the floor all the time," "I wished it would stop raining," and "The earthquakes we felt frightened me." More to the point, perhaps, as a serious comment was the statement by an American participant who had experienced many varied and stimulating intercultural events in his life: he felt that this workshop was one of the most important professional and personal opportunities which he had ever involved himself in. I would agree.

EPILOGUE

In *Cultural Dialogue*, we have addressed ourselves to a large number of issues, questions, and areas which should concern us as regular cultural communicators. We have considered the role played in cultural communication by such issues and questions as similarities and differences, conflict, control, technology, cultural stability versus change, and cultural imperialism versus dependency. We have attempted to understand the impact which such components of communication as the message, the communicators at various levels, linguistic and nonverbal codes of communication, and the media and channels of communication have in developing ethnographically a community or culture's social discourse. We have offered from among the possible cultural components which could be chosen an understanding of cultural orientations, of language in its cultural role, values, and as an aspect of subjective culture, perception and its relations to other aspects of subjective culture. Frequently, throughout the book, we have attempted to link the initial sets of issues and questions with the communicative and cultural components as they serve to provide the "said of social discourse." We have offered extended examples of these linkages in considering the relationship of such initial issues and questions as conflict, control, and attitudinal and social change to the communications media and channels. Finally, we have provided a detailed example of the principle of similarities and differences which affects intercultural communication through the autobiographical presentations of a Japanese living in transition in the United States, and by my perceptions of an actual cultural dialogue between Japanese and American teachers, professionals, and students in Japan. This dialogue applies many of the synthesized statements in the earlier part of *Cultural Dialogue*, either directly or indirectly. By using such a dialogue with two nearly opposite cultures, whose members at the same time have much in common, we can see more clearly both the opportunities and problems which arise out of intercultural communication.

Perhaps you had believed that everyone communicates and that there is thereby no real need to study communication as a separate subject. Perhaps, too, you could readily acknowledge that all communication has cultural components, and that naturally when people from different cultures interact, there will be certain problems because of cultural differences. The point which has been stressed in *Cultural Dialogue* is that both communication and culture are fairly complicated processes. Their interaction occurs not only in a happenstance fashion, but also in a highly systematic manner, especially as technology increases the importance of the initial issues and questions which we have raised. The simplicity of a primitive oral-aural society, the postfigurative culture of which Margaret Mead speaks, is not present for most of the potential readers of such a book. Indeed, such simplicity is no longer present for most of the peoples of the world. Just as technology is irreversible and geometric in its progression, so too is intercultural and crosscultural interaction. Because of your present or potential elite status, simply by virtue of your education and the technological advances which are available to you, you have no choice but to involve yourself continuously and intensely in social interaction within and between cultures.

Some of you are also likely, by your positions or travel, to serve as cultural spokesmen or spokeswomen. Some of you are already bilingual and bicultural. Others will develop such skills when they are needed, much as Mr. Osuzawa in our Japanese-American dialogue reported learning English at age forty-two when he needed to do so. Some of you will remain pseudobilinguals and pseudobiculturals, but others will develop the tendencies of genuine bilingualism and biculturalism. You may find yourselves working with members of other cultures; teaching students from other cultures; having clients or patients from other cultures; traveling among persons from other cultures; living next to members of other cultures; or marrying members of other races or cultures.

A few of you will also find yourselves as multicultural men or women—persons on the boundary between your culture and other cultures—in a state of tension between the values, norms, customs, traditions and subjective culture provided you by your own cultural setting and that of other cultures in which you are involved. Perhaps, too, you will seek to become cultural change agents, either for your own culture, or for others. You may undertake further detailed study and experience in other cultures as many of our academic disciplines point in such directions. Unless you wish to remain totally isolated, you will involve yourselves actively in cultural dialogue for the rest of your lives. Even if you wish to remain isolated, you have little chance of success.

Culture is dependent on our very humanness. Your own subjective culture helps to shape who you have been and who you will become. This subjective culture has been shaped by your cultural setting, and more importantly by the social interaction which takes place regularly between members of your culture and all the others, past and present, geographically and through space. You have no choice. You must be either a cultural communicator or totally without culture. As Clifford Geertz has argued: "Without culture—no men; but without men—no culture." The purpose of *Cultural Dialogue* thus has been to provide a better understanding of how communication and culture interact both at the theoretical and practical levels, so that we might together better comprehend the "said of social discourse," the dialogue which takes place in our own cultural dialogue.

GLOSSARY*

Activity value orientation the way in which a culture is oriented toward "doing" types of behaviors. For example, North American society is characterized as a "doing" society. It is highly active with a "let's-get-it-done" attitude. In contrast, the Filipino society is a "being" society, with a generally passive attitude toward activity.

Action language nonverbal communication which embraces all movements that are not used exclusively as signals. Examples include walking, drinking, and sitting.

Actor-orientation view of conflict resolution conflicts help the individual actor in a conflict to realize his or her individual interests and potential. For example, every participant in a conflict seeks to win the conflict if possible.

Adaptation a concept related to the theoretical orientation toward culture described as cultural ecology in which humans adapt their environment to their culture while animals must adapt to their environment.

Basic problems common to all human groups Kluckhohn and Strodbeck hypothesize that basic universal problems include: the character of innate human nature; the relation of humans to nature and supernature; the temporal focus of human life; the modality of human activity; human relations with other humans; and the human

---

*The glossary includes the key terms utilized in *Cultural Dialogue* with basic operational definitions. Fuller definitions can be found in the text itself.

conception of time and space, and the individual's place in it. These first five problems formed the basis of their research among five American Southwest communities. The sixth problem was formulated but not tested. These problems lead to the notion of value orientations or preferences for all cultural groups.

Belief and perception beliefs form an important expression of values and value orientations and are structured out of experiential perceptions. Perceptions lead to beliefs, and beliefs lead to values. The reverse is also possible.

Biculturalism the true bicultural individual has the ability to live comfortably in two cultures, while the pseudobicultural individual usually only knows one culture well but attempts to operate in two cultures.

Bilingualism the true bilingual individual has the ability to speak two languages with perfect ease, and can think, develop abstractions, and use other specialized forms of each language equally well. The pseudobilingual individual attempts to operate in two languages without knowing both languages equally well.

Body motion a term used in nonverbal communication to describe gestures, movements of the body, facial expressions, eye behavior, and posture. It is also referred to as kinesics.

Channels of communication the means by which the communication process is carried out: for example, sound waves, media, and satellites.

Class communication that communication which takes place within and between distinct class groups. It is often more difficult to communicate across class barriers than across cultural barriers when similarities bind together those crossing the cultural barriers .

Codes rules, guidelines, or norms by which a system functions, as exemplified by cultures as codes, laws, languages, or guiding principles. All codes have a structure or grammar, and a vocabulary.

Cofigurative culture It is present-oriented, and often is passed on by near peers, often parents who are only one short generation older than their children, or by exact peers. While the grandfather may still be present, he is not likely to have the authority which might be prevalent in the postfigurative culture.

Cognitive anthropology that anthropological orientation which holds that all culture is subjective; that is, it depends upon what is held in the minds of a culture's members, such as beliefs, perceptions, values, and thought-patternings.

Cognitive learning in contrast to affective learning which is largely experiential, it is that learning which is obtained by use of reasoning systems and general principles of intelligence.

Collective communication   that interaction which tends to be one-way in its direction; that is, from a small group to a larger group. It tends to be more systematic, routinized, and formalized, with less chance for spontaneous feedback than is usually true with interpersonal communication.

Collective phenomena in language   a notion which relates to the Sapir-Whorf hypothesis of language, it emphasizes aspects of the cultural environment in connection with aspects of the language of the culture. For example, if all members of a particular culture perceive specific colors in the same way, this characteristic is reflected in the language generally of all the members of the culture.

Communication   seen as a process in contrast to communications which are seen as the channels or media by which the process functions. Although many definitions of communication exist, the two chief ones utilized here emphasize that all behavior in the perceived presence of another is communicative on one hand, and on the other hand, the concept that much communication is purposeful, intentional, and instrumental.

Communication breakdown   a failure which causes the process not to work properly. It can also include failures in the intended coding of the message-sender or the decoding of the message-receiver, or in the message itself, or in the channels or media by which the message is transmitted.

Communication event   a component of communication which describes a situation within a culture or community in which much of the resources of the community are involved. It includes those who might participate in the situation, the messages which might be provided, the topics and settings for such messages, the codes in which such messages may be framed, and the channels or media by which messages may be transmitted. Examples in the American setting include the Watergate situation, a presidential campaign, the Cambodian protests and the civil rights protests. Multicultural examples include the imposition of strict censorship in India, the Middle Eastern tensions, and the Canadian debates on bilingualism and biculturalism.

Communication networks   channels or media of communication linked in such a way as to provide a chain. A channel with many sources and destinations is considered a network. Examples include telephone, telegraph, and satellite networks.

Communication-process orientation   interaction which has as its goal simply communicating: for example, when people gather with no definable goals.

Communication-task orientation interaction which has specific goals to accomplish: for example, to make a specific decision or to solve a specific problem.

Competence in language the ability of a speaker to know and to apply the rules of language with a conscious understanding. This differs from performance in language which indicates the actual vocal noises uttered and heard by a speaker, but with no relationship to a conscious understanding of the rules. It is possible for a bilingual individual to perform adequately without knowing the rules. In contrast, it is possible to be competent in a language without being able to perform in the language.

Components of communication all the aspects which make up a communicating community, including the event, participants messages, codes, and channels. The ethnographic study of communication uses the method of studying a culture or community as closely as possible by focusing on those aspects which relate to its interactional processes.

Consensus gentium an acceptance of the notion of cultural universals, or characteristics which appear with regularity in virtually every culture. It could also be expressed as the agreement of all humanity on certain universal norms, values, and priniciples.

Countercultural communication the interaction which occurs when a particular cultural group or subculture rejects the dominant values, beliefs, and assumptions of the dominant culture with which it would normally have contact. Examples include the Amish or Hasidic Jews (who reject modern life), and at the other end of the spectrum, such groups as the Black Panthers or Sybionese Liberation Army (who have sought in the past to destroy the dominant culture around them.)

Crosscultural communication it is defined herein as that communication which takes place between members of whole cultures in contact with each other, or between cultural spokespersons, or in the context of making a comparative base between cultures. It is also called transcultural communication. Crosscultural communication tends to be collective, with one-way directionality, and much planned and systematic interaction, generally only with routinized or ritualized response.

Cultural bias toward communication the notion that every culture or civilization has a particular thrust toward specific types of communication processes and channels. Examples are preliterate societies which have a dominant oral-aural approach to communication, script-oriented societies, technologically oriented societies which emphasize the electronic media, and satellite-oriented societies which emphasize instantaneous crossing of spacial and temporal barriers.

Cultural change   all societies are change-oriented in practice, but some societies appear to change very slowly. Since the static society is typically dying, change must occur, but all societies must change enough to survive, and yet change slowly enough that they don't lose their guiding principles and values. The cultural change agent seeks to speed up the changes taking place in the society.

Cultural communication   interaction which is generally interpersonal in nature, but with the added opportunities and problems of differences in language, nonverbal codes, assumptions, beliefs, values, and thought-patternings. Here we define intercultural communication as interaction at the interpersonal level, and crosscultural communication as the interaction at the collective level, either between the spokespersons for different cultures or whole cultures in contact with each other, or considered on a comparative basis.

Cultural components   those aspects which are essential for the understanding of culture; that is, what makes culture what it is. They include individual processes of culture such as perception, attitudes, stereotypes, and prejudices, as well as deeply cultural characteristics such as values and value orientations. Linguistic and nonverbal codes also apply, but are used herein primarily as communicative components.

Cultural conflict   the continuing tension within and between cultures which leads to communication breakdowns and ineffective interaction. Such conflict occurs within a culture when cultural change agents are seeking to effect change in the culture while other members of the culture seek to prevent such change. Such conflicts often occur when behavior relating to deep-seated values and beliefs of one culture is in tension with the behavior for similar reasons in an opposing culture. Members of a "doing" society often try to force members of a "being" society to accept the principles which they hold, and such action often leads to conflict.

Cultural control   the attempt within or between cultures to exercise regulatory functions over others. Control is a key definition of culture itself, since one of the ways that a culture's norms and values are passed down to succeeding generations is to provide control over their behaviors, attitudes, beliefs, and values.

Cultural ecology   an orientation toward culture which stresses our interaction with our cultural environment, with an emphasis on how cultural systems adapt to their total environments, and as a consequence, how the institutions of a given culture adapt or adjust to one another. An example consists of the relations between members of governments, families, labor forces, educational institutions, and religious institutions as they interact within the guidelines of a specific culture.

Cultural evolutionism an orientation toward culture which stresses the cumulative, collective experience of humankind, sometimes called *Culture Writ Large*. The emphasis could be placed on the human ability progressively to build and use such culture-bearing products as symbols and tools, and the progressive development of the institutions of culture as they interrelate within and between cultures. The notion is that all that is past is prologue for all of human culture, in contrast to the specific evolution of a particular culture, which is sometimes called *culture writ small*.

Cultural functionalism the dominant recent emphasis in anthropological research, it is the cultural orientation which stresses the society or culture as a working and functioning system. The ethnographic worker often attempts to see a culture or community as a functioning unit, as in the example of the American studies of "Middletown." A basic notion is that all cultures have certain functions, or necessary conditions of existence, if the system itself is to continue to work. The concept of cultural universals is closely tied to this orientation.

Cultural history an ethnographic study of the history of a culture as seen through the documents and materials which were contemporary to the culture at one time. All study of culture is a study of contemporary history for the period that it is being studied.

Cultural imperialism the tendency of members of a culture to seek dominance over other members of the culture or over members of different cultures. The cultural imperialist is expansive in pushing outward his or her own values, beliefs, assumptions, and often his or her codes of communication, such as language. Cultural imperialism also requires cultural dependency, and often seeks control over others.

Cultural maximizers those persons in a culture, such as parents, educators, philosophers, scientists, and political leaders, who help to pass down the values and norms of the culture or who help to influence others to accept these norms and values. They help to assure the culture's survival, especially when cultural conflict occurs because they are the most powerful members of the culture whom others either wish to follow or have no choice but to follow.

Cultural placenta the interaction which people engage in through social discourse. On one side of the placenta, Americans place the full range of individual experience; on the other side, the total cultural system is seen as important. It can be described as that framework within a culture in which interaction can take place. Thus in a culture which emphasizes group and family contexts, the restraints on the interaction may be set by group and family norms, while in North American culture, the individual may be the guiding norm.

Cultural quantum of communication   the direct interaction between communication and culture, emphasizing the totality of the interacting communicative and cultural components within and between cultures. Since the term "communication" is defined and utilized differently from culture to culture, assumptions about it also vary from culture to culture. The totality of communication possibilities in the North American culture where the individual receives dominance contrasts sharply with the context within a Marxist society where stress is placed on communication as an aspect of the whole society.

Cultural stability   the maintenance of cultural values and norms in a relatively static situation. In a sense, every cultural change agent is culture bound; that is, he or she is encumbered with all of the cultural baggage provided by the existent culture, whose chief objective is to remain the same as much possible.

Cultural units   the aspects of culture through which its characteristics are transmitted. Cultural units include, among others, cultural maximizers; the quantum of culture; cultural universals; the cultural placenta; the cultural quantum of communication; and the specific cultural bias toward communication which each culture or civilization has. *See individual concepts.*

Cultural universals   those characteristics which are shared from culture to culture, past and present, such as customs relating to the cycles of life: birth, adolescence, courtship, marriage, maturation, and death; bodily care; relations with others; and customs relating to the supernatural.

Culture   among the variety of definitions possible, three are emphasized here: the notion that it is through culture that traditions, norms, values, perceptions and thought-patternings are passed from generation to generation; the concept that culture, like communication, is a constantly changing process; and the concept that humans act upon their cultural environment instead of simply being passively acted upon by it. In this sense culture is synonymous with control. As Clifford Geertz suggests, without culture, no humans, but without humans, no culture.

Culture Writ Large   a concept of the cultural evolutionism orientation. It suggests an interest in all of world culture and its characteristics since the beginning of time to the present. The idea can be contrasted with *culture writ small*, which emphasizes the cultural evolution of a specific culture over time and space.

Deep structure in language   an aspect of the deterministic theory of language, also called generative or transformational grammar, that while languages differ widely on the surface, when one moves below the surface to its deep structure, underlying similarities are present both in the structure and also at times in the semantic meanings.

Descriptive grammar in contrast to prescriptive grammar, which attempts to prescribe how grammar ought to work, descriptive grammar simply describes how it actually does work within a particular language and among related languages.

Deterministic theory of language also called generative or transformational grammar. The theory is a dominant one held by scholars of language today, and argues that language universals which have the same characteristics across languages or across related sets of languages can be isolated. By knowing the underlying structure of language, one can generate new grammars. It is the opposite from the relativistic or Sapir-Whorf theory of language, which stresses that every language positively and firmly shapes its culture, thus making every system at least partially different from the next.

Directiveness in value orientations the dominant behavior which results in a culture from definitely patterned or rank-ordered principles to direct their activities toward specific ways in solving common human problems, while members of another culture may be pointed in a different direction in solving the same type of problems. An example can be seen in the way that specific members of cultures direct their activities toward time and space. Members of one culture may direct their efforts toward the past and toward the preservation of spatial monuments, while members of another culture direct their activities toward the present and to a disposable view of their space.

Dominant value orientations those orientations toward values which a dominant number of members in a culture or between cultures hold and promote. For example, if members of a society place heavy emphasis on family and group relationships, this would suggest that a dominant value orientation is present. At the same time, there are always likely to be some members of the culture who would deviate from that widely held view and would place special emphasis on the individual in contrast to the group or family.

Dyadic communication that interpersonal communication which takes place between two persons. The direction of the communication is two-way; it is frequently spontaneous and unplanned; and much feedback is possible.

Ethnocentrism the tendency of members of a culture to believe that for one reason or another their culture is better or superior to other cultures.

Ethnographic research the attempt to map a culture or community by its chief characteristics. Thick ethnographic details include as many detailed facets as possible about the culture or community, while thin ethnographic details include somewhat superficial attention to the facets of the culture or community.

Ethnography of communication   the attempt to map a culture or community by studying its communication events, and the various components of communication which interact in the event itself. Such components include the message, the participants in communication, codes (such as language or nonverbal cues), and media or channels, to name a few.

Experiential learning   that learning developed from perceptions based on past or present experiences. In contrast to learning cognitively, or through possibly abstract processes, one learns by being directly involved. Part Four offers an illustration.

Focused interaction   that willingness to supply cues, at least briefly, for others to act on; to be reasonably responsive to the cues provided by others; and to be capable of weaving these two coding activities into an acceptable pattern.

Generative grammar   *See* **Deterministic theory of language.**

Global communication   that interaction, generally at the collective level, which transcends national and cultural barriers. While such communication often is affected by problems of language, attitudes, values, and thought-patterning, there is generally some mutually uniting factor for such communication to take place effectively. An example is the unifying nature of Islamic thought for Moslems all over the world which allows them to communicate effectively with each other despite other barriers.

Grammar   the structure or syntax by which any code operates. In the case of language, this grammar consists of the rules by which sentences are built, since sentences are the major component of the human ability to communicate.

Hierarchical sets of communication participants   the model offered here is one which includes five levels of communication participants: intrapersonal, interpersonal, cultural, collective, and global levels, and their subsets. Each level subsumes characteristics of the earlier levels and adds more specialized characteristics.

Homo faber   man (or woman) the maker, both of symbols and of tools, the two human characteristics upon which culture is built.

Human nature value orientation   seeks to define innate human nature and its character. Some cultures conceive human nature as evil and unalterable, or evil and perfectable, or as good and unalterable, or as good and corruptible. Still others see it as a mixture subject to both positive and negative influences. Most societies in the world hold the last orientation, though there are societies at each extreme of the spectrum.

Individual processes of culture   those processes which are unique to each individual, often called subjective culture. These processes include individual beliefs and values which are not necessarily characteristic of the whole culture, plus perceptions which are experientially based for each individual within the culture.

Intercultural communication sometimes also called crosscultural communication or transcultural communication. Here it is defined as the interpersonal communication which has the added characteristics of similarities and differences in language, nonverbal cues, attitudes, perceptions, norms, values, and thought-patterning. It is subsumed in the cultural level of the hierarchical model and is related to such subsets as intra/interracial, intra/interethnic, countercultural, and intracultural communication. While intercultural communication is seen as much more spontaneous and unplanned with a relatively small number of persons, crosscultural communication is considered the interaction on a much more formal, planned, and routinized basis. Intercultural communication is considered much more two-way communication, while crosscultural communication is considered one-way, from a small group to a larger group.

Interpersonal communication involves a small number of people, typically with much two-way communication, much unplanned, spontaneous interaction, and with considerable opportunity for feedback.

Intuitional reasoning considered to be the type of reasoning adhered to by much of the Eastern world. It stresses the organic harmony between the whole and its parts and utilizes many arguments from analogy and ancient authority. Such reasoning is also important in the nationalistic state.

Language while speech is the basic coding procedure, language is the secondary coding system. It is abstract and is made real by vocalized utterances. Language symbolizes and catalogs our perceived reality, and is the symbolic characteristic of humans which gives them their truly human character.

Language planning the development of a written language system based on past oral usage, as when bilingualism was promoted in Canada as an official policy, or when a once-living language, such as Gaelic in the modern Irish state, or Hebrew in modern Israel, is reinstated.

Language universals summary statements about all human speakers, language universals serve to provide the most general laws of linguistics. They offer a similar logical structure from language to language and similar substantative content. They help one to move from one language to another with expectations of certain characteristics always operating. Language universals are a key concept in the deterministic theory of language.

Linguistic relativity theory   also called the Sapir-Whorf theory, or the Whorf theory, it holds that language is a self-contained, creative, symbolic organization. It not only refers to experience largely acquired without its help, but actually defines experience for us by its structure and by our acceptance of the language's ability to influence our experience by shaping our symbolic meanings for us. It is the guide to social reality.

Man/nature value orientation   explains the human's interaction with nature, and sometimes also supernature, and emphasizes that some cultures believe that humans are subjugated to nature, while others believe that they must create harmony with nature, and still others believe that they are destined to master nature. Although many North Americans believe that they can have mastery over nature, many Native Americans believe that they are one with nature, and Filipinos tend to believe that they cannot overcome nature, as it has mastery over humans.

Mass communication   also called mass communications, it is a form of collective communication which typically is directed by a small group toward a large group. Messages tend to be planned and systematic, and feedback is routinized or ritualistic.

Media   *see* **Channels of communication**

Message   a key component in communication, as it subsumes all other components, according to Dell Hymes. Messages are sent between communication participants, generally coded in a specific way, and through specific channels or media. Messages may serve a neutral function, such as providing information; they may provide emotional releases; they may seek to influence other communication participants; they may provide a united symbolic presentation through poetry, painting, or music; or they may serve to keep open channels of communication. Messages may take different forms and shapes and may have different topics or settings.

Metacommunication   the human ability to communicate about communication. While animals can communicate, they cannot reflect on their communication. This is a special characteristic of humans.

Metalanguage   the human ability to utilize language to discuss language. Only humans can reflect on their language.

Multicultural person   described as the person able to move in and out of several cultures with relative ease. Often such a person is on the boundaries of both an old and a new culture. With increasing contact between cultures, it is now possible for some persons to move frequently in and out of cultures at a substantial rather than superficial level. Tension in values is often present.

Nominalistic reasoning utilizes heavily the inductive approach to logic so prevalent among many North Americans. It is distrustful of "pure reason" and broad categories, but emphasizes instead empirical data, often developed by reliance on industrial and technological societies. It is highly empirical.

Nonverbal communication may be considered to include all human coding except language, and generally serves as a complement to linguistic codes and patterns. It includes body motion, the involvement of the senses in a balanced ratio, and various artifacts of human culture.

Objective culture in contrast to subjective culture which consists of the mental aspects of culture, objective culture refers to cultural objects such as ornaments, documents, artifacts, etc.

Perception the most individual process of subjective culture, perception is formed by the memory of past structured, stable, and meaningful experiences. Perception is an individual process while intelligence is more of a universal characteristic. Each culture provides different ways of developing perceptions based on past experiences. While a child may know cognitively in certain cultures how to wink, he or she must learn the actual process by experiential learning.

Postfigurative culture often an oral-aural society, such a culture is grandfather-oriented with key figures of authority being the elderly members of the culture as the ones who pass on the traditions, and control the activities of the young members of the culture. Such a culture is typically past-oriented.

Prefigurative culture Margaret Mead describes such a culture as one which has developed since World War II because of the drastic shrinkage in time and space, the ability to be aware of what happens almost instantly in vastly different parts of the world, or to move quickly across cultural barriers. She calls it an erratic, unpredictable, and rapidly changed situation from what older cultural members knew and expected previously.

Prescriptive grammar grammar which prescribes certain rules and identifies incorrect use of structural and syntactical rules of the grammar.

Relational value orientation describes the human's relation to other persons. Relational orientations includes how members of cultures handle the problems of ancestral lineage, collateral relations or group interdependence within the culture, and individualistic norms and goals as autonomous persons. While all cultures are concerned with each of these aspects, members of some cultures prefer one of the aspects. For example, much of the Eastern world has important ties to ancestral lineage; North Americans stress individualism; and cultures with extended families as the norm stress the collateral or group orientation.

Ritual   serves as the acting out of the "subjective content of culture" and symbolizes the culture's values of truth and reality. Ritualistic communication is common to most forms of collective interaction and is common to most cultures. Examples are religious and nationalistic beliefs and values, expressed by specific behavior.

Sapir-Whorf hypothesis   *see* **Deterministic theory of language**

Social discourse   the means by which most cultural traditions, norms, perceptions, and values are transmitted. Since culture assumes the social context, it is also a prerequisite for culture.

Space-value orientation   deals with how humans handle space and the values which they hold toward it. For example, North Americans have a visual linear perception of lines, right angles, and rectangles, while members of a culture living in a tropical rain forest see space as curving and flowing shapes without precise beginnings or endings.

Speech   the basic coding procedure for humans which provides them with the ability to communicate effectively by building and using symbols, and by being able to use speech to build and use another critical element of culture, tools, and tool-making tools.

Structure   *see* **Grammar**

Subjective culture   *see* **Individual processes of culture**

Symbols   arbitrary ways to express and catalog preceived reality. They are "stand-ins" for the actual things. For example, the word "rain" is not rain, nor is purple cloth royalty. In language, words are symbols. Signs, however, do bear real relationships to the things for which they stand. For example, high fever is a sign of sickness rather than an arbitrary stand-in for sickness itself.

Syntax   *see* **Grammar**

Technology   called the metaphysics of the twentieth century, it has always existed in culture, but is defined herein as a fundamental influence on contemporary society. Technological progress is irreversible once it begins, and is geometric in its spreading influence.

Theoretical orientations toward culture   several have been identified herein, including cultural evolutionism, cultural functionalism, cultural history, and cultural ecology. Additionally, we have suggested cognitive anthropology or subjective culture as an added and related orientation. See **Individual concepts.**

Thought-patterning   the way in which members of a culture tend to think, based on the shaping of the culture and often its language. Examples include the nominalistic reasoning of North Americans in general, the universalistic reasoning of the French, the intuitive reasoning of those from Eastern traditions, and the dialectical reasoning of Russians. Language helps shape these patterns.

Time value orientation   the way in which members of a culture view their relation to the concept of time. Some are past-oriented, some are present-oriented, and others are future-oriented. The postfigurative culture represents a type of past-orientation; the cofigurative culture represents a type of present-orientation; and the prefigurative culture represents a type of future-orientation.

Transcultural communication *see* **Crosscultural communication**

Transformational grammar   *see* **Deterministic theory of language**

Uniqueness attributes   perceptual ways of viewing or emphasizing one's personal uniqueness, through such characteristics as naming, perceptions of the self, scarcity of information, experiences, resources, and individual performance.

Universalistic reasoning   logic which moves from broad and often sweeping premises to specific examples; it is characteristic of members of cultures speaking French and other Romance languages.

Values and value orientations   values are the most deep-seated aspects of culture and often cause the greatest cultural conflict when they impede upon cultural communication. They lead to behavior which seems irrational to those who do not share the same values. Value orientations are the dominant ways in which members of culture operate toward certain basic human problems, such as the role of humans in nature, their place in it, their relations to other humans, their use and relations to time and space, and their orientation toward activity.

Whorf hypothesis   *see* **Linguistic relativity theory.**

REFERENCES

Aberle, David F., et al., 1950. "The Functional Prerequisites of a Society." *Ethics* 60, 100-111.

Adam, George, ed. 1976. *Journalism, Communication and the Law.* Englewood Cliffs, New Jersey: Prentice Hall.

Alder, Peter S., 1974. "Beyond Cultural Identity: Reflections on Cultural and Multicultural Man." In *Topics in Learning,* August, 23-40.

Alexander, Hubert G., 1967. *Language and Thinking: A Philosophical Introduction.* Princeton: Princeton University.

Alexander, Hubert G., 1969. *Meaning in Language.* Glenview, Illinois: Scott, Foresman.

Allport, G. W. 1954. *The Nature of Prejudice.* New York: Macmillan.

Allport, G.W. 1961. *Pattern and Growth in Personality.* New York: Macmillan.

Aranguren, J.L., 1967. *Human Communication.* Translated by Frances Partridge. New York: McGraw-Hill .

Bach, E. and R. T. Harms, eds., 1968. *Universals in Linguistic Theory.* New York: Holt.

Badami, Mary Kenny, 1977. "Interpersonal Perceptions and Outcomes of Communication in a Simulation Game of Intercultural Contact." Unpublished Ph.D. dissertation, Northeastern University.

Baier, Kurt, and Nicholas Rescher, 1969. *Values and the Future.* New York: Free Press.

Bailey, Alfred G., 1972. *Culture and Nationality.* Toronto: McClelland.

Barnlund, Dean,1968. *Interpersonal Communication: Survey and Studies.* Boston: Houghton Mifflin.

Barnlund, Dean, 1974. "The Public Self and the Private Self in Japan and the United States." In *Intercultural Encounters with Japan: Communication Contact and Conflict.* Edited by John C. Condon and Mitsuko Saito. Tokyo: Simul Press.

Barnouw, Victor, 1973. *Culture and Personality.* Homewood, Illinois: Dorsey.

Basu, A. K. and R. G. Ames, 1970. "Cross-Cultural Contact and Attitude Formation." *Sociology and Social Research* 55 (October), 5-16.

Bateson, Gregory, 1944. "Human Dignity and the Varieties of Civilization." In *Conference of Science, Philosophy, and Religion, 3rd Symposium.*

Beals, Alan R., with George and Louise Spindler, 1973. *Culture in Process.* New York: Holt.

Bell, Daniel, 1970. "The Cultural Contradictions of Capitalism." In *The Public Interest.* September.

Beltran, Luis Ramiro, 1975. "Research Ideologies in Conflict." *Journal of Communication* 25 (Spring), 187-193.

Benedict, Ruth, 1934. *Patterns of Culture.* Boston: Houghton Mifflin.

Benjamin, Robert L., 1970. *Semantics and Language Analysis.* Indianapolis: Bobbs-Merrill.

Benson, Thomas W., 1973. "Violence: Communication Breakdown?" In *Intercommunication among Nations and Peoples.* Edited by Michael H. Prosser, New York: Harper & Row.

Berelson, Bernard and Morris Janowitz, eds. 1950, 1953. *Reader in Public Opinion and Communication: Enlarged Edition.* New York: Free Press.

Berlo, David K., 1960. *The Process of Communication.* New York: Holt.

Bernstein, Basil, 1964. "Elaborated and Restructed Codes: Their Social Origins and Some Consequences." *American Anthropologist* 6: part 2. 55-60.

Bersheid, Ellen and Elaine Hatfield Walster, 1969. *Interpersonal Attraction.* Reading, Massachusetts: Addison-Wesley.

Birdwhistell, Ray L., 1967. "Some Body Motion Elements Accompanying Spoken American English." In *Communication: Concepts and Perspectives.* Edited by L. Thayer. Washington, D.C.: Hayden.

Birdwhistell, Ray L., 1970. *Kinesics and Context: Essays on Body Motion Communication.* Philadelphia: University of Pennsylvania.

Birney, Robert C., and Richard C. Teevan, 1962. *Measuring Human Motivation.* Princeton: Princeton University.

Blublaugh, Jon A., and Dorthy L. Pennington, 1976. *Crossing Differences: Interracial Communication.* Columbus, Ohio: Merrill.

Blumer, Herbert, 1950. "The Mass, The Public, and Public Opinion." In *Reader in Public Opinion and Communication.* Edited by Bernard Berelson and Morris Janowitz. New York: Free Press.

Boas, Franz, 1938. *The Mind of Primitive Man.* New York: Free Press.

Bock, Philip K., 1970. *Culture Shock: A Reader in Modern Cultural Anthropology.* New York: Knopf.

Bogart, Leo, 1976. *Premises for Propaganda: The United States Information Agency's Operating Assumptions in the Cold War.* New York: The Free Press.

Bosmajian, Haig A., 1971. *The Rhetoric of Nonverbal Communication: Readings.* Glenview, Illinois: Scott, Foresman.

Bostian, Lloyd R., 1973. "The Two-Step Flow Theory: Cross-Cultural Implications." In *Intercommunication among Nations and Peoples.* Edited by Michael H. Prosser. New York: Harper & Row.

Brandt, J. M. and H. L. Fromkin, 1974. "Number of Similar Strangers and Feelings of Undistinctiveness as Limits for the Similarity Attraction Relationship." Unpublished paper presented at the Midwestern Psychological Association Convention. (May). Chicago.

Breen, Myles P., 1975. "Severing the American Connection: Down Under." *Journal of Communication.* XXV. 2. (Spring). 183-186.

Brembeck, Cole S., and Walker H. Hill, 1973. *Cultural Challenge to Education.* Lexington, Massachusetts: Lexington Books.

Brislin, Richard W., Stephen Bochner, and Walter J. Lonner, 1975. *Cross-Cultural Perspectives on Learning.* New York: Halsted.

Brislin, Richard W., Walter J. Lonner, and Robert M. Thorndike, 1973. *Cross-Cultural Research Methods.* Foreword by Leonard Doob. New York: Wiley.

Broadbent, D. E., 1958. *Perception and Communication.* New York: Pergamon.

Browne, Ray B., Richard H. Crowder, Virgil L. Lokke, and William T. Stafford, 1968. *Frontiers of American Culture*. West Lafayette, Indiana: Purdue University.

Browne, Robert S., 1968. "Dialogue between the Races: A Top Priority." *Today's Speech*, 16;5-8.

Bryson, L., ed., 1948. *The Communication of Ideas*. New York: Institute for Religious and Social Studies.

Buber, Martin, 1965. *Between Man and Man*. New York: Macmillan.

Budd, Richard W. and Brent D. Ruben, eds., 1972. *Approaches to Human Communication*. Rochelle Park, New Jersey: Hayden.

Burgoon, Judee K., and Thomas J. Saine, 1978. *The Unspoken Dialogue: An Introduction to Nonverbal Communication*. Boston: Houghton Mifflin.

Burk, Jerry L., 1975. "The Effects of Ethnocentrism upon Intercultural Communication: Functional and Dysfunctional." Paper prepared for the Speech Communication Association Convention. Houston.

Burk, Jerry L., 1974. "An Explication and Evaluation of Cognitive Anthroplogy." In *International and Intercultural Communication Annual*, I, 24-38.

Burke, Kenneth, 1964. *Terms for Order*. Edited by Stanley Edgar Hyman, Bloomington, Indiana: Indiana University.

Burke, Kenneth, 1969. *A Rhetoric of Motives*. Berkeley: University of California.

Burling, Robbins, 1970. *Man's Many Voices: Language in Its Cultural Context*. New York: Holt.

Burton, John W., 1969. *Conflict and Communication: The Use of Controlled Communications in International Relations*. London: Macmillan.

Busignies, Henri, 1972. "Communication Channels." In *Communication, A Scientific American Book*. San Francisco: Freeman.

Caplow, Theodore, 1968. *Two against One: Coalitions in Triads*. Englewood Cliffs, New Jersey: Prentice-Hall.

Carey, James W., 1975. "Canadian Communication Theory: Extensions and Interpretations of Harold Innes." Paper presented at the Association for Education in Journalism Annual Meeting. Ottawa, Canada.

Carpenter, Edmund, 1973. *Oh What a Blow That Phantom Gave Me*. New York: Holt.

Carpenter, Edmund, and Marshall McLuhan, eds., 1960. *Explorations in Communication.* Boston: Beacon Press.

Casmir, Fred, ed., 1974, 1975, 1976. *International and Intercultural Communication Annual.* Vols. 1, 2 and 3. Falls Church, Virginia: Speech Communication Association.

Casmir, Fred L., 1973. "International, Intercultural Communication: An Annotated Bibliography." Speech Communication Module, Eric Clearinghouse on Reading and Communication Skills. Falls Church, Virginia: Speech Communication Association.

Cassata, Mary and Molefi Asante, 1977, eds., 1977. *The Social Uses of Mass Media.* Buffalo: The State University of New York.

Chaffee, Clarence C., 1971. *Problems in Effective Cross-Cultural Interaction.* Columbus, Ohio: Battle Memorial Institute.

Chapple, Eliot Dismore, 1970. *Culture and Biological Man.* New York: Holt.

Chas, Yuen Ren, 1968. *Language and Symbolic Systems.* Cambridge, Massachusetts: Cambridge University.

Cherry, Colin, 1957. *On Human Communication: A Review, a Survey and a Criticism.* Cambridge, Massachusetts: M.I.T.

Cherry, Colin, 1971. *World Communication: Threat or Promise?* New York: Wiley.

Chomsky, Noam, 1967. "The Formal Nature of Language." In *Biological Foundations of Language.* Edited by Eric H. Lennenberg. New York: Wiley.

Chomsky, Noam, 1966. "Three Models for the Description of Language." In *Communication and Culture: Readings.* Edited by Alfred Smith. New York: Holt.

Clay, V. S., 1966. "The Effect of Culture on Mother-Child Tactile Communication." Ph.D. dissertation, Teachers College, Columbia University, New York.

Cohen, Rosalie, Gerd Fraenkel, and John Brewer, 1967. "Implications for 'Culture Conflict' from a Semantic Feature Analysis of the Lexicon of the Hard Core Poor." In *Linguistics* (Winter).

Cole, Michael, John Gay, Joseph A. Glick, and Donald W. Sharp, 1971. *The Cultural Context of Learning and Thinking: An Exploration in Experimental Anthropology.* New York: Basic Books.

College of Communication Arts, Michigan State University, 1972-73. *Human Communication: International and Cross-Cultural Implications.* East Lansing.

Condon, E. C., 1973 a. *Conflicts in Values, Assumptions, Opinions: Human Relations in Cultural Context: Teacher Training Materials.* New Brunswick: Rutgers University.

Condon, E. C., 1973b. *Introduction to Cross-Cultural Communication: Human Relations in Cultural Context: Series C: Teacher Training Materials.* (Reference Pamphlets on Intercultural Communication). New Brunswick: Rutgers University.

Condon, John C., 1974. *Semantics and Communication,* 2nd ed. New York: Macmillan.

Condon, John C. and Fathi Yousef, 1975. *An Introduction to Intercultural Communication.* Indianapolis: Bobbs-Merrill.

Condon, John C. and Mitsuko Saito, eds. 1976. *Communicating across Cultures for What? A Symposium on Humane Responsibility in Intercultural Communication.* Foreword by Kenneth E. Boulding. Tokyo: The Simul Press.

Condon, John C. and Mitsuko Saito, eds., 1974. *Intercultural Encounters with Japan: Communication-Contact and Conflict.* Tokyo: Simul Press.

Cook, Albert B., III., 1969. *Introduction to the English Language: Structure and History.* New York: Ronald.

Dance, Frank E. X., ed., 1967. *Human Communication Theory: Original Essays.* New York: Holt.

Dasgupta, Satadal, 1973. "Communication and Innovation in Indian Villages." In *Intercommunication among Nations and Peoples.* Edited by Michael H. Prosser. New York: Harper & Row.

Davis, A. L., ed., 1972. *Culture, Class and Language Variety.* Urbana, Illinois.

Davis, Flora, 1971. *Inside Tuition: What We Know about Nonverbal Communication.* New York: New American Library.

Davis, Kingsley, 1959. "The Myth of Functional Analysis as a Special Method in Sociology and Anthropology." *American Sociological Review* 24, 752-772.

Davison, W. Phillips, 1974. *Mass Communication and Conflict: The Role of the Information Media in the Advancement of International Understanding.* New York: Praeger.

deBoer, Richard James, 1967. "The Netsilik Eskimo and the Origin of Human Behavior." *MSS,* (1969) 8.

de Cardona, Elizabeth, 1975. "Multinational Television." *Journal of Communication* (Spring). XXV, 2, 122-127.

de Saussure, Ferdinand, 1959. *Course in General Linguistics.* Translated by Wade Baskin. New York: McGraw-Hill.

Deutsch, Karl W., 1966. "On Social Communication and the Metropolis." In *Communication and Culture: Readings.* Edited by Alfred Smith. New York: Holt.

Deutsch, Karl W., 1953. *Nationalism and Social Communication.* Cambridge, Massachusetts: M.I.T.

Deutsch, Karl W., 1966. *The Nerves of Government: Models of Political Communication and Control.* New York: Free Press.

Deutsch, M. and associates, 1967. *The Disadvantaged Child.* New York: Basic Books

DeVito, Joseph, 1970. *The Psychology of Speech and Language: An Introduction to Psycholinguistics.* New York: Random House.

DiStefano, J. J., 1972. "A Conceptual Framework for Understanding Cross-Cultural Management Problems." Unpublished paper, The University of Western Ontario.

Dizard, Wilson P., 1964. "American Television's Foreign Markets." In *Television Quarterly,* 3 (3).

Dodd, Carley H., 1977. *Perspectives on Cross-Cultural Communication.* Dubuque: Kendall/Hunt.

Doob, Leonard, 1961. *Communication in Africa: A Search for Boundaries.* New Haven: Yale University.

Douglas, Mary, 1973. *Natural Symbols.* New York: Vintage Books.

Downs, James F., 1971. *Cultures in Crisis.* Beverly Hills, California: Glencoe.

Dube, S.C., 1967. "A Note on Communication in Economic Development." In *Communication and Change in the Developing Countries.* Edited by Daniel Lerner and Wilbur Schramm. Foreword by Lyndon B. Johnson. Honolulu: East-West Center.

Duncan, Hugh Dalziel, 1962. *Communication and Social Order.* New York: Bedminister.

Duncan, Hugh, 1968. *Symbols in Society.* New York: Oxford University.

Durkheim, Emile, 1951. *The Division of Labour in Society.* Translated by G. Simpson. Glencoe, Illinois: Scott, Foresman.

Eakins, Barbara, and Gene Eakins, 1978. *Differences in Human Communication.* Boston: Houghton Mifflin.

Eapen, K. E., 1973. *The Media and Development.* Leeds, England: J.A. Kavanaugh.

Edelstein, Alex S., 1974. *The Uses of Communication in Decision-Making: A Comparative Study of Yugoslavia and the United States.* New York: Praeger.

Edmonson, Munro S., 1973. "The Anthropology of Values." In *Culture and Life: Essays in Memory of Clyde Kluckhohn.* Edited by Walter W. Taylor, John L. Fischer, and Evon Z. Vogt. Carbondale, Illinios: Southern Illinois University.

Efron, David, 1972. *Gesture, Race, and Culture.* The Hague: Mouton.

Eisenberg, Ralph, and Ralph Smith, 1971. *Nonverbal Communication.* Indianapolis: Bobbs-Merrill.

Ekman, Paul and Wallace V. Friesen, 1975. *Unmasking the Face.* Englewood Cliffs, New Jersey: Prentice Hall.

Ekman, P., W.V. Friesen, and T. J. Tausig, 1969. "VID-R and SCAN: Tools and Methods in the Analysis of Facial Expression and Body Movement." In *Analysis of Communication Content.* Edited by G. Gerbner, O. Holst, K. Krippendorff, W. Parsley, and P. Stone. New York: Wiley.

Ellul, Jacques, 1964. *The Technological Society.* Introduction by Robert K. Merton. Translated by John Wilkinson. New York: Knopf.

Ellul, Jacques, 1966. *Propaganda: The Formation of Men's Attitudes.* Introduction by Konrad Kellen. Translated by Konrad Kellen and Jean Lerner. New York: Random House.

Emmert, P. and W. D. Brooks, 1970. *Methods of Research in Communication.* Boston: Houghton Mifflin.

Epps, Edgar G., ed., 1974. *Cultural Pluralism.* Berkeley: McCutchan.

Ervin-Tripp, Susan M., 1973. *Language Acquistion and Communicative Choice: Essays.* Selected and introduced by Anwar S. Dill. Stanford: Stanford University.

Fagen, Patricia, 1974. "Media in Allende's Chile: Some Contradictions." *Journal of Communication,* 25 (Winter), 59-70.

Fagen, Richard, 1966. *Politics and Communication.* Boston: Little, Brown.

Fast, Julius, 1971. *Body Language.* London: Pan Books.

Felstehausen, H. M., 1971. "Conceptual Limits of Development Communication Theory." Paper prepared for presentation at the annual meeting of the Association for Education in Journalism. Columbia, South Carolina (August).

Ferguson, Charles A., 1971. *Language Structure and Language Use: Essays.* Selected and introduced by Anwar S. Dill. Stanford: Stanford University.

Fersh, Seymour, ed., 1974. *Learning about Peoples and Cultures.* Evanston, Illinois: McDougal.

Fieg, John P. and John G. Blair, 1975. *There Is a Difference: 12 Intercultural Perspectives.* Washington, D. C.: Washington International Center.

Fischer, Heinz-Dietrich and John C. Merrill, eds., 1970. *International Communications: Media, Channels, Functions.* New York: Hastings.

Fischer, Heinz-Dietrich, and John C. Merrill, eds., 1976. *International and Intercultural Communication.* New York: Hastings.

Fishman, Joshua A., 1972. *Language in Sociocultural Change: Essays.* Selected and introduced by Anwar S. Dill. Stanford: Stanford University.

Fishman, Joshua A., 1966. "A Systemization of the Whorfian Hypothesis." In *Communication and Culture: Readings.* Edited by Alfred Smith. New York: Holt.

Foa, U.G. 1971. "Interpersonal and Economic Resources." *Science.* 171. 345-351.

Foster, George M., 1962. *Traditional Cultures and the Impact of Technological Change.* New York: Harper.

Foster, Thomas, William K. Katz, and Henry J. Otto, 1966. *Value Orientations in Four Elementary Schools.* Austin: University of Texas.

Freire, Paulo, 1971. *Pedagogy of the Oppressed.* New York: Seabury.

Fried, Charles, 1970. *An Anatomy of Values: Problems of Personal and Social Choice.* Cambridge, Massachusetts: Harvard.

Fromkin, H. L., 1973. *The Psychology of Uniqueness: Avoidance of Similarity and Seeking of Differences.* Paper No. 438. West Lafayette, Indiana: Institute for Research in the Behavioral, Economic, and Management Sciences, Krannert School of Industrial Administration, Purdue University.

Fromkin, H. L., and B. Demming, 1967. "A Survey of Retrospective Reports of Feelings of Uniqueness." Unpublished manuscript. Ohio State University.

Fromm, Eric, 1941. *Escape from Freedom.* New York. Ivington.

Fuchs, Lawrence H., 1967. "The Role and Communication Task of the Change Agent—Experiences of the Peace Corps Volunteers in the

Philippines." In *Communication and Change in the Developing Countries*. Edited by Daniel Lerner and Wilbur Schramm. Foreword by Lyndon B. Johnson. Honolulu: East-West Center.

Geertz, Clifford, 1973. *The Interpretation of Cultures*. New York: Basic Books.

Geertz, Clifford, 1971, ed., *Myth, Symbol, and Culture*. New York: W. W. Norton.

Gerbner, George, 1966. "On Defining Communication: Still Another View." In *Journal of Communication*, 16, 99-103.

Gerbner, George, Larry Gross, and William H. Melody, eds., 1973. *Communications Technology and Social Policy: Understanding the New Cultural Revolution*. New York: Wiley.

Glazer, N. and Daniel P. Moynihan, 1963. *Beyond the Melting Pot: The Negroes, Puerto Ricans, Jews, Italians and the Irish*. Cambridge, Massachusetts: M.I.T.

Gleeson, Patrick, and Nancy Wakefield, eds., 1968. *Language and Culture*. Columbus, Ohio: Merrill.

Glenn, Edmund S., 1954. "Semantic Difficulties in International Communication." In *Etc.* 11, 163-180.

Glenn, Edmund S., 1972. "Meaning and Behavior: Communication and Culture." In *Intercultural Communication: A Reader*. Edited by Larry Samovar and Richard Porter. Belmont, California: Wadsworth.

Goffman, Erving, 1963. *Behavior in Public Places*. New York: Free Press.

Goffman, Erving, 1967. *Interaction Ritual: Essays in Face-to-Face Behavior*. Chicago: Aldine.

Goffman, Erving, 1959. *The Presentation of Self in Everyday Life*. Garden City, New York: Doubleday.

Goffman, Erving, 1969. *Strategic Interaction*. Philadelphia: University of Pennsylvania.

Goodenough, Ward, 1961. "Comments on Cultural Evolution." In *Daedalus*, 90, 521-528.

Goodenough, Ward, 1963. *Cooperation in Change*. New York: Russell Sage Foundation.

Goodheart, Eugene, 1973. *Culture and the Radical Conscience*. Cambridge, Massachusetts: Harvard.

Goodman, M. E., 1967. *The Individual and Culture*. Homewood, Illinois: Dorsey.

Grabowski, Stanley M., ed., 1972. *Paulo Freire: A Revolutionary Dilemma for the Adult Educator*. Syracuse, New York: Syracuse University.

Greenberg, B., and B. Dervin, eds., 1970. *Use of the Mass Media by the Urban Poor*. New York: Praegar.

Greenberg, Joseph H., 1971. *Language, Culture and Communication: Essays*. Selected and introduced by Anwar S. Dill. Stanford: Stanford University.

Greenberg, Joseph H., ed., 1963. *Universals of Language*. Cambridge, Massachusetts: M.I.T.

Gregson, Robert, 1975. *The Psychometrics of Similarity*. Chicago: Academic Press.

Greyser, Stephen A., 1973. *Cultural Policy and Arts Administration*. Cambridge, Massachusetts: Harvard.

Gross, R., and P. Osterman, 1971. *Individualism: Man in Modern Society*. New York: Dell.

Gumperz, John J., 1971. *Language in Social Groups: Essays*. Selected and introduced by Anwar S. Dill. Stanford: Stanford University.

Hachten, William, 1971. *Muffled Drums: The News Media in Africa*. Iowa City: University of Iowa.

Hailey, Lord, 1957. *An African Survey—Revised 1956*. London: Oxford University.

Hall, Edward T., 1976. *Beyond Culture*. Garden City, New York: Doubleday.

Hall, Edward, 1966. *The Hidden Dimension*. Garden City, New York: Doubleday.

Hall, Edward, 1959. *The Silent Language*. Garden City, New York: Doubleday.

Hall, Edward T. and G. L. Trager, 1953. *The Analysis of Culture*. Washington, D. C.: American Council of Learned Societies.

Hall, Peter M. and John P. Hewitt, 1973. "The Quasi-Theory of Communication and the Management of Dissent." In *Intercommunication among Nations and Peoples*. Edited by Michael H. Prosser, New York: Harper & Row.

Hallowell, A.I., 1972. "Cultural Factors in the Structuralization of Perception." In *Intercultural Communication: A Reader*. Edited by Larry Samovar and Richard Porter. Belmont, California: Wadsworth.

Hallowell, A. Irving, 1964. "Ojibwa Ontology, Behavior, and World View." In *Primitive Views of the World*. Edited by Stanley Diamond. New York: Columbia University.

Harms, L. S., 1973. *Intercultural Communication*. New York: Harper & Row.

Harrington, Michael, 1962. *The Other America.* New York: Macmillan.

Harris, Marvin, 1971. *Culture, Man and Nature.* New York: Crowell.

Hastorf, Albert H., David J. Schneider, and Judith Polefka, 1970. *Person Perception.* Reading, Massachusetts: Addison-Wesley.

Haugen, Einar, 1972. *The Ecology of Language: Essays.* Selected and introduced by Anwar S. Dill. Stanford: Stanford University.

Henle, Paul, 1958, 1965. *Language, Thought and Culture.* Ann Arbor, Michigan: University of Michigan.

Henry, Jules, 1963. *Culture against Man.* Middlesex, England: Penquin.

Herberichs, Gerard, 1973. "On Theories of Public Opinion and International Organization." In *Intercommunication among Nations and Peoples.* Edited by Michael H. Prosser, New York: Harper & Row.

Herder, J. G., 1969. *Social and Political Culture.* London: Cambridge University.

Hiebert, Ray Eldon, Donald F. Ungurait and Thomas W. Bohn, 1974. *Mass Media: An Introduction to Modern Communication.* New York: McKay.

Hildum, Donald C., ed., 1967. *Language and Thought: An Enduring Problem in Psychology.* Princeton: Princeton University.

Hinde, Robert A., 1972. *Nonverbal Communication.* Cambridge, Massachusetts: Cambridge University.

Hockett, Charles F., 1958. *A Course in Modern Linguistics.* New York: Macmillan.

Hockett, Charles F., 1960. "The Origin of Speech." In *Scientific American,* CCIII, 89-96.

Hockett, Charles F., 1963. "The Problem of Universals in Language." In *Universals of Language.* Edited by Joseph H. Greenberg. Cambridge, Massachusetts: M.I.T.

Hoffman, Arthur S., ed., 1968. *International Communication and the New Diplomacy.* Bloomington, Indiana: Indiana University.

Hoggart, Richard, 1972. *On Culture and Communication.* New York: Oxford University Press.

Hoijer, Harry, ed., 1954. *Language in Culture.* Chicago: University of Chicago.

Hoijer, Harry, 1972. "The Sapir-Whorf Hypothesis." In *Intercultural Communication: A Reader.* Edited by Larry Samovar and Richard Porter. Belmont, California: Wadsworth.

Holton, Gerald, ed., 1967. *Science and Culture.* Boston: Beacon Press.

Homans, George C., 1950. *The Human Group.* New York: Harcourt Brace Jovanovitch.

Hoopes, David W., ed., 1971, 1972, 1973, 1974, 1975. *Readings in Intercultural Communication.* Volumes 1-5. Washington, D.C.: SIETAR, Georgetown University.

Hopkinson, Tom, 1967. "Newspapers Must Wait in Priority Queue." *IPI Report* 16 (June), 18.

Hymes, Dell H., 1964. *Language in Culture and Society: A Reader in Linguistics and Anthropology.* New York: Harper & Row.

Hymes, Dell , 1973. "Toward Ethnographies of Communication." In *Intercommunication among Nations and Peoples.* Edited by Michael H. Prosser. New York: Harper & Row.

Illich, Ivan D., 1971. *Celebration of Awareness.* Garden City, New York: Doubleday.

Imada, Shigeko Y., 1974. "A Brief Introduction to Japanese Phonology and Writing." In *Intercultural Encounters with Japan: Communication—Contact and Conflict.* Edited by John C. Condon and Mitsuko Saito. Toyko: Simul Press.

Inkeles, Alex, and David H. Smith. 1974. *Becoming Modern: Individual Change in Six Developing Countries.* Cambridge: Harvard University Press.

Innis, Harold, 1973. *The Bias of Communication.* Toronto: Univeristy of Toronto.

Innis, Harold A., 1972. *Empire and Communications.* Revised by Mary Q. Innis. Foreword by Marshall McLuhan. Toronto: University of Toronto.

Inose, Hiroshi, 1972. "Communication Networks." In *Communication: A Scientific American Book.* San Francisco: Freeman.

Ishii, Satoshi, (N.D.) "Japanese Nonverbal Communicative Signs: A Cross-Cultural Survey." Unpublished paper, Otsuma Women's University, Tokyo.

Jain, Nemi C., ed., 1977. *International and Intercultural Communication Annual.* Volume IV. Falls Church, Virginia: Speech Communication Association.

Jain, Nemi C., Michael H. Prosser, and Melvin H. Miller, eds., 1974. *Intercultural Communication: Proceedings of the Speech Communication Association Summer Conference, X,* Falls Church, Virginia: Speech Communication Association.

Jain, Nemi C. and Richard L. Cummings, eds., 1975. *Proceedings of the Conference on Intercultural Communication and Teacher Education.* Milwaukee: Milwaukee Urban Observatory, University of Wisconsin-Milwaukee.

James, William, 1950. *The Principles of Psychology.* New York: Peter Smith.

Jandt, Fred E., 1973. *Conflict Resolution through Communication.* New York: Harper & Row.

Jerome, Judson, 1970. *Culture out of Anarchy: The Reconstruction of American Higher Learning.* New York: Herder and Herder.

Johnson, Nicholas, 1973. "What Can We Do about Television?" In *Mass Media: The Invisible Environment.* Edited by Robert J. Glessing and William P. White. Chicago: Science Research Associates.

Jones, James M., 1972. *Prejudice and Racism.* Reading, Massachusetts: Addison-Wesley.

Kakonis, Tom E. and James C. Wilcox, eds., 1971. *Now and Tomorrow: The Rhetoric of Culture in Transition.* Lexington, Massachusetts: Heath.

Kaplan, David, and Robert A. Manners, 1972. *Culture Theory.* Englewood Clifts, New Jersey: Prentice-Hall.

Katz, Elihu, 1966. "Communication Research and the Image of Society: Convergence of Two Traditions." In *Communication and Culture: Readings.* Edited by Alfred Smith. New York: Holt.

Katz, Elihu, 1957. "The Two-Step Flow of Communication: An Up-to-Date Report on an Hypothesis." In *Public Opinion Quarterly,* 21, 61-78.

Katz, Elihu and Paul F. Lazarsfeld, 1955. *Personal Influence: The Part Played by People in the Flow of Mass Communications.* New York: Free Press.

Keltner, John W., 1977. *Interpersonal Speech Communication: Elements and Structures.* Belmont, California: Wadsworth.

Kiesler, Charles A., and Sara B. Kiesler, 1970. *Conformity.* Reading, Massachusetts: Addison-Wesley.

Kimball, Solon, 1974. *Culture and the Educative Process: An Anthropological Perspective.* New York: Teachers College.

Kimball, Solon T. and Jacquetta H. Burnett, 1973. "Learning and Culture." Proceedings of the 1972 Annual Spring Meeting of the American Ethnological Society. Seattle.

King, Stephen W., 1975. *Communication and Social Influence.* Reading, Massachusetts: Addison-Wesley.

Kleinjans, Everett, 1975. *Communication and Change in Developing Countries.* No. 12. Honolulu: East-West Center.

Kluckhohn, Clyde, 1958. "The Scientific Study of Values and Contemporary Civilization." In *Proceedings of the American Philosophical Society,* 102, 469-76.

Kluckhohn, C., 1962. *Culture and Behavior: Collected Essays of Clyde Kluckhohn.* Edited by Richard Kluckhohn. New York: Free Press.

Kluckhohn, Florence Rockwood and Fred L. Strodbeck, 1961. *Variations in Value Orientations.* Evanston, Illinois: Row, Peterson.

Knapp, Mark, 1972. *Nonverbal Communication in Human Interaction.* New York: Holt.

Koide, Fumiko, 1974. "Some Observations on the Japanese Language." In *Intercultural Encounters with Japan: Communication—Contact and Conflict.* Edited by John C. Condon and Mitsuko Saito. Tokyo: Simul Press.

Koivumaki, Judith Hall, 1975. "Body Language Taught Here." In *Journal of Communication,* 25.1 (Winter), 26-30.

Kopan, Andrew, 1974. *Rethinking Educational Equality.* Edited by Andrew Kopan and Herbert Walberg. Berkeley, California: University of California.

Lacy, Dan Mabry, 1965. *Freedom and Communications.* Urbana, Illinois: University of Illinois.

Lambert, Wallace E., 1972. *Language, Psychology and Culture: Essays.* Selected and introduced by Anwar S. Dill. Stanford: Stanford University.

Langer, Suzanne, 1942. *Philosophy in a New Key.* Cambridge, Massachusetts: Harvard.

Lazarsfeld, Paul F., Bernard Berelson, and Hazel Gaudet, 1948. *The People's Choice.* 2nd ed. New York: Columbia University.

Leach, Edmund R., 1965. "Culture and Social Cohesion: An Anthropologist's View." In *Science and Culture.* Edited by Gerald Holton. Boston: Beacon Press.

Leacock, Eleanor B., 1971. *The Culture of Poverty: A Critique.* New York: Simon & Schuster.

Lee, Dorothy D., 1959. *Freedom and Culture.* Englewood Cliffs, New Jersey: Prentice-Hall.

Lee, Irving J., 1941. *Language Habits in Human Affairs: An Introduction to General Semantics.* Foreword by Alfred Korzybski. New York: Harper.

Lerner, Daniel, 1967. "International Cooperation and Communication in National Development." In *Communication and Change in Developing Countries.* Edited by Daniel Lerner and Wilbur Schramm. Foreword by Lyndon B. Johnson. Honolulu: East-West Center Press.

LeVine, Robert Alan, 1973. *Culture, Behavior and Personality.* Chicago: Aldine.

MacAndrew, Craig and Robert Edgerton, 1970. "Man without Culture." In *Cultural Shock: A Reader in Modern Cultural Anthropology.* Edited by Philip K. Bock. New York: Knopf.

McCormack, Thelma, 1973. "Social Change and the Mass Media." In *Intercommunication Among Nations and Peoples.* Edited by Michael H. Prosser. New York: Harper & Row.

McLuhan, Herbert Marshall, 1970. *Culture Is Our Business.* New York: New American Library.

McLuhan, Marshall, 1962. *The Gutenberg Galaxy: The Making of Typographic Man.* New York: New American Library.

McLuhan, Marshall, 1964. *Understanding Media: The Extensions of Man.* New York: New American Library.

McNeil, David, 1970. *The Acquisition of Language: The Study of Developmental Psycholinguistics.* New York: Harper & Row.

McNelly, John, 1967. "Media Accessibility and Exposure in Developing Urban Societies: Some Directions for Communication Research." Paper presented at the Conference on Research Needs: Communication and Urbanization. Honolulu.

Maletzke, Gerhard, 1970. "Intercultural and International Communication." In *International Communication: Media, Channels and Functions.* Edited by Dietrich Heinz-Fischer and John C. Merrill. New York: Hasting House.

Mandelbaum, David G., ed., 1949. *Selected Writings of Edward Sapir in Language, Culture, and Personality.* Berkeley: University of California.

Markham, James W., ed., 1970. *International Communication as a Field of Study.* Iowa City: University of Iowa.

May, Rollo, 1969. *Love and Will.* New York: Norton.

Mead, George H., 1967. *Mind, Self and Society.* Chicago: University of Chicago.

Mead, Margaret, 1970. *Culture and Commitment*. Garden City, New York: Doubleday.

Mehrabian, Albert, 1971. *Silent Messages*. Belmont, California: Wadsworth.

Merrill, John C. and Ralph Lowenstein, 1971. *Media, Messages and Men: New Perspectives in Communication*. New York: McKay.

Merritt, Richard L., ed., 1972. *Communication in International Politics*. Urbana, Illinois: University of Illinois.

Miller, George A., 1951. *Language and Communication: A Scientific and Psychological Introduction*. New York: McGraw-Hill.

Miller, Gerald R. and Herbert W. Simons, ed., 1974. *Perspectives on Communication in Social Conflict*. Englewood Cliffs, New Jersey: Prentice-Hill.

Montagu, Ashley, 1971. *Touching: The Human Significance of the Skin*. New York: Columbia.

Morsbach, Helmut, 1973. "Aspects of Nonverbal Communication in Japan." In *Journal of Nervous and Mental Disease*, 157, 262-277.

Mowlana, Hamid, 1971. *International Communication: A Selected Bibliography*. Dubuque: Kendall/Hunt.

Mowlana, Hamid, 1976. "A Paradigm for Mass Media Analysis." In *International and Intercultural Communication*. Edited by Heinz Dietrich-Fischer and John C. Merrill. New York: Hastings House.

Mowlana, Hamid, 1977. "Social and Political Implications of Communication Satellite Applications in Developed and Developing Countries." In *Communication Yearbook I*. Edited by Brent Ruben. New Brunswick: Transaction Books.

Mukasa-Bilikuddembe, Jospeh, 1968. "The Mirror." In *Short East-African Plays*. Edited by David Cook and Miles Lee. London: Heinemann.

Muramatsu, Masumi, 1974. "Symposium on Conference Interpreting and Problems of Translation." In *Intercultural Encounters with Japan: Communication—Contact and Conflict*. Edited by John C. Condon and Mitsuko Saito. Tokyo: Simul Press.

Murdock, George, 1945. "Common Denominator of Cultures." In *Science of Man in the World Crises*. Edited by R. Linton. New York: Columbia.

Murphy, Robert D., 1977. *Mass Communication and Human Interaction*. Boston: Houghton Mifflin.

Nakane, Chie, 1972. Human Relations in Japan (Summary Translation of "Tateshakai no Ningen Kankei." *Personal Relations in a Vertical Society).* Tokyo: Ministry of Foreign Affairs.

Nan Lin, 1973. *The Study of Human Communication.* Indianapolis: Bobbs-Merrill.

Naroll, R., 1973. "The Culture-Bearing Unit in Cross-Cultural Surveys." In *Handbook of Method in Cultural Anthropology.* Edited by R. Naroll and R. Cohen. New York: Columbia.

Newcomb, Theodore M., 1966. "An Approach to the Study of Communicative Acts." In *Communication and Culture: Readings.* Edited by Alfred Smith. New York: Holt.

Nida, Eugene A., 1975. *Language Structure and Translation: Essays.* Selected and introduced by Anwar S. Dill. Stanford: Stanford University.

Nieburg, Harold L., 1973. *Culture Storm: Politics and the Ritual Order.* New York: St Martin.

Nierenberg, Gerard V., and Henry H. Calero, 1973. *How to Read a Person Like a Book.* New York: Pocketbooks.

Norbeck, Edward, Douglass Price-Williams, and William M. McCord, 1968. *The Study of Personality: An Interdisciplinary Appraisal.* New York: Holt.

Nyerre, Julius K., 1970. "All Mankind Is One." In *Sow the Wind, Reap the Whirlwind: Heads of State Address the United Nations.* Edited by Michael H. Prosser. New York: Morrow.

O'Brien, William V., 1973. "International Propaganda and the Minimum World Public Order." In *Intercommunication Among Nations and Peoples.* Edited by Michael H. Prosser. New York: Harper & Row.

O'Doherty, E. F. 1958. "Bilingualism: Educational Aspects." In *Advances in Science,* 56, 282-286.

Oliver, Robert T., 1971. *Communication and Culture in Ancient India and China.* Syracuse: Syracuse University.

Oliver, Robert T., 1962. *Culture and Communication: The Problem of Penetrating National and Cultural Boundaries.* Springfield, Illinois: Charles C. Thomas.

Ong, Walter J., S.J. 1977. *Interfaces of the Word.* Ithaca: Cornell University Press.

Ong, Walter J., S.J. 1967a. *In the Human Grain: Further Explorations of Contemporary Culture.* New York: Macmillan.

Ong, Walter J., S.J., 1967b. *The Presence of the Word: Some Prolegomena for Cultural and Religious History.* New Haven: Yale.

Osgood, Charles E., George J. Suci, and Percy Tannenbaum, 1957. *The Measurement of Meaning.* Urbana, Illinois: University of Illinois.

Osgood, Charles E., William H. May, and Murray S. Miron, 1975. *Cross-Cultural Universals of Effective Meaning.* Urbana, Illinois: University of Illinois.

Oswalt, Wendell H., 1970. *Understanding Our Culture: An Anthropological View.* New York: Holt.

Pace, R. Wayne, Robert R. Boren, and Brent D. Peterson, 1975. *Communication Behavior and Experiments: A Scientific Approach.* Belmont, California: Wadsworth.

Parsons, Talcott and Edward A. Shils, eds., 1962. *Toward a General Theory of Action.* Cambridge, Massachusetts: Harvard. *Patterns of Communication in and out of Japan: 20 Original Studies of Japanese Communication—in the Family, in Public, and Across Cultures,* 1974. (Senior Thesis Study Group of International Christian University, Tokyo.)

Patton, Bobby R., and Kim Griffen, 1974. *Interpersonal Communication: Basic Text and Readings.* New York: Harper & Row.

Pederson, Paul, Walter J. Lonner and Juris G. Draguns, 1976. *Counseling Across Cultures.* Honolulu: East-West Center Press.

Peterson, Theodore, William L. Rivers, and Jay W. Jenson, 1965. *The Mass Media.* New York: Holt.

Piaget, Jean, 1969. *The Mechanisms of Perception.* Translated by G. N. Seagrim. New York: Basic Books.

Poiret, Maude, 1970. *Body Talk: The Science of Kinesics.* New York: Universal.

Porter, John, 1965. *The Vertical Mosaic: An Analysis of Social Class and Power in Canada.* Toronto: University of Toronto.

Pribram, Karl, 1949. *Conflicting Patterns of Thought.* Washington, D.C.: Public Affairs Press.

Price-Williams, D., 1972. "Cross-Cultural Studies." In *Intercultural Communication: A Reader.* Edited by Larry Samovar and Richard Porter. Belmont, California: Wadsworth.

Prosser, Michael H. ed., 1977a. "Communications Media and Attitudinal and Social Change." In *The Social Uses of Mass Communication.* Edited by Mary B. Cassata and Molefi K. Asante. Buffalo: State University of New York at Buffalo.

Prosser, Michael H., ed., 1969. *An Ethic for Survival: Adlai Stevenson Speaks on International Affairs, 1936-1965.* New York: Morrow.

Prosser, Michael H., 1978. "Intercultural Communication: Major Constructs. An Overview." In *Communication Yearbook II.* Edited by Brent Ruben. New Brunswick: Transaction.

Prosser, Michael H., ed., 1973a. *Intercommunication among Nations and Peoples.* New York: Harper & Row.

Prosser, Michael H., 1973b. *Major Books on Intercultural Communication.* Washington, D.C.: SIETAR, Georgetown University.

Prosser, Michael H., ed., 1970. *Sow the Wind, Reap the Whirlwind: Heads of State Address the United Nations.* 2 Vols., New York: Morrow.

Prosser, Michael H., ed., 1974 (1975). *Syllabi in Intercultural Communication* Charlottesville, Virginia: Department of Speech Communication, University of Virginia.

Prosser. Michael H., 1975. "Teaching Intercultural Communication: An Illustrative Syllabus and Bibliography." In *Speech Teacher,* XXIV, 3 (September), 242-250.

Prosser, Michael H., ed., 1977b. *USIA Intercultural Communication Course: 1977 Proceedings.* Washington, D.C.: USIA.

Pye, Lucian W., ed., 1963. *Communications and Political Development.* Princeton: Princeton University.

Rao, Y. V. Lakshmana, 1966. *Communications and Development: A Study of Two Indian Villages.* Minneapolis: University of Minnesota.

Rattray, Robert S., 1923. *The Ashanti.* London: Oxford University.

Reich, Charles A., March 8, 1971. "Beyond Consciousness." *New York Times,* p. 311.

Reich, Charles A., 1970. *The Greening of America.* New York: Bantam.

Renwick, George, in progress. *Intercultural Communication: A Bibliography on Intergroup, Ethnic and Race Relations.* Washington, D.C.: SIETAR, Georgetown University.

Rich, Andrea, 1974. *Interracial Communication.* New York: Harper & Row.

Riesman, D., 1954. *Individualisms Reconsidered.* Glencoe, Illinois: Scott, Foresman.

Rivers, William L., Theodore Peterson and Jay W. Jensen, 1971. *The Mass Media and Modern Society.* San Francisco: Rinehart Press.

Robertson, Stuart and Frederic G. Cassidy, 1954. _The Development of Modern English._ 2nd edition. Englewood Cliffs, New Jersey: Prentice-Hall.

Robinson, Gertrude Jock, 1977. _Tito's Maverick Media: The Politics of Mass Communication in Yugoslavia._ Urbana: The University of Illinois Press.

Rogers, Carl R., 1961. _On Becoming a Person._ Boston: Houghton Mifflin.

Rogers, Everett M., 1976. _Communication and Development: Critical Perspectives._ Beverly Hills: Sage.

Rogers, Everett M., 1973._Communication Strategies for Family Planning._ New York: Macmillan.

Rogers, Everett M., in association with Lynn Svenning, 1969. _Modernization Among Peasants: The Impact of Communication._ New York: Free Press.

Rogers, Everett M., and F. Floyd Shoemaker, 1971. _Communication of Innovations: A Cross-Cultural Approach._ New York: Free Press.

Romulo, Carlos P., 1977. _Economic Decolonization: The New Imperative of Our Time._ Manila: National Media Production Center.

Rosenberg, Bernard, and David Manning White, 1971. _Mass Culture Revisited._ New York: Free Press.

Roshco, Bernard, 1976. _Newsmaking._ Chicago: University of Chicago Press.

Roszak, Theodore, 1968. _The Making of a Counter Culture._ Garden City, New York: Doubleday.

Roszak, Theodore, 1972. _Where the Wasteland Ends._ Garden City, New York: Doubleday.

Roy, Prodipto, Fredrick B. Waisanen, and Everett M. Rogers, 1969. _The Impact of Communication on Rural Development: An Investigation in Costa Rica and India._ Paris: National Institute of Community Development.

Ruben, Brent D., 1977, 1978. _Communication Yearbook_ I, II. New Brunswick: Transaction Books.

Ruesch, Jurgen, and Gregory Bateson, 1951. _Communication: The Social Matrix of Psychiatry._New York: New York.

Ruesch, Jurgen, and Weldon Kees, 1956, 1970. _Nonverbal Communication: Notes on Visual Perception of Human Relations._ Berkeley: University of California.

Ruhly, Sharon, 1975. "The Major Triad Revisited: A Potential Guide for Intercultural Research." Paper presented at the Speech Communication Association Convention. Houston.

Ruhly, Sharon, 1976. *Orientations to Intercultural Communication.* Chicago: Science Research Associates.

Russell, Bertrand, 1959. *My Philosophical Development.* New York: Simon and Schuster.

Salomon, Louis B., 1966. *Semantics and Common Sense.* New York: Holt.

Samovar, Larry and Richard E. Porter, eds., 1972, 1976. *Intercultural Communication: A Reader.* First and second editions. Belmont, California: Wadsworth.

Sapir, Edward, 1958,1964. *Culture, Language and Personality.* Berkeley: University of California.

Sapir, Edward, 1949. *Selected Writings of Edward Sapir in Language, Culture and Personality.* Edited by David G. Mandelbaum. Berkeley: University of California.

Sarason, Seymour Bernard, 1971. *The Culture of the School and the Problem of Change.* Boston: Allyn and Bacon.

Sarason, Seymour B., 1972. *The Creation of Settings and the Future Societies.* San Francisco: Jossey-Buss.

Scheflen, Albert E., 1967. "On the Structuring of Human Communication." In *Communication and Culture: Readings.* Edited by Alfred Smith. New York: Holt.

Schelling, Thomas C., 1960. *The Strategy of Conflict.* Cambridge, Massachusetts: Harvard.

Schiller, Herbert I., 1969. *Mass Communications and American Empire.* New York: M. Kelly.

Schiller, Herbert I., 1973. *The Mind Managers.* Boston: Beacon Press.

Schneider, Marie, 1971. "How Others See Us." *Daedalus.*

Schramm, Wilbur, 1967. "Communication and Change." In *Communication and Change in the Developing Countries.* Edited by Daniel Lerner and Wilbur Schramm. Foreword by Lyndon B. Johnson. Honolulu: East-West Center Press.

Schramm, Wilbur, ed., 1960. *Mass Communications.* Urbana, Illinois: University of Illinois.

Schramm, Wilbur, 1964. *Mass Media and National Development: The*

Role of Information in the Developing Countries. Stanford: Stanford University.

Schramm, Wilbur, and Daniel Lerner, eds., 1976. *Communication and Change: The Last Ten Years -- and the Next.* Honolulu: The East-West Center.

Scott, Michael D., and William G. Powers, 1978. *Interpersonal Communication: A Question of Needs.* Boston: Houghton Mifflin.

Sebeok, Thomas A., Alfred S. Hayes, and Mary Catherine Bateson, eds., 1964. *Approaches to Semiotics.* The Hague: Mouton.

Seelye, H., Ned, and V. Lynn Tyler, eds., 1977. *Intercultural Communicator Resources.* Provo: Brigham Young University.

Segall, Marshall H., Donald Campbell, and Melville J. Herskovitz, 1966. *The Influence of Culture on Visual Perception.* Indianapolis: Bobbs-Merrill.

Semour-Ure, Colin, 1974. *The Political Impact of Mass Media.* London: Constable.

Service, Elman Rogers, 1971. *Cultural Evolutionism.* New York: Holt.

Shannon, Claude E., and Warren Weaver, 1949. *The Mathematical Theory of Communication.* Urbana, Illinois: University of Illinois.

Sherif, Muzager, and Carolyn Sherif, 1964. "Social Settings and Reference Groups." in *Small Group Communication: A Reader.* Edited by Robert S. Cathcart and Larry A. Samovar. Dubuque: William C. Brown.

Simons, Herbert, 1974. "The Carrot and Stick as Handmaidens of Persuasion in Conflict Situations." In *Perspectives on Communication in Social Conflict.* Edited by Gerald R. Miller and Herbert W. Simons. Englewood Cliffs, New Jersey: Prentice-Hall.

Simons, Herbert W., 1973. "Interpersonal Perception, Similarity, and Credibility." In *Advances in Communication Research.* Edited by C. David Mortensen and Kenneth K. Sereno. New York: Harper & Row.

Simons, Herbert W., 1975. "Communication and Social Change: The Technoculture, the Counterculture and the Futureculture." Paper presented at the Speech Communication Association. Houston.

Sinauer, E. M., 1967. *The Role of Communication in International Training and Education.* New York: Praeger.

Singer, Marshall, 1971. "Culture: A Perceptual Approach." In *Readings in Intercultural Communication,* I. Pittsburgh: University of Pittsburgh.

Singer, Marshall R., 1972. *Weak States in a World of Powers: The Dynamics of International Relationships.* New york: The Free Press.

Sitaram, K. S., 1972. "What Is Intercultural Communication?" In *Intercultural Communication: A Reader.* Edited by Larry Samovar and Richard Porter. Belmont, California.

Sitaram, K. S., and Roy T. Cogdell, 1976. *Foundations of Intercultural Communication.* Columbus, Ohio: Merrill.

Skinner, B. F., 1971. *Beyond Freedom and Dignity.* New York: Knopf.

Smith, Alfred, ed., 1966. *Communication and Culture: Readings in the Codes of Human Interaction.* New York: Harper & Row.

Smith, Arthur L., ed., 1972. *Language, Communication, and Rhetoric in Black America.* New York: Harper & Row.

Smith, Arthur L., 1973. *Transracial Communication.* Englewood Cliffs, New Jersey: Prentice-Hall.

Smith, Bruce Lannes, and Chitra M. Smith, 1966. *International Communication and Political Opinion.* Princeton: Princeton University.

Smith, Delbert D., 1969. *International Telecommunication Control: International Law and the Ordering of Satellite and Other Forms of International Broadcasting.* New York.

Smith, Jeannette, April 19, 1975. "Television and the Latino Image." *Washington Post.* D 1-2.

Spencer, John, ed., 1963. *Languages in Africa.* Cambridge, England: Cambridge University.

Spradley, James P., 1972. *The Cultural Experience.* Chicago: Science Research Associates.

Starosta, WIlliam J., 1974, 1975, 1976. "A Critical Review of Recent Literature." *International and Intercultural Communication Annual.* Volumes I, II, III. Falls Church, Virginia: Speech Communication Association.

"Starpower", 1973. Simulation game. La Jolla, California: Simile Co.

Stent, Madelon D., William R. Hazzard, and Harry N. Rivlin, eds., 1973. *Cultural Pluralism in Education: A Mandate for Change.* New York: Appleton Century Crofts.

Steward, Julian, 1955. *Theory of Cultural Change.* Urbana, Illinois: University of Illinois.

Stewart, Edward C., 1971. *American Cultural Patterns: A Cross-Cultural Perspective.* Washington, D.C.: SIETAR, Georgetown University.

Stewart, Edward C., 1965. "Individual Decision-Making Across Cultures." Unpublished paper.

Stewart, Edward C., 1975. "A Logic of Diffusion in Communication." Paper presented at the International Studies Association Convention. Toronto.

Stewart, Edward C., 1973. "Outline of Intercultural Communication." Mimeograph released by the Business Council for International Understanding. Washington D. C.: American University.

Stewart, Edward C., 1974a. "An Overview of the Field of Intercultural Communication." Mimeograph. Washington, D.C.: SIETAR, Georgetown University.

Stewart, Edward C., 1974b. "Outline of Intercultural Communication." Expanded unpublished version of 1973 "Outline." Washington D. C.: American University.

Suleiman, Michael W., 1973. The Arabs and the West: Communication Gap." In *Intercommunication Among Nations and Peoples.* Edited by Michael H. Prosser. New York: Harper & Row.

Susman, Warren Irving, ed., 1973. *Culture and Commitment: 1929-1945.* New York: Braziller.

Szalay, Lorand B., 1974. "Adapting Communication Research to the Needs of International and Intercultural Communications." In *International and Intercultural Communication Annual,* I, 1-16. Falls Church, Virginia: Speech Communication Association.

Taylor, Walter W., John L. Fischer, and Evon Z. Vogt, eds., 1973. *Culture and Life: Essays in Memory of Clyde Kluckhohn.* Carbondale, Illinois: Southern Illinois University.

Tillich, Paul, 1966. *The Future of Religions.* New York: Greenwood.

Toffler, Alvin, 1970. *Future Shock.* New York: Bantam.

Triandis, Harry C., 1972. *The Analysis of Subjective Culture.* New York: Wiley.

Triandis, Harry C., 1964. "Cultural Influences Upon Perception." In *Advances in Experimental Social Psychology.* Vol. 1. Edited by Leonard Berkowitz. New York: Academic.

Triandis, Harry C., 1974. "Subjective Culture and Interpersonal Communication and Action." *International and Intercultural Communication Annual,* I, 17-23. Falls Church, Virginia: Speech Communication Association.

Tversky, Amos, 1977. "Features of Similarity." *Psychological Review.* 84:4 (July).

Tylor, Vernon Lynn, 1974. "Dimensions, Perceptives, and Resources of Intercultural Communication." In *International and Intercultural Communication Annual*, I, 64-73. Falls Church, Virginia: Speech Communications Association.

Ueda, Keiko, 1974. "Sixteen Ways to Avoid Saying 'No' in Japan." In *Intercultural Encounters with Japan: Communication—Contact and Conflict*. Edited by John C. Condon and Mitsuko Saito. Tokyo: Simul Press.

United States-Japan Trade Council, 1973. *Japan and America: How We See Each Other*. Washington D. C.

van den Dan, A. W., 1964. "A Revision of the Two-Step Flow of Communication Hypothesis." *Gazette*, 10, 237-250.

van den Ban, A. W., 1973. "Interpersonal Communication and the Diffusion of Innovations." In *Intercommunication Among Nations and Peoples*. Edited by Michael H. Prosser. New York: Harper & Row.

Voegelin, C. F. and F. M. Voegelin, 1964. "Languages of the World: Native America Fascicle One." In *Anthropological Linguistics*, 6, 6, 2-45.

Wagner, Richard V. and John J. Sherwood, eds., 1969. *The Study of Attitude Change*. Belmont, California: Wadsworth.

Wagner, Roy, 1975. *The Invention of Culture*. Englewood Cliffs, New Jersey: Prentice Hall.

Wallace, Anthony F., 1970. *Culture and Personality*. New York: Random House.

Walsh, John E., 1973. *Intercultural Education in the Community of Man*. Honolulu: East-West Center Press.

Watson, Q. Michael, 1970. *Proxemic Behavior: A Cross-Cultural Study*. The Hague: Mouton.

Watzlawick, Paul, and Jane Beavin, 1967. "Some Formal Aspects of Communication." In *The American Behavioral Scientist*, April, 4-8.

Watzlawick, Paul, Jane H. Beavin and Donald D. Jackson, 1967. *Pragmatics of Human Communication*. New York: Norton.

Weakland, John, 1967. "Communication and Behavior—an Introduction." In *The American Behavioral Scientist*, April, 1-4.

Weaver, Gary, 1978. *Crossing Cultural Barriers*. Dubuque: W. C. Brown.

Weber, Max, 1948. *The Protestant Ethic and the Spirit of Capitalism*. London: Scribner.

Weinberg, Alvin M., ed., 1968. *Criteria for Scientific Development: Public Policy and National Goals.* Cambridge, Massachusetts: M.I.T.

Westley, Bruce H. and Malcolm S. MacLean, Jr., 1966. "A Conceptual Model for Communications Research." In *Communication and Culture: Readings.* Edited by Alfred G. Smith. New York: Holt.

White, Leslie, 1959. *The Evolution of Culture.* New York: McGraw-Hill.

White, Leslie, 1949. *The Science of Culture.* New York: Farrar, Strauss.

Whitney, Fredrick C., 1975. *Mass Media and Mass Communication in Society.* Dubuque: W.C. Brown.

Whorf, Benjamin, 1952. *Collected Papers on Metalinguistics.* Washington, D.C.

Whorf, Benjamin, 1956. *Language, Thought and Reality: Selected Writings of Benjamin Lee Whorf.* Edited by J. Carroll. Cambridge, Massachusetts.

Wiener, Norbert, 1966. "Cybernetics." In *Communication and Culture: Readings.* Edited by Alfred Smith. New York: Holt.

Williams, F., 1970. *Language and Poverty: Perspectives on a Theme.* Chicago: Markham.

Williams F., and Lindsay, H., 1970. *A Readership Survey of the Human Opportunities Corporation Newsletter: A Study in Ethnic and Social Class Differences in Communication.* Austin, Center for Communication Research, University of Texas at Austin.

Williams, Raymond, 1962. *Communications.* London: Penguin.

Wilmot, William W., 1975. *Dyadic Communications: A Transactional Perspective.* Reading, Massachusetts: Addison-Wesley.

Wilson, David, 1968. *The Communicators and Society.* New York: Pergamon.

Windlesham, David James, and George Hennessy, 1966. *Communication and Political Power.* London.

Wright, C. R., 1959. *Mass Communication: A Sociological Perspective.* New York: Random House.

Zaltman, Gerald, Philip Kotler, and Ira Kaufman, 1972. *Creating Social Change.* New York: Holt.

Zimbardo, Philip, and Ebbe B. Ebbesen, 1970. *Influencing Attitudes and Changing Behavior.* Reading, Massachusettes: Addison-Wesley.

Zunin, Leonard, 1972. *Contact: The First Four Minutes.* New York: Ballantine.

NAME INDEX

331

SUBJECT INDEX